WHY NATIONS REALIGN:
FOREIGN POLICY RESTRUCTURING
IN THE POSTWAR WORLD

Why Nations Realign:
Foreign Policy Restructuring
in the Postwar World

K. J. Holsti
University of British Columbia

with

Miguel Monterichard
Ibrahim Msabaha
Thomas W. Robinson
Timothy Shaw
Jacques Zylberberg

London
GEORGE ALLEN & UNWIN
Boston   Sydney

George Allen & Unwin (Publishers) Ltd,
40 Museum Street, London WC1A 1LU, UK

George Allen & Unwin (Publishers) Ltd,
Park Lane, Hemel Hempstead, Herts HP2 4TE, UK

Allen & Unwin Inc.,
9 Winchester Terrace, Winchester, Mass 01890, USA

George Allen & Unwin Australia Pty Ltd,
8 Napier Street, North Sydney, NSW 2060, Australia

First published in 1982

British Library Cataloguing in Publication Data

Holsti, K. J.
    Why nations realign: foreign policy restructuring
in the postwar world.
1. World politics–1945-
I. Title
327′.09′04   D843
ISBN 0-04-351062-0

Set in 10 on 11 point Plantin by Preface Ltd, Salisbury, Wilts.
and printed in Great Britain by Mackays of Chatham

Contents

To Matthew and Liisa

Introduction

This volume completes a trilogy of essays about some of the conventional wisdom in international relations and foreign policy theory.[1] I have long been convinced that many Western analyses of international politics and foreign policy reflect certain views about the world which are not shared globally, and which distort or evade certain realities. Writers about the state of the contemporary international system have projected on to the world some of the main characteristics of the relations between the industrial states of the West. Theories of economic integration on the EEC model, and of growing global interdependence, provide perspectives of international relations which sometimes hide more than they reveal. No one disputes the potential economic, political and social benefits resulting from increased communications and from movements of political and economic integration. While the optimistic assumption that these trends or developments will lead to peace needs to be scrutinized very critically even in the Western context, a mounting body of evidence, some of which is related in this volume, supports an insight offered 200 years ago by Rousseau: as nations draw more closely together, and particularly where the relationships are dramatically asymmetrical, conflict, tensions and war – rather than peace and understanding – are possible results. The case studies offered in this volume reveal clearly that in some instance high interdependence or dependence cause nationalist, 'moat-building' behavior – foreign policies that are designed to assert national independence and autonomy. I did not launch this volume attempting to substantiate this point. But most of the cases leave it as an inescapable conclusion.

In fact, this study has as its genesis an interest in an aspect of foreign policy which has received little attention in the theoretical literature, namely, foreign policy change. A review of current writings reveals that the sources of foreign policy – public opinion, decision-making, misperceptions, the personality drives of key policy-makers, and the like – have received more attention than actual policies.[2] And even where policy (seldom defined) is reviewed, rather static pictures emerge; continuity of the major powers' general foreign policy orientations seems to be the norm. Dramatic change, such as China's break from the Soviet Union or Egypt's realignment with the United States in the 1970s, are often described, but not with the aim of analyzing a *type* of foreign policy behavior. This study focuses, then, on a particular type of foreign policy change – the dramatic, wholesale alteration of a nation's pattern of external relations. I have termed this behavior foreign policy 'restructuring'. The chapters explore restructuring by a disparate group of states, possessing a variety of attributes. When we raise *why* questions – why did these nations seek to alter their foreign policies across a range of issues – certain similarities emerge. Foreign policy restructuring is often a response to a threat – but not always a military threat. The threats of the modern era contain cultural, informational and economic components; and many of them derive from the processes associated with 'growing interdependence'. Foreign policy restructuring, in short, is basically an attempt to assert autonomy, to control transnational processes, to destroy the residues of colonialism, to escape from the embrace of a hegemon. To put it in a crude formulation, many cases of dramatic foreign policy change are a manifestation of nationalism in a world popularly characterized as 'beyond nationalism', where growing 'interconnectedness' between societies is supposedly on the verge of creating a global community.[3]

The studies also reveal that overhauling a nation's pattern of relations is easier announced than carried out. Despite the serious commitments of leaders to change their roles and partners in the international or regional systems, the results are often meager, the costs often very high. This suggests that the old metaphor of international politics as a field on which are located independent, sovereign states that make and break alliances and alignments with impunity is inappropriate in the present era. But the competing metaphor of a spider's web international system[4] where a variety of state and non-state actors interact, 'process' issues and 'manage' interdependence is equally off the mark. Whatever the outcome of the great debates about dependence, centre—periphery relations and other pessimistic characterizations of north—south relations, several of the cases lead to the conclusion that these pictures of the world contain some essential truths. The economic costs of attempting to break out of a dependence relationship may indeed be very high. Yet the list of cases in the postwar world as well as recent events in Iran and elsewhere reveal that nationalist impulses, resulting in policies of isolation or extreme self-sufficiency, have by no means been muted by some mythical global interdependence.

At a minimum, readers should find the cases interesting. Our purposes are more fully achieved if the studies confirm that foreign policy change is a subject worthy of systematic analysis. And more ambitiously, if this foray into a little-understood subject generates refinements, and discussion and debate about the nature of the contemporary international system and the theory of foreign policy, a more ambitious objective will have been achieved.

Two graduate student research assistants, Lee Ann Otto and Douglas McNaughton, helped in a preliminary study of Tanzania and with certain sections of the studies on Canada and the introductory essay. The University of British Columbia's Research Committee in the Humanities and Social Sciences provided funds for research assistance and typing. Leo Rose of the University of California was gracious in helping me to secure interviews with Bhutanese officials and offering comments on two chapters. Interviews with Burmese officials, who must remain anonymous, and with Professor James Barrington of the University of Alberta, were especially useful. To them I am very grateful. Various members of the Inter-University Seminar on International Relations, meeting in Ottawa in January 1977, made many criticisms and suggestions. The typists, Grace Cross and Dory Urbano, waded through messy drafts with skill and good humor.

Notes: Introduction

1 K. J. Holsti, 'Underdevelopment and the "gap" theory of international conflict', *American Political Science Review*, 69 (September 1975), pp. 827–39; Holsti, 'Change in the international system: interdependence, integration, and fragmentation', in Ole R. Holsti, Randolph M. Siverson and Alexander George (eds), *Change in the International System* (Boulder, Co.: Westview Press, 1980), pp. 23–53.
2 Reviews of the literature which underscore this point are in Maurice A. East, Stephen A. Salmore and Charles F. Hermann (eds), *Why Nations Act: Theoretical Perspectives for Comparative Foreign Policy Studies* (Beverly Hills, Calif.: Sage Publications, 1978).
3 The thesis of a growing world society is spelled out in Alex Inkeles, 'The emerging social structure of the world', *World Politics*, 27 (July 1975), pp. 467–95.
4 Cf. John Burton, *Systems, States, Diplomacy and Rules* (Cambridge: Cambridge University Press, 1968), esp. p. 8.

1

Restructuring Foreign Policy: A Neglected Phenomenon in Foreign Policy Theory

K. J. Holsti

Between 1963 and 1965 the government of Burma undertook a series of domestic measures and foreign policy decisions which fundamentally altered its orientation toward the outside world. Except for maintaining essential trade and participating in several minor foreign aid projects, the Burmese government drastically reduced its external contacts and imposed a variety of measures which were designed to end external penetration into Burmese society, economics and politics. Foreign aid officials, missionaries, foreign academics and researchers, correspondents and tourists were expelled from the country. Foreign-owned enterprises were nationalized and the government established strict censorship over incoming mail, films and magazines. The Burmese government shunned all invitations to join various regional economic and functional undertakings, vetoed a proposal to build the India–Singapore highway through its territory, became inactive in international organizations and, with a few minor exceptions, took little part in the meetings and diplomacy of the non-aligned states. These actions constituted a radical departure from Burma's traditional foreign policy undertakings which had been actively involved in the non-aligned movement in the United Nations, and in various programs of regional cooperation.

Burma is only one of many interesting cases of a government undertaking to reorient its foreign policy. This book examines this important foreign policy phenomenon, a type of political behavior that has been largely neglected in international relations theory, and only recently alluded to in analyses of Third World states' foreign policies.[1] The substantive chapters constitute case studies of fundamental foreign policy reorientation. These describe the actions and policies of six nations, and seek to explain why reorientation was attempted. Most of the cases concern Third World countries (Tanzania, Bhutan, Burma and Chile), but since we want to understand a type of foreign policy phenomenon that has occurred in all areas of the world we do not limit our inquiry to a particular region or class of states. China and Canada are therefore included as well. In our sample, then, we have developed and developing countries, major powers and small states, democracies and authoritarian regimes. Our concluding chapter will assess the extent to which these basic attributes of states influence the type and style of foreign policy reorientation.

The term *reorientation* refers to the *intentions* of policy-makers to *restructure* their nation's relationships with other countries. For most countries, external relations – the numerous actions and transactions a government and society enter into with others – are not randomly directed toward the outside world. Virtually all accounts of nations' trade figures, UN voting, visits of tourists, communications, numbers and location of diplomatic establishments, military commitments and other acts and transactions reveal that external ties are *patterned*. Naturally these patterns change over the years, as government officials and thousands of private individuals respond to new conditions and opportunities in the external environment. Over a period of a decade, for example, country A's trade with B may grow by 50 percent, while its trade with C may diminish by a similar amount. Likewise, A may decide to provide more external assistance for X, while reducing its commitments to Y. Such changes are normal and are probably more indicative of natural adjustments to changing conditions than to any intent fundamentally to alter a country's relations within a region or in the global system. They do not constitute foreign policy restructuring.

The study is concerned with a type of foreign policy behavior where governments seek to change, usually simultaneously, the *total* pattern of their external relations. The changes usually occur both in the pattern of partnerships (for example, Cuba's trade shifts from the United States to the Communist bloc in the early 1960s) and in the type of activity (for example, a country withdraws from an international organization). The sectors, in brief, may be either geographic or functional. The countries in this study have sought to create essentially different or new patterns of relations in both sectors. Where the intent (reorientation) has been followed by alteration of the total pattern of external actions and transactions, we can say that a country has successfully restructured its foreign policy. We thus distinguish normal foreign policy change, which is usually slow, incremental and typified by low linkages between sectors (for example, a change in foreign aid policy would not be reflected in foreign trade policies), and foreign policy restructuring, which usually takes place more quickly, expresses an intent for fundamental change, is non-incremental and usually involves the conscious linking of different sectors.

The case studies will show how and why restructuring took place. The method, while not free of data problems, is basically simple. It describes each nation's pattern of foreign relations at t_1 and the actions taken to establish new patterns. A second 'photograph' at t_2 indicates the degree of change. The more difficult task is to explain why, given the considerable costs often involved, governments undertake to restructure their foreign relations. This is a particularly important question for developing countries, because in today's world it is primarily these countries that display the most dissatisfaction with the structures and patterns of relationships that they inherited after World War II and the early post-colonial experience.

Yet foreign policy reorientation is certainly no new phenomenon in international politics. Balance of power theory requires governments to align themselves militarily only so long as a particular distribution of capabilities exists. If that distribution is threatened, governments must be willing to establish new commitments. Military threats were historically the common condition underlying such alterations. The famous 'renversement d'alliance' of 1756 ensued from a variety of incompatible interests – and Kaunitz' wiles – but at the core of the diplomatic revolution was Austria's earlier loss of Silesia to Prussia and its elaborate plan of retribution against King Frederick. One hundred and sixty years later the United States abandoned its policy of non-involvement in European quarrels and joined the Entente against Germany. The subsequent decision not to join the League of Nations – the return to 'normalcy' – demonstrated that American isolationism had been abandoned primarily because of a military emergency. Perhaps the most dramatic recent historical example of foreign policy restructuring occurred in 1939, when the Soviet Union abandoned its anti-Nazi foreign policy in order to sign the Non-Aggression Treaty with Hitler's regime. Prior to that agreement, the Soviet Union had played a reluctant, though not destructive, role in the League of Nations, collaborated with France in guaranteeing Czechoslovakia's independence, generally eschewed revolutionary policies abroad, and identified Nazi Germany as the main threat to the Soviet Union's security and to world peace. Though Russia's trade was small, its destinations were diverse.

After August 1939, the Soviet Union completely reversed its previous patterns of activity. Attacks on the Baltic States and Finland (sanctioned in the secret protocols of the Non-Aggression Pact) led to the Soviet Union's expulsion from the League of Nations; Soviet trade was drastically redirected toward Germany, and propaganda tirades became directed predominantly against the Western democracies. Within a matter of weeks, the Soviet Union had altered the role of champion of anti-Nazism and international peace to one of military aggressor and accomplice in Germany's grand design to carve up Europe.

The reasons for this dramatic change are not difficult to pinpoint. Basically, Stalin's disillusionment over British and French appeasement, the Western democracies' vacillation over a proposed alliance with the Soviet Union, and Poland's stiff refusal to allow Soviet troops to transit its territory in case war broke out over Czechoslovakia, led the dictator to conclude that Russia's security interests could best be assured by buying time with the main threat, which was Nazi Germany. In brief, security consideration dictated foreign policy restructuring.

The examples of post-World War II foreign policy restructuring are more difficult to analyze. While military and strategic concerns are underlying factors in some, most have resulted from, or have been responses to, more complex domestic and external conditions. Economic vulnerability, the social consequences of modernization, dependence, ideological disputes between factions, xenophobia, neo-colonialism and nationalism are relevant. China's turn toward self-sufficiency and break with the Soviet Union occurred long before security issues and territorial disputes came to the fore. Similarly, Burma's turn toward isolationism during the mid-1960s can be understood more adequately as a response to extreme foreign penetration and domestic turmoil than to a Chinese or general cold war threat. Canada's attempts to diversify trade and cultural contacts and to regulate the amount of American penetration during the 1970s had nothing to do with military concerns. If threats are perceived, they are of a distinctly economic and cultural character.

A Typology of Foreign Policy Restructuring

Types of reorientation and restructuring can be distinguished on the basis of significant changes in (a) the *levels* of external involvement, (b) the policies regarding types and sources of external penetration, (c) direction or pattern of external involvement and (d) military or diplomatic commitments. While these criteria do not cover all aspects of foreign policy, they should indicate the major directions of actions, transactions and commitments. The following types, with distinguishing characteristics, result.

Isolation. Characterized by extremely low level of external involvement, combined with comprehensive exclusionist policies. All military and diplomatic commitments are avoided. Since externally directed transactions are few, direction is relatively unimportant, and there are few discernible patterns in actions and transitions.

Self-reliance. Trade, diplomatic and cultural contacts are diversified, but levels of transactions are generally low. Any patterns suggesting dependence or vulnerability are scrupulously avoided. Some selective exclusionist policies – usually in the form of import substitution programmes – are instituted. Military commitments which involve dependence conditions (for example, great vulnerability to cessation of arms shipments) or support for other states' interests which are not similar to one's own, are avoided.

Dependence. Externally directed actions and transactions are at a fairly high level, and are characterized by high concentration toward another state or group of similar states (for example, EEC). Essential economic, technical, communications and military requirements come from abroad, usually from a single country. The state is highly penetrated by outside actors, in the form of government advisers, foreign investment, tourists, educators, communications and possibly military personnel. Security is provided by a mentor power, often in return for base rights.

Non-alignment-diversification. This type is characterized by extensive externally directed actions and transactions, but they are well scattered among many states and groups of states. External penetration is often notable, but the government attempts to maintain balance of diversity between numbers and types of foreign agents. The government strictly avoids military commitments to any actual or potential mentor.

When one surveys the states of the contemporary world, it is clear that few fit these types perfectly. The categories are based on continua of involvement, diversification, commitments and exclusion of foreign penetration. Hence, it is possible that states could rank high or low on some of them, but not on all. But there are also examples of states that rank high or low on *all* dimensions simultaneously so that they typify the

Change to → / Change from ↓	isolation	self-reliance	dependence	diversification
isolation	X			
self-reliance		X		
dependence			X	
diversification				X

Figure 1.1 *Possible types of foreign policy restructuring.*

otherwise arbitrary categories. Burma in the mid-1960s and Bhutan until the late 1950s certainly are examples of isolated states, for they rank extremely low on all the continua. China in the early 1960s fits the self-reliance type reasonably well. The Ivory Coast since independence perhaps epitomizes the dependent state, while Tanzania since at least 1967 has systematically sought to reduce its ties with the former mentor to diversify its external contacts and sources of aid, and selectively to exclude foreign agents or processes which might re-establish patterns of dependence or somehow threaten the ruling party's domestic priorities. Most other states could not be so easily categorized.

The problem, however, is not only to delineate state A's pattern of foreign relations at time X, but to describe and explain change from one type, even if it doesn't fit perfectly, *toward* another type. By combining the four ideal types, there are twelve theoretical possibilities for change. Figure 1.1 outlines these. One is hard pressed to find post-World War II examples of each type of change. The cases in our study thus do not represent an example of each theoretical type. Nor are the cases a specific sample of the total universe of attempts to restructure foreign policy since World War II. Without completing the meticulous research required to categorize all known or suspected cases, it is not possible to define the universe of foreign policy restructuring. At the level of foreign policy studies, illustration of types is more significant than sample size. But for those who might be interested in the consequences of foreign policy change on the structure and pattern of transactions in the international *system*, full information on the incidence, location and frequency of foreign policy restructuring would be essential.

It might be interesting, nevertheless, to present a non-exhaustive list of post-World War II cases of foreign policy restructuring. In addition to the twelve theoretical possibilities of change, a further category of abortive attempts is included. Changing from one dependence to another ('switching partners') is also added. Table 1.1 does not include foreign policy restructuring which resulted from victory or defeat in World War II (for example, Finland since 1944), or from the postwar communist revolutions in East Europe.

Table 1.1   *Foreign Policy Restructuring, 1945–79*

Type of change	Countries	Approximate dates, begin and complete
From isolation to:		
(1) self-reliance	none known	
(2) dependence	Nepal	1948–50
	Bhutan*	1964–7
(3) diversification	China*	1970–3
From self-reliance to:		
(1) isolation	China*	1966–9
(2) dependence	none known	
(3) diversification	none known	
From dependence to:		
(1) isolation	Albania?	1977–9
(2) self-reliance	China*	1959–66
(3) dependence		
('switching partners')	Guinea	1958–60
	Iraq	1958–?
	Albania?	1960–76
	Cuba	1960–3
	Indonesia?	1962–5
	South Yemen	1971–?
	Ethiopia	1977–8
(4) diversification	Yugoslavia	1948–
	Rumania	1960s
	France	1962–8
	Tanzania*	1967–72
	Libya?	1967–?
	Iran	1970–4
	Guyana?	1970s
	Canada*	1972–8
From diversification to:		
(1) isolation	Burma*	1963–5
	Iran	1979–
(2) self-reliance	none known	
(3) dependence	Israel?	1948–50
	Brazil	1965–
Abortive attempts:		
	Guatemala	1953–4
	Hungary	1956
	Chile*	1971–3

*denotes cases studies in the project
?denotes marginal case or lack of data

The provisional list indicates that a majority (sixteen of twenty-eight) of the actual or suspected cases involve countries that are normally defined as belonging to the Third World. Conspicuous by their low numbers are countries in the 'First World'. Only France – a debatable case – and

Canada, whose attempts are too recent to be judged successful or not, appear in the list. No particular inference can be drawn from this fact, but it does suggest either that the developed countries are more 'satisfied' in the basic pattern of their foreign relations than are the developing states, or that the costs of restructuring are inordinately high for industrial countries. Why the developing countries should be dissatisfied with their lot is now well known; among the reasons are concern over a situation that contains many characteristics of neo-colonialism. Thus, foreign policy restructuring is not only directed toward establishing a *new* set of relationships, but often requires the destruction of old patterns. Following Anglin, we can designate these actions as 'disengagement'.

Prelude to Foreign Policy Restructuring: Disengagement

In many cases, countries that adopt a new foreign policy orientation systematically destroy old patterns of diplomatic, commercial, cultural and military relations. For some, it is forced upon them by the boycotts, embargoes and expulsions of mentor powers. For example, the reorientation of Yugoslavia and Cuba, and to a lesser extent Guinea, was partly a necessary response to the mentor power's step to cut traditional ties. The old relationships had been terminated for them by the Soviet Union, the United States and France. For countries emerging from isolation, disengagement is not involved because their external relations were so limited and sporadic as to constitute no barrier to establishing new sets of relationships. Nepal prior to 1948 and Bhutan before 1958 are cases in point. But isolation is not the only condition where disengagement is not involved. As the study of Canada's relations with the United States reveals, restructuring can be attempted by selective measures to reduce penetration and vulnerability, combined with vigorous actions aimed at establishing balancing economic, diplomatic and cultural links abroad – all without fundamentally altering or severing ties to the mentor.

Where disengagement does precede restructuring – or takes place simultaneously – it can usually be understood as a response to perceptions of dependence and/or to extensive external penetration. By dependence, we mean a situation where the 'smaller' state can act in its domestic and/or external policies only with the implicit or explicit consent of another state, and where the capacity to threaten or reward in the relationship is highly asymmetrical. To put it another way, the major power – what we call the mentor – establishes the parameters for the political and economic actions of the dependent state, and has the means to ensure conforming behavior. Although there has been considerable controversy over the precise meaning of dependence and the types of indicators that should be used to measure it,[2] this working definition should adequately suggest the essential nature of a dependent relationship. Highly asymmetrical patterns of transactions between two states (for example, 70 percent of A's trade goes to B, but only 5 percent of B's trade goes to A) provide clues to the potential availability of coercive instruments; in this example, B possesses economic leverage and a capacity (though not necessarily intention) to threaten or carry out economic pressure against A. Such patterns also imply asymmetrical vulnerabilities. Vulnerability is one consequence of a dependent relationship; not only does the mentor possess coercive capabilities, but if they are applied, the costs will be asymmetrical. B can hurt A, while the reverse is not possible. Moreover, because of a high degree of economic integration, B's domestic policies may significantly harm A's interests, without B even intending such harm. Efforts to restructure foreign policy often have as a major objective the reduction of vulnerability.[3]

Disengagement may also be a policy response to extensive external penetration. Characteristically, the bureaucracies of penetrated states are supervised by hordes of foreign advisers and, in many cases, high civil service positions are actually held by foreign nationals. Industrial, educational and cultural organizations are often owned or staffed by non-citizens, as are the media. And the political process in the penetrated state is often subject to manipulation, bribes and pressures from foreign agents. Not all these characteristics exist simultaneously, but they are widespread enough in many states to cause nationalist responses in the form of demands for exclusionist domestic policies and termination of asymmetries. Leaders may conclude, for example, that despite the economic benefits of foreign aid or private investment from a mentor power, the structural constraints imposed by such programmes are not compatible with sovereignty, national dignity or some other value. Such calculations, along with the sense of vulnerability and perceptions of other types of threats, combine to produce demands for terminating penetration and/or dependence.

International Relations Theory and Foreign Policy Restructuring

We may ask, then, why such events – often dramatic, and often generating intense international conflict – have not commanded attention. Numerous answers could be advanced, but three intellectual perspectives in recent international relations literature deserve attention in particular: (1) emphasis on the cold war and its associated problems; (2) narrow interpretation of the concept of threat in diplomacy; and (3) the concentration on 'interdependence' and integration as inevitable and progressive trends, with a concomitant neglect of nationalism and disengagement.

Much of the literature on international relations during the last three decades has focused on the cold war and problems associated with it. Our 'maps' of the world have commonly featured only three kinds of states: the communist, Western and non-aligned. Movement from one type to the other was almost impossible because of the sanctions bloc leaders could impose on the wayward or recalcitrant. Indeed, it was not until the 1960s that the concept of non-alignment met with any enthusiasm in Washington or Moscow. The world, then, was rigidly structured into patrons and clients, with non-aligned states being assiduously courted by the superpowers. Underlying these analyses of international politics, whether studies of deterrence, bargaining, alliances or economic development, was a pronounced, if often unstated, concern for values, namely, the preservation of freedom against the onslaughts of revolutionaries and subversives. The defections of Yugoslavia and Cuba from their respective mentors caused much discussion, but these were seen as significant aberrations from the normal diplomatic line-ups, and certainly not events upon which to theorize.

A literature with a particularly Third World outlook has developed only recently. As détente has become a relatively fixed feature of international life, international theory has become increasingly concerned with the problem of inequality. Dependence may have been an acceptable state of affairs in a world confronted with military threats and possible nuclear war. It is no longer accepted with equanimity today. The quest for greater equality and drives to end dependent relationships are important characteristics of contemporary diplomatic life; dependence theory, appropriately, developed initially in Latin America in the 1950s and 1960s but did not become a standard perspective in international relations theory until the 1970s. Its great popularity among North American social scientists is symptomatic of growing concern over the plight of the small and weak state. Only very recently have writers begun to explore foreign policy change as a response to conditions that have no connection with the cold war.

Emphasis on military and subversive threats has been a second important bias of our 'maps' of international relations. The international system has been portrayed as basically benign except for the fulminations and plots of communists, or the military build-ups of the two major communist states. Writers have commonly assumed that once these threats were dispelled through preventive war, nuclear supremacy, stable deterrence, alliances, arms control, or even through unilateral disarmament, the world could return to a condition of peace and stability with an orderly growth of interdependence. Western academics and statesmen have ignored until recently the idea that small, weak and/or vulnerable states could also face a variety of *non-military threats* from the external environment, threats that have little to do with the cold war in general or the moves of great powers in particular.

However, in the past several years spokesmen from the developing world have made the point that their countries' political independence, cultural integrity and economic fortunes are threatened by a variety of non-military conditions in the international system, including new developments in technology, communications and business enterprise. Despite all the talk in Western industrial capitals about the mutually beneficial consequences of growing international interdependence, about the potential for development through private foreign investment, aid and tourism, and the advantages accruing to all through a truly global communications system, many radicals in the developing countries have interpreted these institutions, trends, or processes as posing threats to a variety of local values. The claims of these radical nationalists have recently won the support of even some conservative regimes in the Third World. The list of actual or potential threats, as seen from the vantage of the developing countries, is lengthy. It has been discussed in detail through a variety of publications and conferences over the past few years. We do not need to dwell on them here.

Much of the dependence literature has reflected the ideological zeal of individual writers more than the perceptions of those who are responsible for public policy. Nevertheless, as the officials view the world around them, the actual and potential threats that loom on the horizon are often not of a military nature, but involve economic and social phenomena. All types of interactions with the industrialized countries extend vulnerabilities and often involve risks, frequent maldistribution of benefits and occasional exploitation. Even where dependent relationships bring notable economic benefits – as is the case of several of the former French colonies in Africa – some factions may find it politically expedient to demand the sacrifice of those advantages in order to gain more political, economic and cultural autonomy. In their campaigns, they frequently portray the foreigners as posing a variety of threats.

For many industrial countries, non-military threats are perceived only intermittently. Europeans have worried about America's technological 'invasion', Canadians constantly complain about the economic and cultural effects of the American presence in the country, and the Arab oil embargo forced some Americans to acknowledge that control over vital resources by hostile governments could constitute a serious threat to United States security. Indeed, some influential Americans have even urged the government to broaden the concept of 'national security', and to begin monitoring the international system for all sorts of potential and actual threats to America's economic position.[4] But it is unlikely that foreign investment, tourism, or foreign television will soon reach such proportions in the United States that Americans will perceive them as constituting a problem demanding exclusionist solutions or dramatic foreign policy change.[5] Yet all these forms of external penetration *have* reached extensive proportions in many developing countries. Governments cope with them in different ways; among them are decisions to reorient the country's foreign policy, to establish more diversified or balanced economic relationships, to exclude all foreign influences to the maximum extent feasible with economic survival, or to glorify self-sufficiency.

Such restrictive reactions are seldom understood by those who continue to portray the world in terms of an inexorable trend toward greater interdependence. But any map which plots the flow of transactions in the world would reveal that interdependence is a characteristic primarily between the industrial countries.[6] Aside from the OPEC countries, the network of transactions shows virtually no symmetry in terms of flows, capacities to coerce, sensitivity, or vulnerabilities. Only in the sense that events throughout the world impinge on each other is the world interdependent.

Even abstract academic models of the 'global system' fail to incorporate the inequitable features of contemporary international life. They too ignore the problem of non-military threats and the restrictive reactions to processes which are termed 'interdependence'. The literature characterizes our world as a 'global system', where all sorts of transaction networks criss-cross in a jumbled spider's web. In these networks, issues are 'processed' and alliances are constructed between transnational actors. This mechanistic image of the world fails to raise a number of critical questions: In which directions do communications flow? In economic transactions, do benefits distribute equally or proportionally among participants? Who 'processes' global issues – that is, who wields influence, control or authority? Are solutions designed to increase global equality in a variety of goods and values, or do they maintain disparities and dependencies? Do processes support variety or homogeneity? From where do the 'inputs' into the system originate? From the strong and developed, or from the weak and underdeveloped? Who commands the capabilities – financial, technical and intellectual – to set up or alter the networks of transactions? Whose values are effectively promoted in the system? Does a system seek 'stability' or homeostasis – often implicitly defined as good? Or, for a system to survive, is radical restructuring of relations necessary? Until recently, statesmen from the industrial countries seldom addressed their thoughts to these problems, unless it was within the context of traditional remedies for underdevelopment, that is, more aid, more trade, more tourism and communication, and more private investment. For a variety of reasons, academics did not raise such questions either until the literature on dependence – despite all its shortcomings – emerged.

Disengagement and foreign policy reorientation have been neglected, finally, because academics have remained largely unconcerned with the phenomenon of nationalism. Somehow, nationalism does not square with the notion that increased interdependence and regional integration are progressive developments or trends. Yet, if anything, the demand for political, economic and cultural autonomy, and exclusion of dominant foreign 'influences', has grown increasingly strident since the end of World War II. One paradox of our age is that as the world 'shrinks', as communications grow and as awareness of the outside world penetrates even into remote villages, the desire for autonomy and separateness appears to have become more pronounced. The fear that local cultures and languages will be overwhelmed by outside forces exists among hundreds of groups and nations, from the Quebecois to the Basques, from Amazon Indians to Ukrainians. To many among these people, integration and 'interdependence' imply cultural dilution and possibly extinction.[7]

Despite these trends, increased interdependence and integration remain notable desiderata in the international relations literature. The voluminous body of theoretical and empirical literature on European integration perhaps reveals this value orientation best. No matter how rigorous the theorizing or empirical work on integration, most studies have explicitly or implicitly applauded forward movement toward eventual political unity in Europe. De Gaulle's concept of a 'Europe of fatherlands' – at best, a loose confederation – was dismissed as reactionary or as a mode of political organization that would assure France's paramountcy on the continent. Those governments which have agreed to customs unions, passport zones and coordination of social and labor policies, as in Scandinavia, are considered poor integrationists because they will not take the final plunge into complete political union.[8] Many observers were shocked when the Norwegians voted narrowly to remain outside the EEC. Yet the vote revealed that many Norwegians were convinced that membership in the Common Market would result in massive foreign penetration into Norway and national economic policies that would eventually destroy farming and fishing. More than money was involved in this calculation, for a good case was made that living standards would improve through membership in the EEC. What was at stake, according to many, were traditional ways of life.

Although high on most indicators of integration, the postwar Canadian-American relationship should have indicated clearly that the political will to integrate is the critical variable explaining forward movement, and that unofficial and unorganized processes leading to economic and cultural integration may lead to a nationalist response demanding a slowdown of those processes.[9] Yet neither the theoretical nor empirical literature on integration has adequately emphasized the logic or emotions underlying the opinions of those who resist integration or more 'interdependence'.[10] Some of the case studies in this book present a preliminary foray into one manifestation of modern nationalism, the attempt to *reduce* integration and interdependence, and to augment autonomy.

Describing and Explaining Foreign Policy Reorientation and Restructuring: a Framework

The cases we have selected all involve major attempts to repattern countries' external relations. Many have also undertaken major changes in their policies regarding types and extent of external penetration. Hence, the dependent variables – what we want to describe and explain – will be defined in terms of (*a*) significant changes in the patterns of externally directed diplomatic, cultural, commercial and military relations, and (*b*) identification of new policies with regard to foreign 'agents' within the country. Where evidence is available, we will also add to our dependent variables the policy-makers' *intent* to restructure foreign policy, that is, foreign policy reorientation.

The distinction between intent to change policies and actual repatterning is important. It also raises several problems. First, governments' foreign policy rhetoric may *not* change, yet in the realm of actions, repatterning is obvious. This is true in the case of Burma, where Ne Win's foreign policy pronouncements in the 1960s changed very little in tone and substance from those of the U Nu government of the 1950s. Non-alignment and 'peace' continued to be the main themes. Yet the pattern of externally directed activities changed fundamentally and, even more important, the Ne Win government literally sealed off Burma from the outside world. In such instances, we must rely extensively upon the 'hard' data to describe foreign policy change.

The reverse problem is where policy-makers give strong evidence of *intent* to restructure policy, but for a variety of reasons, fail to bring about degrees or types of change that are distinguishable from the slow, incremental changes observed in the actions and policies of all states. Mexico under the presidency of Echevarria may be one example. Political rhetoric suggested reorientation, but aside from Mexico's pattern of voting in the

United Nations and a few symbolic acts designed to identify Mexico as a leading 'Third World' nation, not much change in the pattern of trade, cultural and diplomatic relations resulted. Most of the cases have been selected on the basis of demonstrated change in actual relations, as identified by the indicators discussed below, rather than on statements of intent. The possible exception is Canada. Intent, as indicated by government documents and political speeches of the highest level policy-makers, appears strong; restructuring of relations is emphasized. But performance in some policy sectors did not extend as far as the statements indicated. Nevertheless, the intent combined with the repatterning of relations and disintegration that *did* take place were sufficient to constitute an example of fundamental change in foreign policy.

The next question follows from the discussion above: how much change is necessary to constitute restructuring and/or disengagement? The definition offered earlier provides part of the answer: restructuring occurs when there is change in many geographical and functional sectors simultaneously. If Tanzania establishes diplomatic relations with China, that act in itself is hardly sufficient to indicate reorientation or restructuring. But if in a reasonably short period of time – let us say within three years – Tanzania drastically diversifies its trade partners, establishes restrictive conditions on foreign investment, ceases accepting aid from Great Britain (its former mentor), terminates long-standing military commitments, and generally reduces the 'foreign presence' within the country, there are grounds for arguing that reorientation was intended, and restructuring was achieved. Obviously, some arbitrary judgement on degrees of change have to be made. It is possible, of course, to establish a priori how much change must be achieved along each dimension before a country is categorized as having changed its foreign policy orientation. But for a variety of reasons it is preferable to work inductively, describing changes in intentions and policies for each case, and allowing the reader to make the ultimate decision. One reason for proceeding in this fashion is that not all types of change are comparable across different types of nations. A country such as Canada, seeking to reduce vulnerability and American penetration, may employ policies and actions quite different from those chosen by China in the early 1960s to reduce its dependence upon the Soviet Union.[11] Change, then, may require different policies for different countries.

At least two types of explanations can be used in accounting for the changes in externally directed actions and policies regarding foreign penetration. First, the study can try to provide evidence about decision-makers' perceptions of the external and domestic conditions which give rise to dissatisfaction with one foreign policy orientation and the desire to restructure external contacts. A variety of factors may be involved, including perceptions of military and non-military threats, calculations of costs and advantages of dependence, domestic political factionalism where creation of an external 'enemy' becomes important, prestige (for example, feelings of guilt about appearing to be dependent), ideological commitments of groups, parties, or factions, cultural values (for example, suspicion of foreigners), personality characteristics of key policy-makers, and the like.

A second type of explanation seeks to answer the question, 'why did the policy-makers choose a particular *type* of new orientation, as opposed to some other?'[12] Where possible, the case studies and concluding chapter attempt to provide evidence to answer this question. But the data do not always provide sufficient clues. Some governments seemingly are more concerned with breaking down old patterns of relations than explicitly defining the goals toward which they are striving. The goals may be vague, or they may vary over time. Bhutan's decision to end isolation was not necessarily predicated on the understanding that the nation should become dependent upon India. Or, even if that calculation was made (but not likely to be admitted publicly), the government probably would argue that dependence is a short-term goal, or a means to creating more diverse foreign contacts later on.

The framework which guided the research into the case studies is represented in Figure 1.2. This framework outlines only the most common explanatory factors. In the research other variables appear, and for many of the cases some conditions are not relevant. Lack of data prevents us from establishing linkages in some instances, and in others, only weak associations can be suggested. The importance of historical and cultural

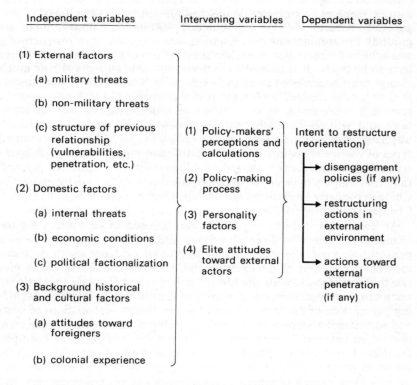

Figure 1.2 *Accounting for foreign policy restructuring.*

variables is notoriously difficult to establish with rigor, but some of the research to date indicates they are significant in conditioning elite and popular attitudes. Policy-makers' psychological needs and personality characteristics can seldom be established as important elements in explaining decisions and actions, except where a single figure is clearly responsible for policy leadership and/or implementation, and where reasonable evidence suggests that without such an individual, intent and actions would have differed significantly.

Organizing the Data

Where available, statements by policy-makers indicate intentions to change foreign policy patterns. Speeches, press conferences, party statements and radio broadcasts serve as the basic sources of information. Where official pronouncements are either misleading (Burma) or rarely available (Bhutan), the studies rely heavily upon hard data and reported government activities. Restructuring of foreign policy is indicated by significant changes in the following types of actions, transactions and/or commitments:

(1) numbers of treaties signed (for example, a significant reduction per annum would indicate isolationist tendencies since the world trend is significantly upward);
(2) numbers and/or states as treaty partners (for example, while maintaining some treaty arrangements with Britain, Tanzania rapidly increased its number of treaties with China, the Soviet Union and East Europe after 1967, indicating a pattern of diplomatic and commercial diversification and an attempt to reduce the relationship with Great Britain;
(3) new commitments of military capabilities abroad, or terminating prior commitments;
(4) significant changes in numbers and destination of students sent abroad to study;
(5) voting patterns in the General Assembly;
(6) direction of foreign trade; degree of trade concentration;
(7) absolute size of trade;
(8) number and direction of visits abroad by head of state or government;
(9) numbers and location of diplomatic missions abroad.

Outward-directed actions and commitments are not the only indicators of foreign policy. Governments also may institute a set of policies which is designed to reduce or increase the amount of foreign penetration, whether official or unofficial. Which foreign governments or non-governmental actors are allowed access to the state, society, or economy? What sorts of policies are fashioned to monitor, control or reduce foreign penetration? In the reverse situation, what sorts of restrictions are reduced or terminated in order to allow in which sorts of foreign influences? Or, does a government literally terminate the diplomatic, cultural and economic presence of one mentor or friendly state, only to allow in the agents and agencies of a new friend or ally? A typical example would be the expulsion of all American influences and institutions in Cuba after 1961, and their replacement by Soviet technicians, party officials, military advisers, foreign aid personnel, literature and films. The indicators in the studies include the following:

(1) expulsion or admission of foreign military personnel, bases and/or equipment;

(2) expulsion of aliens living in the country; restrictions on new aliens entering the country; lifting such prior restrictions;

(3) new restrictions on the size of foreign diplomatic establishments or on the movement of foreign diplomats within the host country; liberalizing such restrictions;

(4) closing the country to tourists from certain other countries, or erecting such administrative barriers as to effectively discourage tourism; terminating such restrictions;

(5) selective or total censorship of incoming books, periodicals, films, radio and television, or lifting such censorship;

(6) restrictions on private investment from abroad, or from particular countries; lifting such restrictions;

(7) nationalization or expropriation of alien property or enterprises;

(8) severe restrictions on numbers of students or academics coming from specific countries; significant alterations to such restrictions;

(9) expulsion of foreign humanitarian, educational, or cultural organizations already in the country or serious restrictions on those attempting to gain access; changing such policies;

(10) restrictions against import of certain commodities from certain countries, where other than economic reasons are given.

Any of these actions taken separately may, of course, be directed toward ends other than fundamentally changing a government's foreign policy. Yet when a number of such policies and actions are taken seriatim or simultaneously, thus fundamentally altering traditional relationships and/or establishing significant new external relationships, we can use these data to demonstrate foreign policy restructuring.

The use of these and other indicators raises some methodological problems. First, the lists are not exhaustive. Since a country such as Canada, whose economy remains highly integrated with that of the United States, may require substantially different policies to alter commercial patterns than would a former colonial territory whose trade ties to the former metropole are weak and confined to a few commodities, other indicators may be more appropriate. Second, limitations on the availability of data make it impossible to employ each indicator for each case study. Moreover, change might be observed in many of the indicators, but not on all of them. Judgement must be used to decide how many indicators must show significant change before we can argue that restructuring is, or has been, occurring. Third, how *much* change must there be across all indicators? Scientific precision might require the researcher to establish benchmarks or 'gates' which must be passed before he could argue that restructuring of foreign policy has taken place. Some might claim, for example, that at least 50 percent of a nation's trade must be redirected before this sector has achieved change. But such a figure would surely be arbitrary. Given the great volume of American-Canadian trade, a change of 10 percent could be considered highly significant, whereas a 30 percent change in Burma's diversified trade pattern would be less noteworthy. And while some indicators are easily quantified, others present more qualitative information. One new military treaty may be more significant than a change of voting patterns in the General Assembly. The case studies therefore present the evidence without a priori definitions of what constitutes sufficient change. We insist only that change occur among a significant number of the dimensions, otherwise we would be dealing with the slow, incremental changes that are typical of any country's foreign policy.

Fourth, should the indicators be weighted? The example of military commitments versus votes in the General Assembly implies that some sorts of actions are more significant than others. But, the importance of various actions depends upon the entire web of relations within which a country operates. It is difficult, therefore, to specify outside of the context of each case study which types of actions are more important than others. A nationalization of foreign property in one nation might be primarily of symbolic importance, whereas in another, its ramifications could spread to the totality of its foreign relations. For Spain to establish an embassy in Moscow or Peking is of greater significance than for Thailand to do so. It would be unwise, therefore, to attach separate weights, a priori, to any of the indicators. The descriptions in each case study include assessments of the relative significance of various policies, but final judgement will remain with the reader.

Finally, what unit of time should be used to measure significant change? Cuba's disengagement and restructuring occurred within a relatively brief span – less than two years. Tanzania's attempts to diversify external contacts and limit foreign penetration have taken much longer, even if the intent to reorient was made known over a relatively brief period in Nyerere's presidency. Although the intent to change was fully enunciated by Canadian officials in 1972, the nature of the Canadian-American relationship is so complex that some patterns – particularly trade – might show no significant modification for several years. We are less concerned with the methodological problems time may raise than with its substantive and theoretical significance: given a certain degree of integration between two economies, is fundamental change for all practical purposes precluded? Or can it be accomplished, but only very slowly? Can developing countries restructure their foreign relations more easily than developed countries? In most of the cases, fundamental change was attempted or occurred in less than five years. But the studies do not set this as an arbitrary limit. The theoretical concern of the study is not the 'suddenness' of change, but the intention or fact of fundamental change. Thus, it is only important to distinguish ordinary foreign policy change from the deliberate intent and attempt of some governments to recast their role in world politics and economics.

Selecting Cases

A definitive study of foreign policy restructuring would examine a large proportion of the cases so that generalization would rest on a large sample. Financial and scholarly resources to conduct in-depth case studies of so many cases would be considerable. The relatively small number of studies in this volume thus makes this no more than an initial excursion into the subject. An alternative approach is to examine at least one case of each *type* of foreign policy restructuring in the expectation that different causal relationships might be involved.[13] The number of cases, using type as a selection criterion, is further reduced by lack of examples and data problems. There are no known examples of the following: isolation-self-reliance; self-reliance-dependence; self-reliance-diversification; diversification-self-reliance. Albania's rupture of relations with China in the late 1970s provides a probable example of change from dependence to isolation, but the researcher soon runs up against a lack of information both in terms of actions and transactions, and causal evidence. Israel, 1948–50 and Brazil in 1965 provide partial examples of change from diversification to dependence, but a preliminary examination revealed that the change was primarily in a single sector (for example, Israel's dependence upon the United States for military support). Moreover, both of these cases violated another selection criterion: government incumbency.

Many of the cases listed in Table 1.1 suggest that foreign policy restructuring resulted quickly after a change (usually violent) in government or upon the achievement of independence. Almost by definition, a revolutionary regime helps to discredit its predecessors by linking them with 'evil' or exploitative mentors; new partners have to be found, or all contacts with foreigners are shunned. With the exception of Chile, all of our cases represent situations where an incumbent government – defined as being in office at least one year – begins to restructure the nation's foreign policy. These regimes had either inherited or established one pattern of relations; the case studies explore why they found those patterns so unsatisfactory that they were willing in most cases to absorb economic and (sometimes) political costs for the sake of creating new orientations. The criterion of government incumbency ruled out examples of 'switching partners'. The requirement was relaxed in the case of Chile for two reasons: (1) we wanted to explore one case of an abortive attempt to restructure, where a relatively weak and dependent country faces a mentor's opposition, and (2) while a great deal has been written in English about Allende's demise and the role of the CIA in destabilizing Chilean politics, much less attention has been devoted to examining the main outlines of Chile's foreign policy during the period of the *Unidad Popular*.

The cases come from all regions of the world except Europe and Russia, and represent states with diverse social, economic and political attributes. Changes were occasioned by a variety of threats and opportunities. The concluding chapter, based on the six studies, demonstrates that a major hypothesis introduced here – the importance of non-military threats in foreign policy change – is confirmed.

Notes: Chapter 1

1 Marshall R. Singer's *Weak States in a World of Powers* (New York: Free Press, 1972) concentrates on the measurement of dependence, but in places it touches upon the problems governments face in reducing dependence through reorienting foreign policy. Douglas Anglin's 'Zambian disengagement from Southern Africa and integration with East Africa, 1964–1972: a transactional analysis', in Timothy M. Shaw and Kenneth A. Heard (eds), *Cooperation and Conflict in Southern Africa: Papers on a Regional Subsystem* (Washington, DC: University Press of America, 1976), pp. 228–89, is the one of the few works which examines empirically one nation's attempt to disengage from a dependent relationship.

2 For theoretical formulae to measure dependence and vulnerability, see James Caporaso, 'Methodological issues in the measurement of inequality, dependence, and exploitation', in James Kurth and Steven Rosen (eds), *Testing Economic Theories of Imperialism* (Lexington, Mass.: D. C. Heath (Lexington Books), 1974), pp. 87–116. For further elaboration see Raymond Duvall, 'Dependence and dependencia theory: notes toward precision of concept and argument', *International Organization*, 32 (Winter 1978), pp. 51–78; and David A. Baldwin, 'Interdependence and power: a conceptual analysis', *International Organization*, 34 (Autumn 1980), pp. 471–506.

3 Integration theory has developed primarily out of the European experience. It has not been applied to colonial or post-colonial relationships. Yet many of the newly independent countries retain some of the features of economic, cultural and political integration that were so prominent in the colonial relationship. Many metropolitan – former colony *economic* relationships are characterized, for example, by liberal trade arrangements (including preferential tariff treatment), free flow of factors of production and harmonization of economic and fiscal policies. These arrangements were made through extensive consultation. *Social* integration at the elite level is also very high between industrial states and former colonial territories: the elites speak the same language, follow similar careers and communicate extensively. In the era of post-colonial tutelage, there are also many characteristics of *political* integration: civil servants of the former colonial power staff bureaucratic, educational, agricultural and business enterprises; much policy is made jointly (policy integration); and in extreme cases, the weak state government may ask its former colonial mentor to intervene militarily on its behalf to cope with indigenous dissidents.

   According to measures offered in the integration literature (Nye in particular), we could argue that many small, weak states in the developing world are still integrated with former colonial mentors. But this observation would seem to place the integration literature into areas for which it was originally unintended. We know that the new countries do *not* intend to integrate with Europe or North America. Yet the facts are there: using virtually any measure offered in the literature, we find that many developing countries remain integrated with former metropolitan powers.

4 Maxwell Taylor, 'The legitimate claims of national security', *Foreign Affairs*, 52 (April 1974), pp. 577–94.

5 There are regions in the United States where foreign penetration has become a local issue, however. For example, Japanese investment in Hawaii has grown rapidly, causing some local residents to call for controls. The amount of foreign investment and ownership in the United States, particularly in banking and purchase of farmland, has caused some observers to demand restrictions. See, for example, John Congers and Marcus G. Raskin, 'Taking over America', *New York Times*, 1 June 1979, p. A 25. In proportional terms, foreign investment in the US is only 10 percent of American investment in Canada.

6 It is significant that empirical studies of growth in transactions and interdependence concentrate only on relations between industrial countries. See Richard Rosecrance *et al.*, 'Whither interdependence?', *International Organization*, 31 (Summer 1977), pp. 425–72. Yet diplomats constantly talk of 'global interdependence'.

7 For elaboration, see K. J. Holsti, 'Change in the international system: interdependence, integration and fragmentation', in Ole R. Holsti, Randolph Siverson and Alexander George (eds), *Change in the International System* (Boulder, Co.: Westview Press, 1980).

8 Cf. Amitai Etzioni, *Political Unification: A Comparative Study of Leaders and Forces* (New York: Holt, Rinehart & Winston, 1965), ch. 6.
9 Joseph Nye has demonstrated in the African context that if integration assumes asymmetrical characteristics, that is, an unbalanced flow of transactions between units, the desire for further integration will wane. See his *Pan Africanism and East African Integration* (Cambridge, Mass.: Harvard University Press, 1965), pp. 259–60. Naomi Black has observed that as economic integration between Canada and the United States mounts, nationalism in Canada will inhibit further integration. 'Absorptive systems are impossible: the Canadian-American relationship as a disparate dyad', in Andrew Axline *et al.* (eds), *Continental Community? Independence and Integration in North America* (Toronto: McClelland & Stewart, 1974), pp. 92–108.
10 An exception is Robert Gilpin's 'Integration and disintegration on the North American continent', *International Organization*, 28 (Autumn 1974), pp. 851–74.
11 I am grateful to Jeanne Laux, University of Ottawa, for suggesting this point. The problem of change on each indicator is discussed below.
12 Jeanne Laux proposed the distinction between the two types of explanation.
13 This more modest strategy was, frankly, affected by financial and time considerations as well.

2

From Isolation to Dependence: Bhutan, 1958–62

K. J. Holsti

On 23 September 1958 Prime Minister Nehru of India rode into the capital of the small Himalayan kingdom of Bhutan. He was the first government leader of any state to make an official visit, in modern history, to the remote land of the *Drukpas*. To get to Paro, Nehru had travelled by car, jeep, pony and yak. Leaving New Delhi, he motored to Gangtok, the capital of Sikkim; from there he went by jeep and then mounted a pony to make the trek across portions of Tibet's Chumbi Valley, over the 14,000-foot Nathu La pass, and finally into Bhutan. The remainder of the trip to Paro involved climbing ridges on yak and descending into fertile river valleys. Nearing Paro, he was met by the king's guards, colorfully garbed in dress more reminiscent of ancient Mongolia than modern mufti. The trip had taken six days – undoubtedly the slowest progress of any prime ministerial travel since the eighteenth century.[1]

The importance of Nehru's trip lay not in the leisurely progress of the Prime Minister's entourage, however. Rather, it helped inaugurate a fundamental revolution in Bhutan's relationship to the outside world. Bhutan was the last physically isolated state in the modern world, the only political entity that was almost totally ignored by that world. Nehru's visit was prompted by developing events in the Himalayas, events which eventually forced the royal government of Bhutan to abandon its isolationism and to accept a degree of dependence on an outside mentor which finds few parallels in modern history. Prior to 1958 Bhutan had no foreign relations as that word is commonly employed. By 1965, it was involved in a rich network of external relationships – although they were focused almost exclusively upon India. This represented a change of orientation from isolationism to dependence and a restructuring of actions and transactions from virtually none to a pattern concentrated on a single mentor.

Five Critical Decisions

Bhutan's location and topographical features help explain the relative ease with which the royal government was able to maintain its isolation throughout most of the twentieth century. Wedged between India and Tibet, its steep mountains and dense jungles along the southern frontier made access to the central valleys, where most of the population is located, very difficult. To the north, Himalayan ridges provide natural barriers between Tibet and Bhutan, although fourteen passes make contact possible. But with no roads the traffic was sporadic, confined primarily to a small number of Bhutanese traders and monks who travelled to Lhasa. The steep mountain ridges and valleys of central Bhutan also kept the Bhutanese separated from each other. Although they speak dialects of the same Dzonkha language, communication between the various regions of the country was confined to a few high civil or religious officials. Until recently, it would have been inaccurate to speak of Bhutan as a 'nation' in the sense that a majority of its people were cognizant of, and identified with, each other.

Estimates vary, but at the time of Nehru's visit, approximately 600,000 (over 1 million today) Bhutanese inhabited a territory the size of Vermont and New Hampshire combined. There were no radios in Bhutan, no roads, no mail service, no newspapers, no wheels, not to mention airports, hospitals, or secular schools. The society was comprised of small land-holders and, until the king's reforms of the 1950s, many serfs. It was a simple society, neither highly stratified nor ridden by class or serious ethnic cleavages. Visitors during the 1960s often characterized it as a happy society which suffered from few of the most debilitating consequences of development. There was little poverty, no malnutrition, few demonstrable social injustices, and certainly no communities resembling the shanty-towns of Bombay, Teheran or São Paulo. The economy was simple but self-sufficient. Unemployment was largely unknown and the Bhutanese were seldom affected by climatic disasters. Pollution was not a feature of the landscape. The most serious problems were a high infant mortality rate, goiter, venereal disease and some underemployment. While Bhutan's society by the late 1950s may not have lived in a Shangri-la, the country was poor only in the sense that fifteenth-century Switzerland was poor. Finally, no Bhutanese had been killed in war since a few border skirmishes with British troops in northern India in the early 1860s.

Between Nehru's visits in 1958, and 1961, the Druk Gyalpo (King) of Bhutan, Jigme Dorji Wangchuk, and his closest adviser (later Prime Minister), Jigme Dorji, made five decisions that ended Bhutan's isolation, led to extensive dependence upon India and inaugurated the modernization of Bhutan's society. The first decision, taken only after considerable soul-searching,[2] was to send some Bhutanese youth to India for modern education. It was anticipated that these students would return to launch and direct the modernization of the country's educational, economic and governmental institutions. The second decision, accepting Nehru's 1958 offer, was to allow the Indians to build a road from Assam to Paro and Thimphu, Bhutan's major towns in the west, thus opening up the country to vehicular traffic for the first time. The third decision, taken six months after the anti-communist rebellion erupted in Tibet in March 1959, closed Bhutan's border with Tibet. The fourth decision, based on the recognition that a few Bhutanese students educated abroad could not by themselves initiate development programs, accepted generous Indian foreign aid offers, including all the trained personnel – bureaucrats, overseers, financial planners, engineers, and the like – that would be required to initiate and bring to successful conclusion a variety of aid projects. Finally, the government in 1959 also decided to request the Indians to equip and train a national Bhutanese army to replace the traditional militia armed with bows, arrows and swords.

Time One: Bhutan as an Isolated State

To understand the critical consequences of these decisions, it is necessary first to describe briefly the nature of Bhutan's contacts abroad prior to 1958. What do we mean by the term 'isolation'? Bhutan offers an example approximating the ideal type. In terms of the two dimensions of foreign policy discussed in the preceding chapter, Bhutan was isolated because its outwardly directed actions were few and mostly intermittent rather than patterned, and because access (penetration) into the country from outside was almost non-existent. This is not to say, however, that Bhutan was always isolated, or that its isolation could be explained exclusively by its geographic remoteness. Prior to the twentieth century, Bhutan had been involved in the 'diplomacy' of the Himalayan region, if not on a regular basis, at least sufficiently to embroil itself in frequent wars and armed forays into neighboring territories. The country's isolation in the twentieth century was a deliberate foreign policy orientation or strategy and not merely the consequence of physical barriers.

As religion and politics in Bhutan were closely intertwined, the foreign activities of the pre-twentieth-century Bhutanese were related to religious issues, including the question of religious obedience to the Dalai Lama (the Bhutanese Drukpa religion is an offshoot of the Tibetan Kagyupa Buddhist sect). Lamas from Bhutan regularly went to Tibet for training and study, and Tibetan forces occasionally invaded Bhutan to ensure religious conformity.[3] In the eighteenth century Bhutan also had been active militarily, occupying parts of Sikkim for a six-year period, and making armed incursions into Bengal and Assam. But when British and Chinese power extended into the Himalayas and Tibet in the nineteenth century, Bhutan's response was to isolate the country and to place strict controls over intra-regional trade between India and Tibet.[4]

For most of the twentieth century until Nehru's visit to Paro, Bhutan's relations with the outside world were confined primarily to religious interchanges with Tibetans. Bhutan also exported 20,000 tons of rice each year over the Himalayan passes; even under the early years of communist control in Lhasa, Bhutan's traders moved freely into the country and, reportedly, had access to medical and educational institutions there. Bhutan also maintained a trade representative in Lhasa.[5] But what of contacts with the British and Indians?

The royal government's contacts with British authority in the pre-independence India were at best intermittent. Several expeditions had managed to get into Bhutan during the nineteenth century, and in 1864 British and Bhutanese forces clashed over possession of territory in the Assam Duars (plains). In the 1865 Sinchula Treaty, Bhutan gave up possession of the contested territory. Little else occurred until 1910 when, faced with increased Chinese pressure in Tibet, Bhutan and England revised the 1865 treaty, Britain guaranteeing non-interference in Bhutan's internal affairs in exchange for Bhutan's agreement to be 'guided' by British advice in regard to its external relations. Britain also granted the Druk Gyalpo (who had just consolidated authority within the realm) an annual subsidy of 100,000 rupees. There is no available record of Britain's 'guidance' of Bhutan's external relations subsequently, probably because Bhutan had few such relations. Indeed, Britain maintained no official representation in Bhutan, Bhutan never became part of the empire or of British India, and the British helped prevent Westerners from visiting the country knowing that the Bhutanese resented any foreign intrusion.[6]

Relations with the Indians were similarly sporadic and inconsequential. After India's independence, Bhutan's status remained basically the same: India simply took over the British role. The 1910 treaty was amended in 1949, but not in its essence. India returned a small strip of territory to Bhutan, promised not to interfere in Bhutan's internal affairs and increased the annual subsidy to the Druk Gyalpo. Bhutan agreed to be 'guided' by India in its foreign affairs and not to import military equipment without India's agreement. India maintained a special agent for Sikkim and Bhutan in Gangtok, but he visited Bhutan only every three or four years. The Bhutanese were reportedly not keen to see him more often than that![7] Only one other Indian official – a high-level administrator in the Indian Foreign Ministry – visited the country prior to Nehru's trip.

There was some trade between Bhutan and India, but the lack of transport facilities prevented the volume from growing into anything significant. Finally, in order to try to modernize Bhutan's army, the Druk Gyalpo had sent a few officers to India for study and training in the mid-1950s. In brief, Bhutan's relations with the outside world were confined to the travels of a few lamas and traders to Tibet, and sporadic contacts with the British and Indians. The intermittent transactions had persisted for decades, with virtually no disruption even during World War II. Bhutan's isolation was not total, but the volume of externally directed transactions, compared to most states, was uniquely low.

On the ingress dimension of foreign policy, however, Bhutan was a hermit nation. No figures are available, but probably fewer than a handful of foreigners (perhaps excluding Tibetan religious officials) visited the country in the 1950s. Aside from the physical impediments to travel, no visitor could enter Bhutan without the king's invitation.[8] Such an invitation was apparently almost impossible to secure, in part because of extreme sensitivity to the diplomatic ramifications of having contacts with outsiders. The Bhutanese even feared that if foreign friends of the major families were allowed into the country, the Indians might ask for equal permission to visit. The visits of the fortunate who did enter the country were kept discreetly quiet.[9] In addition to excluding all but a handful of foreigners, Bhutan also repeatedly turned down Indian offers of economic and technical assistance.[10] Regarding ingress, then, there was no *pattern* of activities, either by type or over time, nothing even as irregular as the treks of Bhutanese lamas and traders to Lhasa. Our photograph of Bhutan at t_1, roughly the first six decades of this century, thus shows very few flows of activity, either going to or from Bhutan. It comes close to being an empty picture.

Only several years later, all had changed. Bhutan's society had become penetrated by numerous Indians, and the royal government had a Foreign Ministry to keep track of the country's multiplying external activities. Our photograph of t_2 is taken during the 1960s, for the most part the first half of the decade.

The Pattern of Dependence and Penetration

The implementation of the five key decisions required fundamental revisions in Bhutan's traditional exclusionist practices. By the mid-1960s teachers, officials, technicians and advisers from India had come in large numbers with the purpose of assisting Bhutan achieve two major objectives: modernization of the economic, governmental and educational system, and building a modern defense capability. The penetration dimension of foreign policy restructuring was not, however, a matter of extensive public discussion; there were apparently no attempts by the royal government to explain to its subjects why, all of a sudden, the country should be frequented by numerous foreigners. The unstated policy, however, was to accept only as many Indians as the Bhutanese thought they needed to achieve their objectives, and not necessarily how many the Indians thought were needed. India's penetration of Bhutan and the royal government's dependence on India can be divided along several dimensions of activity: military, economic aid, communications, government personnel, teachers, trade and currency, and diplomatic intervention in Bhutan's domestic affairs.

Bhutan initially believed it could organize a modern military force by sending a few officers to India's military academies; it vigorously opposed inviting Indians to Bhutan for training purposes.[11] By 1959, however, Chinese activities in Tibet and along Bhutan's northern border had become so provocative that Jigme Dorji, the king's major adviser, went to New Delhi to ask for an unequivocal Indian commitment of military aid in case of Chinese aggression.[12] Within two years, Bhutanese and Indian officials were involved in joint defense planning and the Indian government was contemplating the possibility of sending Indian troops to Bhutan in case of an emergency.[13] In 1962, Bhutan established its own military academy, but it was under the supervision of an Indian colonel; Indian army officers made up a large portion of the instructing staff.[14] By the middle of the decade virtually the entire effort to create a modern Bhutanese army was under the direction of an Indian Military Training Team.[15]

There were limits to the Indian military presence, however. The Druk Gyalpo consistently refused to allow India to station troops permanently in Bhutan, despite Indian suggestions that this course of action would best provide for Bhutan's security against Chinese encroachments.[16] Such action would also have served India's security interests. Even at the height of the Sino-Indian 1962 war, Bhutan never officially allowed in Indian troops for purposes other than training Bhutan's army. But this was only official policy. Rumors of Indian troop movements abounded, and correspondents wrote of seeing truckloads of Indian troops on the Indian-built road from Phuntsoling to Paro and Thimphu. According to one observer, an entire Indian division of 15,000 men was stationed in Bhutan.[17] The exact number or purposes of the Indian military presence in Bhutan during the 1960s will probably never be published, but whether it was 5,000 or 15,000, either figure is a dramatic increase over 1959 when there were none.

Bhutan's objective of economic and social modernization involved no less Indian penetration and Bhutanese dependence. At first, only a few Indian technicians came to conduct geographic surveys and to help the inexperienced Bhutan government draft five-year development programs. The number of advisers and officials swelled in the 1960s as it became increasingly clear to the Indian government that the Bhutanese did not possess the trained manpower and bureaucracy necessary to implement development projects. By the end of the decade the Indian government had virtually taken over the entire planning function for Bhutan. It had established a Planning Commission which not only drew up the five-year plans, but also monitored progress on all development projects.[18] India provided most of the funds for the projects: the costs of the three five-year plans running from 1961 to 1976 differ according to source[19] but there is general agreement that approximately 90 percent of the funds were provided by India. The total number of Indian aid officials who operated in Bhutan is unavailable; we can assume, however, that a large portion of the 5,000 officially acknowledged Indians in Bhutan in the early 1970s were connected with various aid projects.[20] As in the typical aid-dependent relationship, the mentor provides the funds and the intellectual and technical skills, while the host provides most of the manual labor.

One of the assumed attributes of sovereignty is government policy-making and administration by nationals. In the case of Bhutan, this attribute was not clearly visible in the 1960s. To be sure, the Druk Gyalpo and his immediate advisers made the fundamental decisions (not without an official Indian adviser in the early 1960s, however), but the day-to-day direction of policy in areas such as development, police, the military and government organization lay mostly in the hands of Indians. No exact figures are available, but one correspondent estimated that 55 percent of Bhutan's bureaucrats were Indians.[21] India's Political Officer to Sikkim and Bhutan stated in 1968, however, that there were 700 Indians serving in the Bhutan government – a figure which would probably add up to more than one-half of Bhutan's officialdom.[22]

To meet its domestic objectives of modernization, Bhutan had little choice but to rely heavily on the Indians. As there was virtually no secular schooling system in the kingdom prior to 1958, Bhutan did not have the trained manpower necessary to administer expanding government programs. Thus, in the 1960s Indians were to be found at all levels of government, holding semi-skilled and clerical jobs, as well as top executive and managerial positions in the Bank of Bhutan, the police and in communications facilities. The Chief Accounts Officer, responsible for preparing the annual budget, control of expenditures, taxation policy, currency, banking and customs, was an Indian.[23] This situation may seem an anomaly to a government which still clung to certain vestiges of isolationism (see below), but the Bhutanese did not see the predominance of foreigners in administration as a permanent condition – nor did the Indians for that matter. Even if temporary for a decade or two, Bhutan's dependence upon Indian personnel was nevertheless exceptionally pronounced.

In the area of communications the pattern of dependence was parallel to administration. Considering the developing events in the Himalayas in 1958, Nehru proposed to the Druk Gyalpo that India build a road connecting the two countries. The king was not prepared to accept the offer at that time, but by 1959 the situation regarding China had deteriorated sufficiently so that he and his advisers saw the necessity of obtaining immediate Indian military assistance. The fateful decision, taken reluctantly[24] in September 1959, reduced the time of travel from India to the heart of Bhutan from six days to six hours. The Phuntsoling–Thimphu–Paro road was completed in 1962. A second road to Tashigang in eastern Bhutan followed soon after, and a third major Indian project linked eastern and western Bhutan by road for the first time. By the end of the decade the Indians had funded, surveyed and built a road network of 10,500 kilometers[25] crossing high mountain passes, deep river valleys, jungles and evergreen forests. After the roads were completed, Indian crews remained in the country to provide maintenance services.

Indians also built the first telephone exchanges in Bhutan (with all external lines leading to India),[26] the postal and telegraphic services, and ultimately the first airport in the country. These installations were manned and maintained primarily with Indian personnel. By the end of the decade, then, Bhutan was theoretically very accessible from the south; all lines of external communication went to India.

In trade, Bhutan's dependence was somewhat less pronounced, primarily because its simple peasant society remained basically self-sufficient. However, the foreign policy reorientation of 1959–61 did create some areas of vulnerability. The decision to stop the export of surplus rice to Tibet created a glut in the domestic market, thus driving down prices. As virtually the only export of any consequence, Bhutan had to find an alternative market for its rice. That market would have to be provided by India. Bhutan also exported some coal, dolomite, vegetable dyes, brass utensils and fruits to India, but the amounts involved were not significant. Yet the pattern of exports reveals the classic characteristics of asymmetry, dependence and some vulnerability: geographic and product concentration and export items which are not critical to the purchaser. Even if Bhutan possessed a largely self-sufficient economy, it still had to obtain some foreign exchange to cover the costs of imports that were not funded by the Indian aid program. Under an arrangement with the Indian government, Bhutan could obtain foreign funds only from the Central Bank of India, thus furthering the economic dependent relationship.[27] Bhutan earned only about $60,000 annually (by sale of stamps to philatelists)[28] in currencies other than rupees. The total amount of exports and imports in

Indo-Bhutan trade represented an insignificant proportion of India's foreign trade activities.

Other economic areas were characterized not only by asymmetry and dependence but also by integration. For example, until 1976 the rupee was the medium of exchange outside the barter economy. That year the Bhutanese *ngultrum* replaced the rupee, but the rupee continues to be used in many transactions and the Bhutanese currency remained pegged to the Indian currency.[29] The high degree of financial integration greatly increased Bhutan's sensitivity to economic fluctuations in India. This, of course, was one price paid for accepting a condition of asymmetrical dependence. A 'steady state' self-sufficient economy is protected against most regional or global economic variations. Once isolation is ended, the small economy can no longer be directed or guided solely by national governments. Hence, the influx of Indian aid, as well as inflation on the subcontinent, had some economically disruptive consequences in Bhutan.[30]

The government of Bhutan initially hoped to develop its secular educational system by sending students to India, who would then return to Bhutan to train more indigenous teachers. The Indian government generously granted scholarships for these students, but most returned to join regular governmental departments rather than the teaching profession. Hence, numerous teachers from India came to staff the small number of Bhutan's new schools. By 1963 there were fifty-three primary schools and fifteen middle schools in which 71 percent of the teachers were Indian.[31] More significant than the numbers, perhaps, were the subjects taught. In addition to English, children learned Hindi and Indian – not Bhutanese – history. Indeed the school system became a virtual replica of Indian models.[32] Such emulation was necessary given the realities of the day, but it resembled almost perfectly the educational patterns found between Britain, France and the United States and their former dependencies. Meanwhile, virtually all of the higher education of Bhutanese students took place in India. Even though some Colombo Plan countries offered scholarships to students from Bhutan, the government did not 'avail itself' of these opportunities on the grounds that the Indian government supplied a sufficient number of funds for study abroad.[33] There is a possibility, of course, that the foreign scholarships offered during the 1960s were turned down primarily so as not to offend the Indians who, as we will see, were extremely sensitive about Bhutan's contacts with third countries.

We can summarize briefly the extent to which Bhutan's society by the mid-1960s had become penetrated and dependent upon India for achieving the objectives of economic modernization and military security. Since many figures are unavailable (India's presence in Bhutan was a delicate issue in both countries; most statistics come from journalists and in some cases their figures do not tally with each other), Table 2.1 should be read as approximations only, and as averages for the decade. While these figures do not show change over the years, they do indicate overall the 'concentration' of Bhutan's dependence as well as the scope of India's presence in the country. They also illustrate how, after 1961, Bhutan's exclusionist policies had been abandoned. Such figures cannot reveal any-

Table 2.1 *The Indian Presence in Bhutan, 1960s*

Activity or program	Percent of total personnel from India	Percent of total funds from India
National budget	—	75
Defense training	100	n.a.
Defense equipment	—	100
Road construction	10a	100
Road maintenance	90a	100
Radio	n.a.	100
Public administration	55	n.a.
Development plans	n.a.	90
University education	—	99
Teachers	50	n.a.

n.a. = no data available
a = rough estimate only
Sources: Patrice DeBeer, 'Le Bhoutan sort du moyen age', *Le Monde*, 3 August 1974; Leo E. Rose, *The Politics of Bhutan*, p. 202; Far East Economic Review, *Yearbooks*, 1961–4, 1971–4; *Countries of the World and their Leaders*, 2nd edn (1975).

thing about the dynamics of Indian-Bhutanese diplomatic relations, however. We must ask as well whether the Indian authorities used their presence and Bhutan's vulnerability to manipulate domestic politics or to apply pressures against the Bhutanese.

Exploiting Penetration and Vulnerability in the Mentor–Client Relationship?

The court politics of Bhutan are difficult to unravel because they include largely unreported family quarrels and personality conflicts. In any case it is not our purpose to go into this question except to illustrate how the Indian authorities were involved.[34] It is clear from the several crises in Bhutan's politics during the 1960s and early 1970s that the Indian government was fully committed to supporting the Druk Gyalpo against the plots of his opponents. Rumors that India was involved in the assassination of the Prime Minister, Jigme Dorji, in April 1964 are not supported by any evidence; quite the contrary. The Prime Minister enjoyed royal and Indian confidence, and when the assassination took place, the Indian government assisted in bringing the Druk Gyalpo, who was recuperating in Switzerland from a heart attack, immediately back to Bhutan to forestall a possible *coup*. The Indian government also alerted paratroopers for possible military action to support the king.[35] The Druk Gyalpo's trust in the Indians was revealed in his subsequent request to the Indian authorities to help identify and capture the assassin. During a court conflict in November 1964 and an assassination attempt against the Druk Gyalpo in August 1965, the Indian government immediately offered the king military assistance if he requested it.[36] Finally, in 1974 the Indians conducted investigations into a rumored plot to take over the Bhutan government by certain exiled Tibetan elements, including the late king's Tibetan mistress.[37] Without its own foreign intelligence service, Bhutan was dependent upon India for investigatory assistance regarding the activities of Bhutanese dissident elements abroad.

Members of the Dorji family, including the deceased Prime Minister's brother (who succeeded Jigme Dorji for several months) and sister, went to Nepal after the November 1965 plot was discovered, and from Katmandu issued numerous anti-Indian statements to the press. Their basic theme was that the Druk Gyalpo was compromising Bhutan's independence by permitting so many Indians into the country and by continuing to eschew diplomatic relations with third countries. These statements and interviews were roundly condemned in the Indian press, so the Indians must have taken them seriously. There may be some grounds to the report, then, that in 1974 the Indian Foreign Minister tried to prevent the fourth Druk Gyalpo, Jigme Singye Wangchuk, from inviting some of the exiles to return from Nepal for a reconciliation of the Dorji and royal families.[38] If the story is accurate, it still provides the exception rather than the rule. Despite India's paramount economic, bureaucratic and military-advisory position in Bhutan, it generally abstained from meddling in Bhutan's domestic politics. Nor is there evidence that India exploited Bhutan's vulnerability to extort personnel or policy changes from an unwilling Druk Gyalpo. This is not to deny the 'anticipated reaction' phenomenon, where the royal government may have avoided certain policies or actions, particularly in relation to third countries, fearing Indian displeasure and possible retaliation. On the whole, however, India's general discretion was certainly not typical of relationships of asymmetrical dependence and penetration. On the contrary, the power of the weak is demonstrated in the Druk Gyalpo's imposition of strict limitations on Indian activities in Bhutan, limitations which occasionally were highly irritating to authorities in New Delhi.

For example, the royal government allowed free access on the new roads only to official cars from India, prohibited Indian taxi services and required all foreign vehicles to obtain special entry permits. It was difficult to obtain one except for reasons of official business.[39] Entry into Bhutan by other means was impossible, so aside from the Indians who were in the country under government-to-government agreements, very few visitors travelled in the country. The number of foreign tourists was considerably greater than pre-1961, but it was still restricted to a few hundred per year, always in group tours with official supervision.

Bhutan also prohibited any form of private investment – from India or elsewhere.[40] Here again, Bhutan's strict control over its resources diverged from traditional colonial or neo-colonial situations. And finally, the Druk Gyalpo consistently refused to allow (officially) the Indians to station troops on Bhutan's territory. Jigme Dorji Wanchuk probably adhered to this policy to avoid annoying the Chinese, who may have wondered about India's intentions in building a military presence in Bhutan. But fear of a negative impact on Bhutan's society by the activities of numerous Indian soldiers may have been a factor as well.

The Pattern of Externally Directed Actions

Declaratory policy by the Druk Gyalpo and Jigme Dorji strongly affirmed Bhutan's close links with India. In their numerous visits to New Delhi and their occasional press conferences, they underlined the view that Bhutan's prospects were dependent upon maintaining close friendly relations with the southern mentor. Relations with other states – a matter of some controversy between Thimphu and New Delhi – were seldom discussed publicly.[41]

As with policy statements, Bhutan's externally directed actions were focused heavily toward India. This can be demonstrated in many ways. While there was no dramatic growth in the number of official visits to India by high-level Bhutanese from 1960 to 1970, it must be remembered that there were virtually none before 1959. In the 1960s there was at least one such visit each year, and in 1969 there were four visits. During this same period neither the Druk Gyalpo nor the Prime Minister visited any other country in an official capacity. Prior to 1959, there was only one treaty between India and Bhutan. By the early 1970s India and Bhutan had signed treaties covering hydroelectric projects, extradition, postal services, exchange of parcels and construction of a cement plant. Bhutan had no bilateral treaties with other states.

The royal government entered the world of institutionalized diplomacy cautiously and slowly. Despite the growing web of relationships with India, Bhutan did not send an official representative with ambassadorial rank to New Delhi until 1972, although there had been an exchange of 'representatives' before then.[42] It is significant, perhaps, that with India's sponsorship Bhutan joined the United Nations and established a mission in New York (1971) before it was willing to send an ambassador to New Delhi.

Despite the lack of a Bhutanese embassy in India until 1972, the royal government consistently supported India's foreign policies. The support may have been somewhat muted in the case of Indo-Chinese relations – it was more a policy of non-involvement except where Bhutan's direct interests were at stake – but in relation to Pakistan, India could count on sympathy from Thimphu. Bhutan was among the first nations to recognize Bangladesh independence and in the United Nations General Assembly Bhutan's and India's votes were almost identical, as Table 2.2 reveals. The Druk Gyalpo predicted such supportive diplomacy in 1971, but insisted that Bhutan's voting positions would be based on similarity of perspectives on international issues rather than on any compulsion from India.[43]

Bhutan's diplomacy throughout the 1960s was thus basically concerned with bilateral relations with India. On the surface, these relations appeared satisfactory to both parties: the Indians obtained certain strategic advantages vis-à-vis China by building up a quasi-ally in the Himalayas, and successfully countered Chinese claims to Bhutanese territory. Bhutan, for its part, obtained unofficial defense guarantees from India, the wherewithall to produce an armed force with at least limited border-protecting capabilities, and the resources necessary to launch economic, social and

Table 2.2   *Bhutan and India General Assembly Votes, 1971–5: Indices of Agreement*

Year	Agreement on Yes and No votes	Agreement on Yes, No and Abstain	Agreement on Yes and No, where Abstain = No
1971	1·0000	·9863	·9063
1972	·9855	·8718	·8718
1973	1·0000	·9552	·9552
1974		No General Assembly voting	
1975	1·0000	·9565	·9710

governmental modernization programs. Bhutan's extensive penetration by Indian officials had certain strict limitations, and there was little evidence of overt Indian interference in Bhutan's internal politics. Bhutan's extreme vulnerability to India after 1962 was certainly felt, and prompted the royal government to emphasize increased self-sufficiency as a policy goal for the 1970s. But Bhutan's restiveness with its overly narrow range of diplomatic relations caused more conflict with New Delhi than did vulnerability or penetration. The question of Bhutan's right to establish relations with third countries was critical because it touched upon the fundamentals of sovereignty, independence and international personality. The Bhutanese may also have believed that penetration, though not dependence, would be a transitory phenomenon and one that could be controlled so as to minimize negative consequences on Bhutan's domestic politics and social life. If, however, India did not admit Bhutan's right to establish relations with third parties, Bhutan would never be regarded by the international community as more than an Indian protectorate.

Bhutan's Dilatory Search for Diversity

Despite an early outbreak of enthusiasm for diversifying diplomatic relations in the early 1960s, the Druk Gyalpo did not really wish to establish diplomatic relations with third countries if that meant that Thimphu would become the home of numerous foreign embassies. The critical requirement was to obtain international recognition of Bhutan's sovereignty and independence and that could be achieved only by extending the royal government's diplomatic activities beyond New Delhi. The issue arose initially over differing interpretations of the 1949 treaty in which Bhutan agreed to be guided by India in its foreign relations. As early as 1959, an official stated at a press conference that Bhutan planned to establish diplomatic relations with foreign countries. Prime Minister Nehru immediately wrote the Druk Gyalpo advising against such a move.[44] The Indians interpreted the 1949 treaty to mean that India's advice or guidance was binding on Bhutan. For their part, the Bhutanese reserved the right to accept or reject that advice. In Jigme Dorji's words, 'Bhutan agrees to be guided by the advice of India in matters of her external affairs, but Bhutan, if she so desires, can conduct her own external relations.'[45] This included the right to receive foreign aid from sources other than India.[46] While no open conflict ensued from these and similar statements, the evidence suggests that the Bhutanese were gravely concerned about establishing their international identity. The Indians, on the other hand, were extremely reluctant to see Bhutan exchange diplomatic representation with other countries, or even to accept aid from other sources, on the grounds that the foreigners would meddle in Bhutan's politics and that the country would become a center of international intrigue. Moreover, it is not entirely certain that India itself was prepared to deal with Bhutan as an independent state, with a status fundamentally different from its Himalayan protectorate, Sikkim. Indian maps of the region, for example, showed until the early 1970s only an administrative border between India and Bhutan, not an international frontier.

Indian pressures on Bhutan (see below), combined with the royal government's own misgivings about having diplomats from other countries in Thimphu, somewhat reduced the vigor of a drive to diversify external contacts after some initial efforts were made in the early post-isolation period. It was rumored, for example, that in 1959 or 1960 Bhutanese agents approached two Western powers to broach the subject of establishing diplomatic relations. On hearing of these overtures, the Indian authorities informed the two governments in question that any positive action on their part would be considered an unfriendly act against India.[47] Subsequent statements with regard to diversifying relations were met with polite Indian suggestions that Bhutan did not yet have the financial resources to establish diplomatic missions abroad.

One way out of the impasse was to seek Indian approval for joining international organizations. Jigme Dorji placed considerable pressure on Nehru to sponsor Bhutan's admission to the Colombo Plan. The Indians agreed, and in 1961 the Prime Minister's sister, Tashi Dorji, headed Bhutan's first official delegation to an international gathering. This is not to say that after 1961 Bhutan began to receive aid from sources other than India. Indeed, while in exile in Nepal in 1965, Tashi accused the Indians of pressuring other Colombo Plan members not to offer aid on the grounds that Bhutan's economy could not absorb it. According to her, Bhutan's membership in the organization had 'become useless'.[48] Whether or not there was substance to her charges is unknown; but aside from India, Bhutan received only very small amounts of aid from Switzerland, Australia and New Zealand throughout the 1960s. However, membership in the Colombo Plan was not sought solely to obtain aid funds and technical assistance. The primary purpose of Dorji's initiative had been more political than economic, namely, gaining Bhutan's exposure to sources of information other than Indian, and recognition of the sovereignty and independence of Bhutan by the outside world.[49]

Later in the decade, India sponsored Bhutan's membership in the Universal Postal Union. The ultimate step – admission to the United Nations – remained several years away. As early as 1965, the Druk Gyalpo had broached the subject while on an official visit to New Delhi. Prime Minister Shastri reportedly advised him to shelve the issue for another fifteen years until Bhutan became more self-sufficient.[50] In the summer of 1966, the king announced that his country was not yet ready to assume the responsibilities and obligations of UN membership; the costs of maintaining a mission in New York were also mentioned as an inhibiting factor. Finally in 1968, the Druk Gyalpo received a written promise from Indira Gandhi that India would sponsor Bhutan's membership to the world organization.

Bhutan joined the United Nations in 1971. Its status as a sovereign state was now beyond dispute. But bilateral relations with others came very slowly indeed. In part, financial limitations continued to inhibit the expansion of diplomatic contacts abroad, but perhaps equally important, along with India's views on the matter, were old isolationist attitudes, the fear of foreign intrusion into a society and a political system that were already troubled with the presence of so many Indians. Two years before his death in 1972, the Druk Gyalpo revealed these fears when justifying his cautious approach to extending diplomatic relations beyond India and the three international organizations. 'We have to go slowly about it. We know the fate of countries that opened up too quickly and exposed themselves to foreign conspiracies.'[51] By the late 1970s, Bhutan had established diplomatic relations (but not exchanged ambassadors) with only one more nation, Bangladesh.

With UN and Colombo Plan membership, Bhutan had achieved its objective of securing international recognition of its sovereignty and independence. But the pattern of external relations remained focused on India. Bhutan's foreign policy was almost synonymous with its Indian policy. The attempts to diversify external contacts had led to membership in three international organizations, but that membership involved primarily a learning role. Bhutan was not yet an international actor in the sense that its foreign policy initiatives (if any) influenced the policies of states beyond India. Thus, while the level of Bhutan-Indian activity grew dramatically in the 1960s, it was not accompanied by a parallel development of Bhutan's relations in other areas of the world. This profile strongly resembles those of classical colonies and dependencies: not only are they extensively penetrated by a single hegemon (though in Bhutan's case, with the important exceptions noted previously), but their externally directed activities find very few outlets aside from the capital of the mentor power. India was the model of emulation; it was the source of funds, government personnel, defense assistance and communications. Like the thousands of African and Asian intellectuals who flocked to London and Paris to learn 'Western' ways, similarly Bhutanese students went abroad to India. At home, the school curricula, the organization of Bhutan's military forces and academy, and bureaucratic procedures were all patterned on the Indian example. Bhutan thus had many of the characteristics of the classical dependency; but in important respects it also diverged. The Druk Gyalpo never lost control of his policy-making authority – which included the right to restrict the amounts and types of Indian presence in the country. If Bhutan's medieval society was going to be modernized – a process launched by the king in the early 1950s – it would be on Bhutan's terms and not those of India. The Indians operated in an atmosphere of intense Bhutanese nationalism or patriotism, a phenomenon not frequently found in the areas colonized by Europeans in the late nineteenth century. Nevertheless, Bhutan abandoned its long successful isolationist policy and accepted a degree of dependence and penetration seldom found today even in the communist bloc. What factors help explain the dramatic restructuring of Bhutan's foreign policy orientation and actions?

Explanations

The five critical decisions were not taken simultaneously, nor was the complex environment in which Bhutan found itself in the late 1950s and early 1960s unchanging. Each of the decisions was conditioned by somewhat different external and domestic circumstances. However, for purposes of analysis, we shall consider the decisions as belonging to the same 'bundle'. Even though the policies or strategies changed somewhat over time, the major objectives of security and modernization remained fixed. The foreign policy reorientation took place between 1958 and 1959, while the restructuring of actions and transactions continued on for several years into patterns that were well established by the mid-1960s.

There are two external and one domestic explanatory variables, as well as the intervening, or decision-making, variables: (1) China's policies and actions in Tibet and on Bhutan's border from 1959 until the Indo-Chinese war of 1962; (2) India's strategic concerns in the Himalayan region and its proposals to Bhutan to 'open up' to Indian influence; (3) the attitudes and opinions of key elites in Bhutan; and (4) the perceptions, socialization, attitudes and political aspirations of the actual policy-makers, the Druk Gyalpo and Jigme Dorji.

The decisions to allow India to build the road into the heart of Bhutan, to end trade with Tibet and to seek Indian military assistance can be traced directly – and primarily – to Chinese actions in Tibet starting with the Tibetan revolt against communist rule in the spring of 1959. The suppression of the rebellion had a particularly telling impact in Bhutan, not only because the country had to accept an inflow of several thousand Tibetan refugees, but also because the Chinese policies had been directed against Buddhist institutions and practices. A society such as Bhutan's, which was permeated with religion in daily life, could not fail to respond strongly to the blatantly sacrilegious actions of the Chinese authorities.[52] By the autumn of 1959 the Chinese began to pose a more direct security threat to Bhutan. No matter how sympathetic the Bhutanese may have felt toward their Tibetan coreligionists, so long as Chinese activities remained confined to Tibet there was no *necessary* reason to abandon isolationism. But in September the Chinese began paying Bhutanese rice traders with worthless paper money and sending some back laden with revolutionary propaganda; the lamas of Bhutan were no longer admitted to Tibet to study at Buddhist institutions; and the Chinese sealed off the Chumbi Valley between Sikkim and Bhutan, thus cutting off the most important route into Bhutan from India.[53] Although Bhutan voluntarily withdrew its trade representative from Lhasa, Jigme Dorji made it clear in an interview that the decision to break off contacts with Tibet (and by implication the necessity of expanding relations with India) was occasioned by the Chinese actions.[54] By early 1960 China began to lay claims to Bhutanese territory and to boast in its internal propaganda that it would liberate the country from its feudal government. These activities were backed up by more concrete measures that led the Druk Gyalpo and Jigme Dorji to seek formal Indian military backing. The Chinese built roads from Tibet right to the Bhutan border and their forces occupied eight frontier hamlets populated by Bhutanese.[55] Under such circumstances, it was clear that neither the old isolationist policy nor Bhutan's primitive armed forces could protect the country's frontiers should the Chinese choose to press their claims by military means. The Tibetan revolt and subsequent menacing Chinese gestures against Bhutan could thus be considered as sufficient conditions to explain the reversal of Bhutan's foreign policy orientation. There seemed to be few alternatives: either turn to India or attempt to appease the Chinese. Given the unpopularity of Chinese actions in Tibet, it is unlikely that the latter option was ever considered seriously. There is some possibility that Bhutan would have 'opened up' for other reasons, as will be suggested below, but certainly the rapidity of change and the extent of dependence on India would not have occurred in the absence of China's activities in Tibet and toward Bhutan.

What of India's role? The evidence suggests that prior to 1958, while the Indians fully appreciated Bhutan's strategic importance,[56] they were cautious in extending a meaningful military guarantee to Bhutan; there is little evidence, furthermore, of strenuous Indian pressures on Bhutan to 'open up' to Indian influences.

By 1958 the Indian government was already beginning to display nervousness about Chinese designs in the Himalayas. Nehru had been originally invited by the communists to visit Lhasa, but the Chinese withdrew the invitation several months before his scheduled departure. Nehru decided to make the Bhutan part of the trip anyway, and his six-day venture on pony and yak underlined to him how utterly remote Bhutan was. If there was relatively easy access to Bhutan from Tibet, while the small country was virtually inaccessible to Indians, China could establish itself easily on the south slope of the Himalayas thus breaching the Himalayan buffer zone that separated the two powers. Nehru's offer in Paro to build roads into Bhutan thus must have been motivated primarily from strategic considerations. Yet Nehru was very sensitive to Bhutan's isolationist tradition, and he personally advised the king not to open up the country to foreigners, not even to Indians. He sought to reassure Bhutanese officials that India wanted the kingdom to develop according to its own priorities, and to treat it as an independent state. He also acknowledged that Bhutan had rejected all his offers of assistance – for the simple reason that the Bhutanese feared foreigners.[57] The way to help Bhutan, then, would be to have Bhutanese come to India rather than send Indians to Bhutan. This strategy coincided with the royal government's desire to achieve security and the beginnings of modernization with the least amount of foreign intrusion.

The events in Tibet in 1959, combined with Chinese territorial claims against Bhutan, made this approach obsolete. In September, Jigme Dorji went to New Delhi to seek a formal commitment of Indian military assistance. Nehru had already announced in the Lok Sabha that a Chinese military attack on Bhutan would be considered an attack on India. But this statement could not have been taken very seriously in Paro. There was little India could do to help defend Bhutan in the absence of any access to the country. A parachute operation would be the only possibility and it would probably be insufficient for coping with anything more significant than limited Chinese border probes. Moreover, under the 1949 treaty India was in no way committed to the defense of Bhutan. Hence the royal government was caught in a bind: it wanted defense assistance, but it did not wish to give the impression that India had any particular rights or responsibilities for defense under the treaty. To accept Nehru's declaratory policy might have compromised Bhutan's status as a sovereign state. Hence, the Druk Gyalpo had to point out publicly that his country was not an Indian protectorate and that there was no reference in the 1949 treaty to a defense commitment.[58] But this comment was issued apparently for publicity only. Dorji in fact did ask the Indians to conclude a military treaty, which the Indians refused to do.[59] They did agree, however, to build the road into Bhutan (work started in January 1960 under the direction of Indian army engineers); military assistance in the form of training and supply of weapons commenced soon after.

As Indo-Chinese relations deteriorated in succeeding months, the Indians began to request the royal government to allow Indian troops to be stationed in its territory. Apparently the Druk Gyalpo did not feel obligated to help protect the mentor's security interests – a common characteristic of small partners in alliances; he wanted assistance to help cope with Bhutan's security problem while remaining uninvolved in the larger Indo-Chinese conflict. He did not believe, by 1961, that Indian troops were needed to cope with the direct threat to Bhutan. By 1962, the Indians were reportedly irritated at Bhutan's persistent refusal to allow Indian troops into the country for reasons other than the training and equipping of Bhutan's army.[60]

While Nehru initially broached the subject of building a road into Bhutan, it is clear that the Druk Gyalpo and Jigme Dorji did not accept the proposal until the Tibetan revolt and the publication of vague Chinese threats of 'liberation' and claims to rectify the Tibet–Bhutan boundary. India's strategic interests required access to Bhutan, but had there been no apparent Chinese threat to Bhutan itself, it is unlikely that the royal government would have even requested the Indians to conclude a military agreement and send a large military training team to organize Bhutan's armed forces. Indian policy and diplomacy cannot, therefore, have been important factors in the key decisions except in the sense that the Indians offered the capabilities to help achieve the security objectives.

The decisions to accept Indian economic aid offers, which involved a significant component of Indian advisers and officials working side-by-side with Bhutanese, can be understood primarily as a recognition by the royal government that the initial strategy of sending Bhutanese to India for education in administration was inadequate to bring about economic and governmental modernization. By 1961 or 1962 it was clear that Bhutan did not possess the human capabilities required to bring about meaningful economic reforms and growth of educational and governmental services. Indian penetration was therefore accepted as a necessary price – but always with the recognition that ultimately Bhutan would achieve a high degree of bureaucratic and educational self-sufficiency. This aspect of foreign policy restructuring was, from the beginning, deemed to be a temporary necessity and not a permanent state of affairs.

The inputs of various domestic political groups and figures are not critical in understanding the decisions to reorient and restructure Bhutan's foreign policy. The five key decisions were made by the Druk Gyalpo and the Prime Minister. The Tshogdu (advisory council of notables) at this time neither initiated policy nor criticized royal decisions – habits that the king himself was trying to change. The Tshogdu later formally supported the modernization policy and all that it implied in terms of relations with India;[61] its role was to legitimize, not to propose.

At the time of Jigme Dorji's assassination in 1964, however, press reports strongly emphasized the opposition of conservative political elements to the Prime Minister's emphasis on modernization.[62] There were officials, of course, who felt threatened by the growing dependence on India, the rising influence of a foreign-educated bureaucratic and officers corps, and the presence of Indians in Bhutan.[63] Almost by definition, secular modernization threatens the leaders of traditional institutions and Bhutan seems to have been no exception. However, there is little evidence that organized opposition existed at the time the decisions were made. The influence of the conservatives was more indirect: the Druk Gyalpo must have been aware of the sensitivities of key elites in the country and tailored the policies as much as possible to obtain their support in the post-decision stage. This is not to suggest that the Druk Gyalpo would have acted otherwise had he complete freedom of choice, because he himself saw the Indian presence and the 'opening up' of Bhutan to the outside world more as a necessity than as a desirable state of affairs (see below).

The socialization, attitudes and perceptions of the two key policy-makers, the Druk Gyalpo and Jigme Dorji, are thus critical factors in understanding Bhutan's foreign policy reorientation and restructuring. Decision-making theories and studies of policy outputs as the result of complex bureaucratic struggles may be appropriate for the analysis of policy in some modern states, but they are of little relevance to the Bhutanese case. At the same time the key decisions were made, policy in Bhutan was initiated solely by the king, with the advice of a few key officials.[64] The king's position in initiating policy was never challenged.

Jigme Dorji Wangchuk was the third Druk Gyalpo (1952–72) of the hereditary monarchy established in Bhutan in 1907. Unlike his two predecessors who were primarily concerned with creating a centralized political system in the country, Jigme Dorji Wangchuk's main energies were devoted to social and political reform.[65] The Druk Gyalpo was educated primarily in Bhutan, but studied shortly in India during the height of the nationalist movement there. In 1950 he spent six months in Europe, mostly in Scotland and England.[66] Unlike the vast majority of his countrymen, he was familiar with some aspects of the modern world. During the first seven years of his reign, he instituted a number of reforms which ended some of the more important feudal characteristics of the country. He abolished serfdom and polyandry, and restricted land ownership (including his own) to 30 acres. Among the political reforms were reorganization of the administration and army, and the establishment of the Tshogdu.[67] It must be emphasized that the Druk Gyalpo personally launched these reforms; he was not acting as a result of domestic pressures for change.

Aware of the outside world and possessing a pragmatic and innovative mind, it is not surprising that the Druk Gyalpo eventually came to appreciate that economic and educational modernization would require some limited forms of contact with societies other than that of Tibet. His nationalism (perhaps unique among leaders emerging from isolationism) and training in Bhutan help explain his strong reluctance to open up the society to foreign influences. His initial choice to send Bhutanese abroad for training rather than inviting in foreigners can be understood as reflecting a strong conviction that the best social and religious traditions of the society could be threatened by waves of foreign advisers, military officials and tourists. Thus, the key decisions to end isolation were never taken with full confidence.

The absence of interview material makes it difficult to reconstruct in detail the Druk Gyalpo's perceptions of the external environment in 1959 or thereafter. Rose[68] suggests that the royal government regarded China's claims to Tibet as spurious and at least considered the possibility that Bhutan would eventually suffer the same fate as the country north of the Himalayas. But later it appears that he became more concerned with the possibility of Chinese subversion than with an outright military invasion. This may help explain his refusal to allow (at least publicly) the Indians to station combat units in the country.[69] At a minimum, the king separated the problems he faced with China from the more general Indo-Chinese conflict.

Jigme Dorji was the most influential member of one of Bhutan's most important families. Unlike the Druk Gyalpo, Dorji, who was ten years senior to the king, lived a good portion of his earlier life in Kalimpong, the home of many progressive missionary schools.[70] He was educated in Darjeeling and Simla and travelled extensively, including the United States. His prime diversion was a stable of race-horses he maintained in Calcutta. Even in the early years as the Druk Gyalpo's main adviser, he spent most of his time in Kalimpong rather than in Paro or Thimphu. Already by 1956 he was convinced that in order to survive as an independent political entity, Bhutan would have to modernize drastically – and that would involve establishing extensive contacts with the outside world.[71] If the Druk Gyalpo held strong reservations about abandoning isolationism, Jigme Dorji did not appear to share them.

Given Dorji's background, we can speculate that he had a strong affinity for the Indians, and in the 1959–61 period perceived the Chinese as posing a serious threat to Bhutan's continued independence. But was he so influential? According to some reports, he strongly argued in favor of opening up extensive ties with India, and he, rather than the king, made the initial decision to seal off the border with Tibet and to try to redirect Bhutan's trade toward India.[72] At a minimum, then, Dorji actively urged the Druk Gyalpo to take the road to reform and to establish contacts with the outside world; and in a few instances Dorji took decisions on his own authority.[73]

Two members of the king's immediate family should also be mentioned. The queen, Ashi Kesang-la, was Jigme Dorji's sister and, by Bhutanese standards, a 'modern' woman. She attended Oxford, the first student from Bhutan to study in England.[74] Although her name was not publicly connected with policy-making, it is possible that she was supportive of the king's decisions by virtue of her exposure to the outside world. The Druk Gyalpo's mistress (the 'second queen') was never mentioned in the press until 1974 when she was named in an anti-government plot. A Tibetan, she became the royal mistress in 1961 and bore the king four children. According to Rose, she was influential in court politics, and members of her family helped organize the assassination of Jigme Dorji in 1964.[75] Yet there is no publicly recorded evidence of her role, if any, in advising on foreign policy matters. Because of her Tibetan origins we can assume that she had an interest in developments in her homeland, but there is no way to link such interests with the five key decisions identified in this chapter.

If we attempt to rank the relative importance of the independent and decision-making variables which account for the reorientation and restructuring of Bhutan's foreign policy, China's actions in Tibet and on the Bhutanese border, as well as its propaganda and territorial claims, must rank first.[76] Without the roads, the claims, the worthless paper currency paid for Bhutanese rice and the brutal suppression of the Tibetans' revolt, it is unlikely that the Druk Gyalpo would have agreed to become so dependent upon India and open the country to an influx of Indian advisers. By 1958 the days of Bhutan's isolation were probably coming to a close, but if there was to be change it would be gradual, pragmatic and designed to keep the country sealed off from most outside influences. Neither Nehru nor the Druk Gyalpo had initial visions of a dramatic transformation; the former was very impressed by the stability and tranquility (and lack of poverty) of Bhutanese society, urged Jigme Wangchuk to go slow, and was obviously sympathetic with attempts to maintain Bhutan relatively free of foreign personnel. The latter was committed to modernization and reform, but not at any price, including extreme dependence upon any single foreign power. But the Himalayan events of 1959 rendered the initial strategy ineffective.

The key decision-makers' perceptions, attitudes and aspirations must come next in importance. Although there is no quoted evidence, Jigme Dorji must have perceived the Chinese activities as an acute threat to Bhutan's continued independence. It is unlikely that he would have sought Indian military support and all that it implied had he estimated that China's intentions involved nothing more than some minor frontier rectifications in its favor. Moreover, Dorji strongly supported Bhutan's alignment with India[77] and appeared to harbor few of the fears of the Druk Gyalpo in regard to opening up the country. Although coming from one of the leading political families in Bhutan, he did not share the training, education and socialization processes of the king. While he may have respected the role of Lamaism and the monarchy, he was no conservative romantic. By the mid-1950s he argued that the isolationist orientation could no longer offer protection to the country. If Bhutan wished to maintain its independence, it would have to obtain international recognition, and such recognition would not be forthcoming unless Bhutan became a full actor in the international system. This would require diplomats, membership in international organizations, a foreign ministry, communications with the outside world and the opening up of the country. Dorji was the Druk Gyalpo's key adviser and, from all accounts, he was very influential in molding the king's views on some issues. It is conceivable that without his advice, the Druk Gyalpo might have been substantially more reluctant to abandon isolationism.

The Druk Gyalpo's perceptions of the Chinese activities were also critical in the key decisions. In 1958 he rejected Nehru's offers; in 1959 he sought both military and economic assistance. His initial strategy for modernization was to send Bhutanese to India for training. By 1961 the Indians had come to Bhutan for the same purposes. The events of 1959 had thus forced him to compromise seriously his original plan of ending isolation very slowly and keeping the country generally free of foreign penetration. His turn to India seems consistent with his background: his travels there and in Europe must have impressed him that a form of parliamentary democracy rather than communism should be the model for Bhutan. Even if he had ever considered a policy of balanced relations between north and south, Chinese actions in Tibet and toward Bhutan certainly reduced his options.[78] But in any event, India's worsening relations with China and its insistence on 'guiding' Bhutan in its foreign relations acted as external constraints that would have precluded alternatives other than aligning with India.

India's actions and policies would rank next in importance. As indicated, despite offers of aid India did not place pressure on Bhutan fundamentally to alter its isolation; Nehru had made it clear in Paro that the Bhutanese should themselves decide which course they would follow. On his return from the visit in 1958, Nehru certainly did not foresee any dramatic change in Bhutan's external orientation. By 1959, however, India began to establish explicit and implicit 'guidelines' which the Bhutanese were expected to follow in their external relations. The Indians acted to prevent Bhutan from turning to other possible sources of assistance and generally advised Bhutan not to extend diplomatic relations to other countries. Every effort the Bhutanese made to establish formal contacts outside of those sanctioned in Delhi were effectively scuttled by the Indians. Indian policies, then, did not explain the end of isolationism (except in the sense that after the offers were made, the royal government knew it could rely on the Indians for assistance), but only the particular form that the new relationship of dependence was going to take. Their importance lies in defining the *post-decision* profile of transactions and orientation of Bhutan.

Finally, domestic political conditions do not loom important in explaining Bhutan's reorientation. The important political figures of the kingdom

generally supported the main lines of the new orientation, understood the
reasons for abandoning isolation and acted primarily as a factor reminding
the Druk Gyalpo that Bhutan's independence could be compromised if too
many Indians appeared in the country and if Bhutan failed to establish
diplomatic relations with international organizations or third countries.
However, the strictly limited forms of penetration (see below) in the
dependence relationship, rather than the reorientation decisions, can be
attributed at least in part to the influence of Tshogdu members and other
officials.

We can summarize the analysis to this point. Chinese policies in Tibet
and toward Bhutan were perceived by two key decision-makers as posing
serious threats to Bhutan's independence and security. Those policy-
makers already were predisposed to end Bhutan's traditional isolationist
foreign policy orientation, but they had planned to follow a strategy of
sending Bhutanese abroad and cautiously opening up the country to
foreigners. The Chinese actions prompted them to turn to India for assistance. This constituted reorientation. The subsequent actions, commitments
and transactions constituted a pattern characterized by pronounced external
dependence and vulnerability, and of internal penetration by the mentor
state.

But the emerging pattern of relations resembled the classical dependency
only in terms of externally directed actions. Bhutan became a penetrated
state as well, but only up to a point. The Druk Gyalpo, supported by
members of the Tshogdu, developed some strict regulations concerning the
extent and types of penetration that are not found in most colonial or
neo-colonial relationships. They included the prohibition against stationing of Indian troops in Bhutan; strict regulations against foreigners travelling in the country (including Indians); prohibitions against private
foreign investment; discouragement of tourism; restrictive regulations concerning research by foreign academics; and uneasiness about establishing
diplomatic relations with other nations. Some of these restrictions can be
explained by lack of capabilities: the Bhutanese did not have and probably
could not afford the amenities most tourists demand, for example. Others
can be explained by India's sensitivity about foreign activity in Bhutan.[79]
More fundamental, however, were the Druk Gyalpo's and numerous
high-level officials' attitudes toward modernization and foreign presence
in the country. As mentioned, the set of attitudes and fears that had
sustained the isolationist orientation for decades did not die out overnight,
not even with the changing military situation in the Himalayas. Unlike the
other forms of foreign policy restructuring and reorientation described in
this volume, the changes undertaken by Bhutan were effectively irrevoc-
able. A policy of diversification or switching dependences need not result
in fundamental social change. Suddenly to open up a country to foreign
influences, to introduce literacy, to import foreign goods never seen
before, to create international awareness of one's existence and to invite in
thousands of foreign advisers involves not only opportunities but great risks
as well. Unlike most of the non-aligned countries in the post-colonial
period, Bhutan had no previous contact with Western ideas, institutions
and economic practices. Little wonder, then, that the Druk Gyalpo was

unhappy with having to make the key decisions to abandon isolationism. The restrictions must be seen as efforts to regulate the pace of change and to try to minimize the negative consequences of modernization. The royal government appears to have accepted the necessity of external economic and military dependence, and a certain amount of cultural penetration. While the educational system was being formed on the Indian model the government made efforts to invigorate and support Bhutanese traditions, including language and literature. According to Travis[80] cultural dependence exists where emulation of the mentor's social habits takes place at the expense of maintaining indigenous cultural patterns. By supporting the positive elements of traditional Bhutanese society, the royal government at least attempted to avoid becoming a cultural dependant of India. But with transistor radios, Hindu films, books and magazines flooding into Bhutan, it may be a losing matter.

Unlike the leaders of many developing countries in the 1950s and 1960s, moreover, the Druk Gyalpo never assumed that industrialization would bring unqualified benefits, or that modernization would not extract some cost in the loss of traditional values. Even as late as 1973, Bhutan's Foreign Minister claimed that 'modernization exacts a high price. I'm not sure it's ideal, but we have no choice. In the modern world you can't live isolated . . . But there is going to be an effect on peoples' values and way of life.'[81] Members of the Tshogdu regularly reminded the king that the benefits of the Indians' largesse were undeniable, but strict care must be taken to preserve what was good in the culture.

In the 1970s, Bhutan's external contacts have slowly increased. Aid has been received directly from several United Nations programs, as well as from Switzerland and France.[82] Bhutan sent delegations to the conferences of non-aligned states in 1974, 1976 and 1979, and to United Nations conferences on housing and water. But in general the pattern of relations established in the 1960s remains largely unchanged: Bhutanese diplomacy means primarily diplomacy toward India. Bhutan's external concerns are characterized less by non-alignment than by non-involvement.[83] The isolationist tradition continues under different guises. Yet Bhutan meets most of the criteria of a dependant; in some respects, though, it is not typical of many developing countries that are more extensively involved in international politics, but also more highly penetrated. As Bhutanization policies are carried out, it may eventually become a more self-sufficient policy, one which will probably continue to remain aloof from regional and global political issues, and relatively inaccessible to most of the outside world. But if past trends continue, the reduction of dependence will not lead automatically to an orientation of extensive diversification combined with a full 'opening up' of the society. Rather, we could expect a foreign policy which uses selective exclusionist measures combined with just enough foreign contacts necessary to bring about modest and measured forms of modernization. If Bhutan is able to undergo the modernization process with fewer costly effects than most developing countries, with its social organization and best traditions still intact, its turn to dependence will have been justified.

Notes: Chapter 2

1 For descriptions of Nehru's trip and quotes from his speeches, see *The Hindu* (Delhi), 24, 27 September, 3 October 1958.
2 'Wangchuk finally took the risk of sending students to study in India, but only after long discussion.' George N. Patterson, *Peking versus Delhi* (London: Faber, 1963), p. 216.
3 Bhutan's early history and relations with Tibet are discussed in detail in Leo E. Rose, *The Politics of Bhutan* (Ithaca, NY: Cornell University Press, 1977), ch. 1.
4 Leo E. Rose, 'Sino-Indian rivalry and the Himalayan border states', *Orbis*, 5 (Summer 1961), p. 204.
5 Pradyuman P. Karan, *Bhutan: A Physical and Cultural Geography* (Lexington, Ky: University of Kentucky Press, 1967), p. 79; Patterson, *Peking versus Delhi*, p. 219.
6 Ram Rahul, *Modern Bhutan* (Delhi: Vikas Publications, 1972), pp. 51ff.
7 *New York Times*, 10 May, 1956, p. 38.
8 Desmond Doig, 'Bhutan builds army as Chinese threat grows', *Daily Telegraph*, 7 September 1959.
9 Patterson, *Peking versus Delhi*, p. 214.
10 In a speech to the National Assembly (Tshogdu) in 1971, the Druk Gyalpo claimed that his father had asked the British for aid numerous times and had been turned down. Portions of the speech are reproduced in Nagendra Singh, *Bhutan: A Kingdom in the Himalayas* (New Delhi: Thompson Press, 1972), pp. 121–2.
11 Desmond Doig, 'Bhutan builds army as Chinese threat grows', *Daily Telegraph*, 7 September 1959.
12 Werner Levi, 'Bhutan and Sikkim: two buffer states', *World Today*, 15 (December 1959), p. 496.
13 Charles H. Heimsath and Surjit Mansingh, *A Diplomatic History of Modern India* (Bombay: Allied Publishers, 1971), p. 220; Sudershan Chawla, *The Foreign Relations of India* (Encino, Calif.: Dickinson Publishing, 1976), p. 121.
14 *The Hindu* (Delhi), 15 October 1962.
15 Leo Rose states that the IMTT numbered about 250 men at its peak in the 1960s. Personal correspondence, 8 March 1978.
16 *Le Monde*, 26 January 1965.
17 Patrice DeBeer, 'Le Bhoutan sort du moyen age', *Le Monde*, 3 August 1974; Rose states, however, that no Indian division was stationed in Bhutan. There may have been occasions when part of an Indian division joined Bhutanese troops for maneuvers. Personal correspondence, 8 March 1978.
18 No official Bhutanese public texts discussed the extent of Indian supervision of Bhutan's development projects, but a statement by Foreign Minister Swaran Singh to the Lok Sabha in 1973 reveals the nature of the relationship: Bhutan's government have 'welcomed the valuable assistance rendered by the [Indian] Planning Commission in framing their five year plans and have accepted the Planning Commission's suggestions for annual review by the Commission of the progress of their plans'. See Satish Kamur (ed.), *Documents on India's Foreign Policy* (Delhi: Macmillan of India, 1976), p. 50. Rose points out, however, that the Indians were generous in allowing the Bhutanese to decide how aid funds would be used. The Indians provided lump-sum grants; the Bhutanese allocated the funds according to their own wishes. See *The Politics of Bhutan*, p. 92.
19 The Far East Economic Review, *Yearbook 1972* estimates total Indian aid for the three five-year plans at $93.9 million. *Countries of the World and their Leaders*, 2nd edn (Detroit: Gale Research, 1975) provides a figure of $180 million.
20 Patrice DeBeer, 'Le Bhoutan sort du moyen age', *Le Monde*, 3 August 1974.
21 ibid. Rose points out, however, that most of the Indians were employed in the Development and Education ministries. The other ministries and departments were mostly staffed by Bhutanese. Personal correspondence, 8 March 1978.
22 *The Hindu* (Delhi), 20 June 1968. By 1972, according to the Minister of Development – the king's daughter – there were 1,000 Indians assisting in administration of the country, and 400 Indian development experts. *Times of India*, 4 October 1972.
23 Far Eastern Economic Review, *Yearbook 1977*, p. 124.
24 Karan, *Bhutan: A Physical and Cultural Geography*, p. 79.
25 Far Eastern Economic Review, *Yearbook 1977*, p. 125.
26 *The Hindu* (Delhi), 15 May 1963.

27 Leo Rose, personal correspondence, 8 March 1978.
28 *The Guardian* (Manchester), 26 June 1974.
29 Far East Economic Review, *Yearbook 1977*, p. 125; Leo Rose, personal correspondence, 8 March 1978.
30 Rose, *The Politics of Bhutan*, pp. 136–7.
31 *Asia Magazine*, 18 August 1963, p. 6. In addition to the Indian teachers, there were a few from other countries, including Canadian Jesuit priests who ran a secondary school in Tashigang. In 1959, Jigme Dorji approached the English to send some teachers; apparently the British government turned down the request for fear of encroaching on India's 'sphere'. *New York Times*, 15 June 1960.
32 Rose, *The Politics of Bhutan*, p. 133.
33 By 1967, a few Bhutanese students were studying in England and other Commonwealth countries. *The Hindu* (Delhi), 28 April 1967.
34 For an account which plays down traditional inter-family rivalries in court politics (generally emphasized in the foreign press) and instead focuses on the role of the king's mistress and her father, see Rose, *The Politics of Bhutan*, pp. 115–24.
35 *Dawn* (Karachi), 19 April 1964. The article presents no evidence of the alert. Generally, Pakistani articles on Bhutan try to emphasize India's domination of the kingdom. The veracity of many of the articles is open to question.
36 *The Hindu* (Delhi), 28 November 1964; *The Times* (London), 2 August 1965.
37 *The Times* (London), 12 June 1974.
38 Daryl d'Monte, 'The day of the dragon', *Guardian* (Manchester), 26 June 1974. An Indian adviser was posted to Prime Minister Dorji's office, on Dorji's invitation. The official no doubt had some influence on Bhutan's domestic politics, but it is not documented. Indian aid officials were forbidden to involve themselves in the political relations between Bhutan and India. See Rose, *The Politics of Bhutan*, pp. 84–7.
39 *The Hindu* (Delhi), 30 May 1962.
40 This policy was amended later to allow a few joint ventures, but Bhutan insisted on maintaining majority control of all investments. Rose, *The Politics of Bhutan*, p. 140.
41 For example, on the occasion of an official visit to Thimphu by India's president in 1970, the Druk Gyalpo declared that his government and people 'will always look to India for guidance and inspiration as we consider our destiny intimately bound up with that of India'. Quoted in Far Eastern Economic Review, *Yearbook 1971*, p. 105.
42 Rose, *The Politics of Bhutan*, p. 88.
43 *The Hindu* (Delhi), 11 April 1971.
44 K. Krishna Murthy, 'Bhutan: thoughts on sovereignty', *Far Eastern Economic Review*, 31 (16 February 1962), p. 297.
45 Girja Kumar and V. K. Arora (eds), *Documents on Indian External Affairs* (Bombay: Asia Publishing House, 1965), p. 337.
46 *New York Times*, 13 June 1960.
47 *Far Eastern Economic Review*, 23 February 1961, p. 297.
48 *Dawn* (Karachi), 2 February 1965.
49 See the statement to this effect by Bhutan's Foreign Minister, Dago Tsering, quoted in Far East Economic Review, *Asia Yearbook 1977*, p. 123.
50 The Observer Foreign News Service, #22575, 26 April 1966. India's attitude toward the issue is revealed in a statement by Mrs Gandhi that 'Bhutan has already been *allowed* to participate in the International Postal Union' (*sic*). *The Hindu* (Delhi), 20 July 1966. My italics.
51 *The Hindu* (Delhi), 27 April 1970.
52 *The Christian Science Monitor*, 1 August 1960; *New York Times*, 13 June 1960.
53 'New roads to the modern world', *The Times* (London), 8 June 1960; *New York Times*, 24 August 1959.
54 *New York Times*, 24 August 1959.
55 Some sources argue that the Chinese made extensive territorial claims on Bhutan, and that Chinese maps depicted these areas, including the town of Punakha, as 'lost territories'. For discussions, see 'Remote Bhutan awakening to the twentieth century', *New York Times*, 13 June 1960; G. S. Bhargava, *The Battle of NEFA: The Undeclared War* (Bombay: Allied Publishers, 1964), p. 64; Karan, *Bhutan: A Physical and Cultural Geography*, p. 19; B. N. Malik, *My Years with Nehru: The Chinese Betrayal* (Bombay: Allied Publishers, 1971), pp. 212, 234; Rahul, *Modern Bhutan*, pp. 100–3. Rose argues that

post-1950s Chinese maps of the region traced Bhutan's boundaries only slightly differently from those in Indian maps. Personal correspondence, 8 March 1978.
56 Any map shows that a Chinese thrust from Tibet's Chumbi Valley to East Pakistan would have isolated all of Assam from the rest of India. Chinese occupation of Sikkim and Bhutan would offer protection to the invasion route.
57 According to Nehru, 'They maintain this kind of seclusion for a very laudable reason . . . because of their desire to maintain their freedom. They thought this might be imperilled if they were too anxious to invite people from outside . . . If I may say so, I advised them to prevent too many outsiders, even from India, coming in . . . ' *The Hindu* (Delhi), 14 October 1958.
58 Neville Maxwell, *India's China War* (London: Cape, 1970), pp. 115–16.
59 Karan, *Bhutan: A Physical and Cultural Geography*, p. 218; Rahul, *Modern Bhutan*, p. 60.
60 *The Hindu* (Delhi), 30 May 1962; Patterson, *Peking versus Delhi*, p. 219. There were, however, numerous Indian soldiers in Bhutan working on the roads. Some may have been engaged in activities other than road construction. Leo Rose, personal correspondence, 8 March 1978.
61 Rose, *The Politics of Bhutan*, ch. 4. Although members of the Tshogdu generally supported the outlines of the Druk Gyalpo's foreign policies, they insisted that Bhutan's traditions must be preserved (p. 164).
62 For example, *Daily Telegraph*, 5 May 1964.
63 Karan, *Bhutan: A Physical and Cultural Geography*, pp. 14–17.
64 Rose, *The Politics of Bhutan*, esp. ch. 4.
65 ibid., p. 151.
66 *The Times* (London), 9 June 1960.
67 Rose, *The Politics of Bhutan*, ch. 4; Rahul, *Modern Bhutan*, ch. 2. Land restrictions have not been observed rigorously.
68 ibid., p. 82.
69 However, there are Indians stationed at each of the border posts of the Bhutan–Tibet boundary. Leo Rose, personal correspondence, 8 March 1978.
70 *Daily Telegraph*, 4 December 1964.
71 *New York Times*, 10 May 1956.
72 Karan, *Bhutan: A Physical and Cultural Geography*, p. 13.
73 Rose, *The Politics of Bhutan*, p. 151.
74 Burt Kerr Todd, 'Bhutan, land of the thunder dragon', *National Geographic Magazine*, 102 (December 1956), pp. 713–54. Todd was a classmate of Ashi at Oxford, and the first American to visit Bhutan.
75 Rose, *The Politics of Bhutan*, pp. 120–2.
76 All accounts of Bhutan's emergence from isolation agree that Chinese policies in the Himalayas in 1959 were the critical factor. There is no way of assessing quantitatively the relative importance of the independent and intervening variables. The rankings are based on judgements deriving from the publicly available evidence.
77 Rose, *The Politics of Bhutan*, p. 86.
78 Rose writes that the royal government did consider a Nepal-like foreign policy of balance, which certain circles in Thimphu promoted, but rejected the option in favor of stronger alignment with India. ibid., p. 82.
79 Access to Bhutan was possible only by transit through Indian territory. Since India had declared the lands adjacent to Bhutan as special security zones, no foreigner could travel to Bhutan without first obtaining special permission from Indian authorities.
80 Tom Travis, 'Toward a comparative study of imperialism', paper presented to 16th Annual Meeting of the International Studies Association, Washington, DC, 1975.
81 *New York Times*, 11 December 1973. By 1973, some costs were already appearing: prostitution had developed in Thimphu and alcoholism was increasing at a rapid rate. Poverty will perhaps be the next residue of development, but generally Bhutan so far has avoided most of the worst effects of widening income gaps. Even many of the younger generation are committed to the preservation of some Bhutanese traditions. Nevertheless, according to one visitor, 'Indépendente ou non, le Bhoutan est en train de devenir un pays presque commes les autres.' Patrice DeBeer, 'Le Bhoutan sort du moyen age', *Le Monde*, 3 August 1974.
82 *New York Times*, 19 August 1976.
83 Rose, *The Politics of Bhutan*, p. 100.

3

From Dependence to Diversification: Tanzania, 1967–77

*Timothy M. Shaw and Ibrahim S. R. Msabaha**

> TANU is involved in a war against poverty and oppression in our country; this struggle is aimed at moving the people of Tanzania from a state of poverty to a state of prosperity. We have been oppressed a great deal, we have been exploited a great deal and we have been disregarded a great deal. It is our weakness that has led to our being oppressed, exploited and disregarded. We now intend to bring about a revolution which will ensure that we are never again victim of these things.
>
> Julius K. Nyerere, *The Arusha Declaration*, 1967 (p. 4)

> Ten years after the Arusha Declaration Tanzania is certainly neither socialist nor self-reliant. The nature of exploitation has changed, but it has not been altogether eliminated . . . our nation is still economically dependent upon the vagaries of the weather, and upon economic and political decisions taken by other peoples without our participation or consent. And this latter is not a reciprocal situation; Tanzania is still a dependent nation, not an interdependent one . . . Few other developing countries . . . are fully self-reliant. What matters is that in the last few years we in Tanzania have taken some very important steps towards our goal, despite adverse climatic and international conditions.
>
> Julius K. Nyerere, *The Arusha Declaration: Ten Years After*, 1977 (p. 1)

Tanzania's 'Arusha Declaration' of 1967 contained the assertion that 'Independence means self-reliance'.[1] This declaration was a critical and novel response to the disillusionment of the first six years of formal 'independence' from foreign rule, in which development remained elusive and autonomy was revealed to be a mirage. Ten years after, in 1977, in a symbolic return to the slopes of Mount Kilimanjaro, scene of the original declaration, President Nyerere admitted that self-reliance and socialism remain elusive goals: a decade is an insufficient period of time in which to build a new political economy in an unequal world system. And he warned that the process of realizing greater independence for Tanzania would be

*An earlier version of this essay was presented at the May 1979 Conference of the Canadian Association of African Studies in Winnipeg. Research assistance from Paul Goulding and critical but helpful comments from Kal Holsti and Arch Ritter are gratefully acknowledged.

both difficult and protracted:

> We cannot expect early reward from our work in the way of increased
> consumption – either of public or personal goods. We must be prepared
> to find our rewards for effort in increased national self-reliance and the
> maintenance of our independence of action. There is a time for planting
> and a time for harvesting. I am afraid for us it is still a time for planting.[2]

This essay examines the intentions and expectations behind the
'planting' and seeks to explain why the 'harvesting' has been rather late and
disappointing thus far for Tanzania. The first decade of Arusha is both a
convenient and appropriate period for analysis because Tanzania was different before 1967 and after 1977, both in terms of policy and in terms of
politics. At Arusha (t_1), the nation's leadership declared a new policy in
response to an inheritance of dependence and an unsatisfactory degree of
development since independence in 1961. At the end of the Arusha decade
(t_2), the incident and impact of subsequent changes in policy and behavior
were considered to be less than expected, as indicated in the second opening citation. And since 1977 many of the assumptions of the previous ten
years have been questioned and revised strategies have emerged.

While dealing with dependence and penetration has proved to be more
difficult than expected at t_1, at least by t_2 some results were apparent.
Without the touchstone of Arusha and the leadership of Julius K. Nyerere
and the Tanganyika African National Union (TANU), Tanzania today
would otherwise probably be considerably more dependent, unequal and
impoverished. As Dr Nyerere himself recognizes, Tanzania has at least
begun the long march toward self-reliance and socialism rather than
retreating into greater dependence and underdevelopment, a common
phenomenon throughout much of Africa:

> although our nation is by no means economically independent, we are
> not becoming more dependent on others as time goes on and develop-
> ment increases. As a result of our socialist policies, it is the people of
> this country – not foreigners – who determine what kind of factories and
> farms shall be established in Tanzania. This means that we can gradu-
> ally increase our control over the Tanzanian economy; we are not being
> bound tighter and tighter into an international capitalist structure which
> we can never hope to control, or even influence.[3]

Time One: the Elusiveness of Development and the Pervasiveness of Dependence

Tanzania lost its innocence between independence and Arusha.[4] But
rather than succumbing to international pressures and domestic demands
for *embourgeoisement*, it abandoned orthodox prescriptions of openness to
market forces and chose instead to turn towards self-reliance and socialism. Tanzania's loss of innocence involved both pragmatism, policy and

principle. Not only was Tanzania unlikely to develop through external aid, investment and technology; even if it did come to achieve such outward-oriented growth, it would not want the typical by-products of this type of strategy, such as domestic inequalities, increased urbanization, rural neglect, conspicuous consumption and social decay.[5]

At independence in 1961 Tanzania was a rather characteristic Third World political economy – highly dependent on external linkages and considerably handicapped by the impact of underdevelopment. Its incorporation within the global economy was based on unequal exchange between center and periphery in which raw materials were traded for manufactured goods and the surplus was accumulated in the center, not in the periphery. The economy of Tanzania had been heavily shaped by external forces.[6] Given the centrality of the economic component in any Third World political economy, this economic dependence meant penetration in several issue areas. Indeed, it is only in the political issue area – particularly within a narrow, legalistic definition of 'political' – that Tanzanian 'independence' had any real meaning in the early 1960s. And it was the obvious and growing gap between economic dependence and political independence that led up to the Arusha Declaration and President Nyerere's decisive statement.

Penetration was most apparent, then, in the *economic* areas of investment and exchange. At independence Tanzania was, at best, a branch-plant economy, and at worst, a primary product producer. Its few manufacturing installations were foreign owned and controlled, either by British interests directly, or via international or local companies in neighboring Kenya. But Tanzania represented a very small and poor market – its 12–13 million people had an average per capita income of only $100 by 1975 – so that multinationals in general were rather 'disinterested' in this territory, the periphery of the periphery. Nonetheless, for particular British and Kenyan interests Tanzania represented an important source of income and profit, and foreign investment in manufacturing averaged about 100 shs million per annum in the late 1960s.

Tanzania's economy was so structured that little capital was either saved or invested internally. Instead, Tanzania was related to the world economy in a number of ways:

(1) exports were characterized by concentration in a few commodities;
(2) dependence on the importation of both consumer and capital goods;
(3) dependence on foreign aid and technical assistance;
(4) dependence on foreign technology; and
(5) dependence on the multinational corporation.[7]

This dependence was not just an exclusively external phenomenon, as it was intrinsically related to 'domestic' institutions such as branch-plants, banks, plantations and entrepreneurs with their transnational linkages. Formal decolonization in 1961 did not by itself change this inheritance; indeed, the process of underdevelopment tended, if anything, to accelerate after independence because of the assertion of national class and regime interests without real control over the process of accumulation or the mode of production. The Arusha Declaration was a response, then, to both external dependence and internal underdevelopment. Nnoli characterizes this first post-colonial period – from independence to Arusha (t_1) – as follows:

> the initial phase was essentially an extension of the pattern of interaction with, and attitude toward, the external environment which prevailed during the colonial period. Its major features were (a) the dominance in the national economy of foreign ownership of the means of production, distribution and exchange; (b) the consequent foreign exploitation of indigenous resources; (c) various forms of socio-cultural and political dependence which sustained these ownership and exploitative relations; (d) the external orientation of the national economy; (e) the confinement of national participation in the international division of labour to primary production for export and the importation of manufactured goods; (f) confidence in the salutary nature of external conditions; (g) high hope of benefits from foreign relations; and (h) appeals to the humanitarian sentiments of the advanced countries, as the major means of international influence.[8]

The perpetuation and even intensification of dependence after independence was apparent not only in Tanzania's growing reliance on foreign aid and personnel, but also in its vulnerability to international diplomatic demands. The 'critical phase'[9] in Tanzania became more acute in the post-independence period because of the coincidence of internal inertia, external threats and increasing domestic demands.[10] The implications of Tanzania's inheritance of dependence became clearer as its attempts to widen its independence through practising nonalignment were challenged by those Western states that were simultaneously also its major benefactors. A series of difficulties with Britain, West Germany and the United States led to a re-evaluation of its traditional foreign policy.[11]

Tanzania's strained diplomatic relations with the Western powers not only cost scarce aid income and technical assistance in the short term; they also pointed to the longer imperative of restructuring the Tanzanian political economy both to reflect national interests and to enhance national power. They led to a fundamental reassessment of both development and foreign policies between 1965 and 1967 (t_1).

The immediate pre-Arusha period (t_1) involved, then, a reassessment of the degree and impact of external dependence and the policy options available to control or reduce it. This chapter consists of a description and explanation of Arusha, with an initial 'snapshot' taken during the period of high levels of dependence and vulnerability leading up to Arusha. T_2 consists of a portrait of the political economy a decade later (1975–7) and an attempt to explain the achievements and constraints of disengagement over the intervening decade. The Arusha Declaration was designed to minimize foreign penetration and maximize governmental control over transnational processes. The successes and failures between t_1 and t_2, analyzed further in the final section, are indicative of the prospects and problems confronting small weak states like Tanzania in shaking off some of the constraints of dependence and poverty.

The Arusha Declaration: the Imperatives of Disengagement and Diversification

The Arusha Declaration proposed several major structural changes in Tanzania's political economy.[12] First, it declared that TANU's policy is to build a socialist state, to maximize the rate and distribution of production: 'Tanzania is a state of peasants and workers, but it is not yet a socialist state. It still has elements of capitalism and feudalism and their temptations. These elements could expand and entrench themselves.'[13] Second, it advocated nationalization of the major means of production, whether they be locally or externally owned. Third, it insisted on relying on domestic resources for development rather than foreign aid or investment on the grounds that independence could not be real if a nation depended upon gifts and loans from others for its development.[14] Finally, Arusha advocated rural, agricultural development rather than urban, industrial growth. Together, these four factors add up to a declaration of self-reliance (an essentially 'external' aspect) as well as of socialism (an essentially 'internal' aspect).

1967 represented, then, an historic conjuncture, a second declaration of independence. As three Tanzanian economists have argued, from independence until Arusha:

> the production and ownership relationships, the structure of the economy, was [sic] still highly biased in favour of the excolonial masters in particular and the capitalist industrial world in general. It is this perverse socio-economic relationship that led the party to declare an economic war against international capitalism . . . It was not until 1967 that Tanzania confronted the problems of economic imbalances, the ownership of means of production and some problems of distortion . . . The Arusha Declaration marked the turning point . . .[15]

The Arusha Declaration was designed to prevent class formation and to reduce, and ultimately eliminate, class, ethnic, regional as well as spatial inequalities. It was also intended to facilitate Tanzania's disengagement from the world capitalist economy and a realignment of its foreign relations to reflect more accurately its policies of non-alignment and socialism. Through Arusha, Tanzania sought to enhance its national power and influence by relying on its own resources rather than being mortgaged to external interests. According to Nnoli's analysis of Arusha, self-reliance became the central aspect of Tanzania's foreign policy. National power and resources were to be augmented to reduce dependence and enhance effectiveness in foreign policy. Ideals alone were not enough; national power was an essential ingredient in successfully exerting influence in world politics.[16]

Kujitegemea: Ujamaa and Mwongozo

Self-reliance (*kujitegemea*) involved the redefinition of transnational relationships which had advanced external penetration. Thus the Arusha Declaration was followed by a series of decisions, pronouncements and debates on how to achieve self-reliance and socialism. The nationalization of the commanding heights of the economy, particularly financial institutions and manufacturing industries, went hand in hand with educational and social reforms, an emphasis on agricultural and rural development, the creation of thousands of *ujamaa* villages, and a reduction of inequalities through income redistribution.[17]

If Arusha was a fairly pragmatic nationalist response to an inheritance of dependence and underdevelopment, then the TANU guidelines of February 1971 (*mwongozo*) were an expression of frustration with, and determination to overcome, the elusiveness of liberation at the several levels of nation (*problématique* of socialism), region (anti-progressive Amin coup in Uganda), continent (resistance to change in southern Africa) and globe (absence of either redistribution or opportunity).[18]

Given the difficulties in achieving self-reliance and socialism – particularly in areas such as the party, security, economic development and foreign policy – *mwongozo* called for a recommitment to the 'spirit' of Arusha:

> The National Executive Committee stresses the implementation of the Arusha Declaration and particularly the need to arouse political consciousness so that every Tanzanian understands our national environment and the importance of safeguarding the security and lives of the people, and of safeguarding our policies, our independence, our economy and our culture.[19]

Mwongozo represented a redefinition of Arusha in more liberationist or *dirigiste* tones, reconceiving of TANU as a 'liberation movement', not just a nationalist party, and the defense forces as a 'liberation army'. It concluded with a ringing appeal for a revolutionary form of self-reliance, a powerful restatement of Arusha:

> we have been oppressed a great deal, we have been exploited a great deal and we have been disregarded a great deal. It is our weakness that has led to our being oppressed, exploited and disregarded. Now we want a revolution – a revolution which brings to an end our weakness, so that we are never again exploited, oppressed or humiliated.[20]

Mwongozo added a new resilience by reformulating Arusha; it reinforced the need for national power to ensure national and continental liberation. Like Arusha, *mwongozo* represented a further stage and learning experience, taking account of the elusiveness of national development, regional integration, continental freedom and international restructuring. As Nnoli notes:

> *Mwongozo*'s predominant focus on tactical considerations supplements both the initial guidelines and the policy of self-reliance by identifying in concrete and specific terms of all the nation's enemies, their major method of operation, and how to mobilize national power against them, as well as for the pursuit of other foreign policy goals.[21]

Mwongozo was a response, then, to the intransigence of dependence and dominance externally and to the elusiveness of socialism and *ujamaa* internally. In particular, it related to several salient themes in Tanzania's post-Arusha development strategy and debate – equality and growth, agriculture versus industry, choice of technology, trade and integration, and the urban–rural dichotomy.[22]

In a critical yet sympathetic review of the difficulties of implementing Arusha, Edmund Clark points to continuities of ministerial and parastatal spending before and after 1967; it is only in the mid-1970s, after *mwongozo*, that government investment begins to concentrate more on rural, agricultural and labor-intensive projects. The considerable time-lag after 1967 before Arusha was effective meant that sectoral distribution of revenue has remained remarkably constant and that foreign capital inflows had tended to increase rather than decrease.[23] Although basic human needs were being met more adequately, the financial commitment and social impact of *ujamaa* villages were limited.[24] And Clark is particularly regretful of the inability of the burgeoning parastatal sector – the central nexus for transnational relationships between multinational corporations and Tanzania – to respond positively to Arusha.[25] There was no developmental innovation on the part of parastatals to make themselves more consistent with the Tanzanian ideology. They tended to want the most modern plants. Turnkey projects, the most obvious example of failure to innovate, have not been uncommon.[26] The apparent inability of Tanzania to escape from external dependence and internal inequalities as typified by the crucial parastatal sector gave rise to a range of critical reactions to which *mwongozo* was an interim response. But the 'super-left'[27] in Tanzania insisted on going beyond Arusha and *mwongozo*, away from the traditional communal notion of socialism expressed in *ujamaa* and toward a more critical, class-based definition.[28] Moreover, Clark and others advocate agricultural- rather than industrial-oriented development to maximize autonomy and accumulation: an 'industrial strategy' characterized by 'use of local raw materials, regional dispersal, rural location, small size, labour intensity'.[29]

The achievement of self-reliance was hindered in the 1970s not only by the absence of a well-defined ideology but also by two sets of external or environmental factors. First, in the early 1970s Tanzania's development activities were skewed by southern African policy, in particular by its informal alliance with landlocked Zambia and its willingness to serve as that state's new transit route. The high cost of the Dar-Ndola oil pipeline, the Dar-Copperbelt road and the Dar-Kapiri Mposhi (Taraza) railway diverted foreign aid, local resources and government attention away from other national problems.[30] Second, the simultaneous drought and energy crisis of 1974–6 diverted attention once again from longer-term planning to short-term crisis management to avoid famine.[31] The Zambia corridor and the food crisis both occurred as post-Arusha plans were beginning to materialize, and constituted further short-term setbacks to Tanzania's attempts to disengagement. Given these interruptions, Clark concludes that despite some structural changes and the expansion of the parastatal sector,

Tanzania remains very dependent upon the rest of the world and, specifically, the capitalist world. The Arusha Declaration and the subsequent behavior of the government and its parastatals has not brought a very rapid decrease in dependence. To someone who views dependency as the critical variable in the development of socialism, this slow change is a cause for concern.[32]

We turn in the next section to an empirical analysis of Tanzania's performance before and after Arusha.

A Decade After the Arusha Declaration: the Difficulties of Disengagement

The Arusha Declaration was Tanzania's initial and determined response to its history of dependence and underdevelopment, subordination and a distorted political economy. But despite the attractions of self-reliance and socialism their realization has remained problematic. Practice has still to catch up with the rhetoric; the transformation between t_1 and t_2 has not been as dramatic or as complete as was anticipated at the time of Arusha. Nevertheless, considerable external diversification and some disengagement are apparent along several indicators as Tanzania has attempted to redefine its place in the world system and to limit external dependence and penetration.

Tanzania's operational definition of self-reliance has involved a diversification of external relationships as well as changes in their content, in addition to domestic restructuring.[33] Given its deficient educational resources at independence, one of its primary goals has been to create a group of educated cadres. Table 3.1 suggests that the reliance on foreign education tended to peak around the time of Arusha, in part because of improved national facilities and because of a redefinition of educational

Table 3.1   *Tanzanian Students Enrolled Abroad*

	1962 (N = 1,326) %	1967 (N = 2,148) %	1971 (N = 1,365) %
Africa	22	25	42
North America	18	13	21
Asia	25	33	n.a.
(of which India)	(23)	(32)	n.a.
Europe	23	19	37
(of which UK)	(15)	(11)	(30)
Oceania	1	2	1
Others	11	8	n.a.
Total	100	100	101

Sources: UNESCO, *Statistics of Students Abroad, 1962–1968* (Paris, 1971), pp. 59–60; UNESCO, *Statistics of Students Abroad, 1969–1973* (Paris, 1976), p. 88.

Table 3.2   *Tanzania: International Treaties Signed, 1961–71*

	1961–7	1968–71
Multilateral	22	3
Bulgaria	1	—
China	10	—
Denmark	3	1
Finland	—	1
France	1	—
East Germany	1	—
West Germany	4	1
Italy	1	—
Japan	1	—
Netherlands	1	1
Poland	1	—
Switzerland	1	—
UK	4	1
USA	4	1
USSR	3	—
World Bank	4	3
Total	62	12

Source: Peter H. Rohn, *World Treaty Index*, Vol. 4 (Santa Barbara, Calif.: American Bibliographical Center, 1974), pp. 576–7.

needs after 1967. Moreover, Tanzania continued to diversify the range of countries to which it sends students, with African states showing a continued growth along with Canada. An increasing proportion also went to England, the former colonial mentor, for education.

A second indicator of increasing diversification is the range of treaties signed. Table 3.2 indicates a rather wide and balanced series of treaties compared with other African states, as well as a dramatic drop-off in the making of new treaties after Arusha. Under the 'Nyerere doctrine', Tanzania refused at independence to accept automatically all colonial treaties made on its behalf, instituting instead a two-year moratorium during which time it would decide selectively on which established treaties to accept or reject.[34] The substantial number of treaties entered into between 1961 and 1963 may be explicable, then, in terms of delayed accession. The decline of new treaties after 1967 – particularly the dramatic decline in agreements with England and the United States – probably reflects Tanzania's determination to be highly selective in entering into new external relations. The high proportion of multilateral and World Bank treaties reflects Tanzania's strategy of diversification, which would be increased if informal regional East African and Pan African accords were included in the tabulation.

A further aspect of routine diplomatic interaction is the exchange of representatives between states. At independence, most foreign missions in

Table 3.3   *Groups of States with Missions Accredited to Tanzania, 1963–78 (selected years)*

	Western industrial countries	Communist countries	Third World	of which African	Total
1963	17	5	4	(3)	26
1967	19	8	22	(16)	49
1973	22	9	29	(18)	60
1978	23	11	44	(27)	78

Source: *The Europa Yearbook: A World Survey*, Vol. II, 1963–78 (London: Europa, annual).

Dar es Salaam were from the rich, industrialized states; by 1967 less than half were Western; and by 1977 less than a third came from the First World (see Table 3.3). By contrast, representation from the socialist states doubled from independence to 1977 and from other Third World states multiplied by a factor of 11. The number of African diplomatic accreditations to Tanzania has also grown dramatically and now is larger than those of the Western group. Although this trend toward diversification was apparent before Arusha, it accelerated afterwards. With most First and Second World countries represented in Tanzania along with about half the African and other Third World states, Dar es Salaam has become an important center in Africa, reflecting external attentiveness to Tanzania's distinctive ideology and experiment. Although all major international actors are represented in Dar es Salaam, Tanzania has been able to afford only a rather selected number of missions abroad itself. As indicated in Table 3.4, it has maintained a relatively high level of visibility in the West and in Africa whilst not increasing the number of its resident missions in either the communist world (Moscow and Peking) or the rest of the Third World (India), either before or after Arusha. So despite external attentiveness to Tanzania, its own distribution of missions abroad would appear to reflect its priorities of African unity and liberation and Western aid and trade; however, the number of its smaller African missions has grown

Table 3.4   *Groups of States in which Tanzania Has Accredited Missions, 1963–78 (selected years)*

Year	Western industrial countries	Communist countries	Third World	of which African	United Nations	Total
1963	4	2	2	1	1	9
1967	7	2	4	3	1	14
1973	8	2	6	5	1	17
1978	9	2	9	8	2	22

Source: *A Year Book of the Commonwealth* (London: HMSO, annual).

faster than those in the West since independence and is likely to continue doing so as the states of southern Africa win their independence.

A fourth indicator of diversification is foreign aid. At independence, Tanzania was highly dependent on Western, especially British, assistance but with the diplomatic rifts of 1964–5 it quickly diversified, initially amongst the Western group and then toward socialist states. Its disillusionment with the inadequate amounts and objectionable terms of aid are reflected in the Arusha Declaration itself. Paradoxically, however, despite Tanzania's proclaimed determination to rely primarily on its own resources, its employment of foreign funds was greater in the post-Arusha Second Five-Year Plan (56 percent of development capital) than in the first (50 percent); without the costs of building the Tanzania–Zambia railroads (Tazara), however, the second plan's percentage would drop to slightly below that of the first – 48 percent.[35] Aid diversification, even since Arusha, has essentially meant moving away from Britain and toward China, Canada, Scandinavia and the multilateral sources (see Table 3.5); assistance from COMECON countries has never been significant. The post-Arusha increase in foreign aid inflows is revealed in Table 3.6, with Netherlands, West Germany and the United States joining Canada, Scandinavia and IDA/UNDP as major donors. Chinese aid has been primarily for Tazara and other donors may have increased their flows in 1974/5 because of the combined drought and oil crises; but local financing has also grown as the state has reduced the outflow of profits and service payments through nationalization, particularly of the banks. Nevertheless, the declaration of self-reliance has not reduced the inflow of aid, although it may have changed its terms, usage and impact. This dramatic reversal is particularly striking in the case of the World Bank, whose own terms changed to favor agricultural development just as Tanzania was

Table 3.5 *Foreign Aid to Tanzania, 1964–73* (shs millions)

	1964–8		1969–73		1964–73	
	Total	%	Total	%	Total	%
Britain	48	7	—	—	48	1
United States	158	22	211	6	369	9
IDA/IBRD	167	24	504	14	671	15
Canada	12	2	202	6	214	5
Nordic	87	12	787	21	874	20
Germany	50	7	226	6	276	6
Israel	10	1	—	—	10	—
USSR & East Europe	1	—	28	1	29	1
China	77	11	1,254	34	1,331	31
Others	99	14	433	12	532	12
Total	709		3,645		4,354	

Source: W. Edmund Clark, *Socialist Development and Public Investment in Tanzania 1964–73* (Toronto: University of Toronto Press, 1978), p. 193.

Table 3.6   *Foreign Aid to Tanzania (US $ millions – selected years)*

	1961	%	1965	%	1967	%	1972	%	1975	%
DAC bilateral total	$38·8	%	$34·9	%	$30·6	%	$56·6	%	$239·1	%
of which:										
Canada	0·02	0·1	0·90	2·6	2·53	8·3	6·1	10·8	32·0	13·4
Denmark	—		0·46	1·3	0·8	2·6	4·6	8·1	24·1	10·0
Finland	—		—		—		2·6	4·6	12·0	5·0
Germany	0·01	0·03	4·2	12·0	3·6	11·7	6·8	12·0	29·2	12·2
Netherlands	—		0·3	0·9	—		3·7	6·5	19·0	7·9
Norway	—		0·3	0·9	0·4	1·3	3·5	6·2	17·2	7·2
Sweden	—		1·6	4·6	2·2	7·2	16·5	29·2	55·1	23·1
UK	33·74	87·0	17·77	50·9	2·75	9·0	4·3	7·6	9·0	3·8
USA	5·0	12·9	9·2	26·3	9·0	29·4	7·0	12·4	34·0	14·2
Socialist bilateral total							7		—	
Multilateral total	$2·9	%	$3·4	%	$5·8	%	$7·8	%	$70·3	%
of which:										
IFC	2·3	79·3	0·1	2·9	—					
IDA	—		1·9	55·9	6·6		2·7	34·6	20·1	28·6
UNDP	6·4	13·8	1·8	52·9	3·0		5·1	65·4	21·0	29·9

Source: OECD, *Geographical Distribution of Financial Flows to Developing Countries 1969–1975* (Paris, 1977), pp. 226–7.

engaged in *ujamaa vijijini*. Although this new penetration of multilateral assistance has been explained by reference to the oil and drought crises,[36] rather than to shared policies,[36] the overall impact of this convergence of interest between IBRD and *ujamaa* is that 'rural development projects in Tanzania are largely creatures of international finance capital'.[37]

A fifth aspect of Tanzania's attempts to diversify relations is revealed in its pattern of arms imports. Until the abortive army mutiny in 1964, Tanzania was largely dependent on British arms and training. It then attempted to diversify by using West German and Canadian equipment and training, but the former was curtailed over the two Germanies' disagreement in 1965. Since Arusha, except for the Canadian air force team, the Tanzanian People's Defence Force has relied mainly on its own local training, Chinese guns and training[38] and, to a lesser extent, on the Soviet Union (see Table 3.7). Despite the threats posed to its sovereignty from both the white regimes and Uganda under Amin, Tanzania's military expenditure has remained remarkably low. As can be seen in Table 3.7, arms imports average about 2 percent of total imports each year and rose only in the early 1970s, largely in response to threats from Portuguese-ruled Mozambique and Amin's Uganda, fears about which are expressed in *mwongozo*.

Table 3.7   *Tanzania: Arms Imports, 1967–76 (US $ millions)*

	1967	1970	1973	1976
Arms imports	2	4	22	36
Total imports	227	318	497	1,640
Arms imports as % of total imports	1	1	4	2

Major sources of arms imports, 1967–76 (in US $ millions): China (75),   USSR (30),   Canada (5),   USA (1),   UK (1), West Germany (1)

Source: World Military Expenditures and Arms Transfers, 1967–1976 (Washington, DC: US Arms Control and Disarmament Agency, July 1978), pp. 151, 159.

A sixth indicator of diversification and realignment is the direction of external trade. Table 3.8 suggests that while Tanzania has reoriented the direction of its exports somewhat since independence, it still relies primarily on markets in Europe and, to a lesser extent, North America and Asia. Australia, Belgium and now Singapore have at times displaced Japan and Hong Kong as major markets, but the only new country to be consistently in the top ten markets is China; and its ranking has slipped since the

Table 3.8   *Tanzania: Ranking of Major Export Markets, 1960–76*

	1960	1967	1973	1976
UK	1	1	1	2
USA	2	6	2	3
West Germany	3	5	3	1
India	4	4	4	7
Netherlands	5	8	9	8
Japan	6	7	7	10
Hong Kong	7	3	5	6
Belgium	8	(11)	10	
Australia	9	(16)	(14)	(13)
Italy	10	10	(12)	5
China		9	6	9
Canada				(12)
Zambia		2	8	
Singapore				4

Sources: M. A. Bienefeld, 'Special gains from trade with socialist countries: the case of Tanzania', *World Development* 3, 5 (May 1975), p. 260; United Nations, *Yearbook of International Trade Statistics, 1976*, Vol. I (New York, 1977), p. 909.

Table 3.9 *Tanzania: Direction of External Trade,*
1967–76 (selected years)

	1967 %	1973 %	1976 %
Imports			
Developed market economies	75	58	64
Developing market economies	15	16	27
Centrally planned economies	6	25	8
Other	4	1	1
Exports			
Developed market economies	64	58	64
Developing market economies	27	34	30
Centrally planned economies	6	7	5
Other	3	1	1

Source: United Nations, *Yearbook of International Trade Statistics, 1977*, Vol. I (New York, 1978), p. 958.

termination of trade to cover Tazara's local costs in the early 1970s. Moreover, although the first period after Arusha was characterized by a degree of diversification, there appears to be something of a regression back to the old established markets.

Table 3.9 shows the source of imports as well as direction of exports since Arusha. Imports appear to show a stronger element of diversification, as First World imports continue to give way to those of the Third World. Once again, imports from China for Tazara peaked in the early 1970s. Most of Tanzania's regular import diversification is with Asia and the Middle East, primarily with Japan, India and the Gulf States. Overall, trade has not been diversified much outside links with the EEC and other industrialized capitalist states. Trade relations with China and India have been less stable, while they have hardly grown at all with the USSR and Eastern Europe. Table 3.10 reveals the resilience of the top ten export markets of 1960 in 1976, although it does suggest a gradual shift away from overreliance on a few major markets, and particularly a reduction in

Table 3.10 *Tanzania: Importance of Top Five or Ten Export Markets,*
1960–76

	1960–3 %	1967–9 %	1974–6 %
Proportion of total export earnings received from:			
The 10 countries most important in 1960	82·6	70·1	60·4
The 5 top countries in each year	64·2	58·1	46·9
The 10 top countries in each year	83·8	78·7	67·1

Sources: adapted from M. A. Bienefeld, 'Special gains from trade with socialist countries: the case of Tanzania', *World Development*, 3, 5 (May 1975), p. 260; United Nations, *Yearbook of International Trade Statistics, 1976*, Vol. I (New York, 1977), p. 909.

Table 3.11   *Tanzania: Export and Import Composition, 1960–73*

	1960 %	1965 %	1970 %	1973 %
Export composition				
Food	37·0	38·2	49·7	50·5
Other agricultural products	44·7	45·7	29·9	28·5
Minerals	5·7	3·5	7·4	11·0
Manufactures and other	12·6	12·6	13·0	10·0
Import composition				
Food and raw materials	23·4	19·4	15·4	24·0
Fuels and lubricants	9·7	2·8	8·6	9·4
Machinery and equipment	24·5	30·3	40·3	34·0
Other manufactured products	43·4	47·5	35·7	32·6

Source: IBRD, *World Tables, 1976* (Baltimore, Md: Johns Hopkins University Press, 1978), pp. 450–1, 458–9.

the percentage of exports going to the top five countries, after the Arusha Declaration.[39]

Tanzania's least impressive domain of diversification has been in external trade composition. Since Arusha exports and imports of food have increased, particularly in the drought period of 1973–4.[40] Moreover, according to Table 3.11, manufactured exports and imports have also declined proportionately since 1967, thus pointing to a perpetual role of primary product exporter. However, mineral exports and machinery imports have risen, indicating the beginning of a somewhat more industrially oriented structure. The one distinctive aspect of Table 3.11 is the decline in other manufactured imports since 1967 (t_1) reflecting a degree of austerity, in terms of elite consumption, uncommon in the Third World.

Unlike many new states, Tanzania is not dependent on just one or two commodities. But as can be seen in Table 3.12, its top five exports have not changed in content, only in ranking. And these changes in order are as much a function of fluctuations in international prices as in level of internal production. As the table indicates, the top five 'colonial' commodities—cotton, sisal, coffee, cashews and cloves—have never constituted less than 60 percent of the value of Tanzania's exports. But these major exports have gradually come closer to each other in terms of volume and value.

One indicator of reliance on the world economy is percentage of GDP constituted by exports. Table 3.13 shows that Tanzania is steadily becoming an increasingly self-reliant economy as exports have fallen from 27 percent GDP in 1964–5 and 25 percent in 1967–70 to about 20 percent in the mid-1970s. However, imports have not fallen as a percent of GDP because of the continued need for external inputs into the development process, as well as the higher price of oil and greater need for food during the droughts. Given these results, Tanzanian economist Kighoma Malima

Table 3.12   *Tanzania: Five Major Community Exports, 1960–74 (shs millions – selected years)*

	1960		1964		1970		1974	
	Rank	Value	Rank	Value	Rank	Value	Rank	Value
Cotton	2	177	3	198	2	247	1	473
Sisal	1	309	1	437	3	179	2	463
Coffee	3	146	2	221	1	312	3	375
Cashews	4	43	4	66	4	137	4	243
Cloves	—	—	5	43	5	109	5	88
Top 5 commodities as % of exports		65		64		60		62

Sources: M. A. Bienefeld, 'Special gains from trade with socialist countries: the case of Tanzania', *World Development*, 3, 5 (May 1975), p. 257; Bank of Tanzania, *Economic and Operations Report* (Dar es Salaam, June 1975), p. 78.

concludes a comparative analysis of Tanzania with other Third World and industrialized states by suggesting that not only is Tanzania's economy relatively more diversified than many less developed countries, both in terms of less dependence on international trade and less concentration of exports on a few commodities, but also its balance-of-payments position was under control up to 1969.[41]

However, because of the recent rise in foreign aid and capital, Tanzania's debt position has worsened since 1967 (t_1), in part, again, as a result of the changed development process. As indicated in Table 3.14, Tanzania's debt quadrupled from the late 1960s until 1975, increasing as a percent of GDP and also rising quite dramatically as a percent of exports. Drought and oil exacerbated this deteriorating situation, which may be ameliorated somewhat by the debt relief being offered by several major donors to least developed countries such as Tanzania. Without debt can-

Table 3.13   *Tanzania's Exports and Imports as Ratios of GDP (at market prices – selected years)*

	1964–5	1969–70	1974–5
Exports of goods and NFS	26·9	24·4	19·7
Goods	24·2	18·3	15·1
Non-factor services	2·8	6·0	4·6
Imports of goods and NFS	24·1	26·4	33·4
Goods	23·1	22·9	30·9
Non-factor services	2·5	3·4	2·5

Sources: M. A. Bienefeld, 'Special gains from trade with socialist countries: the case of Tanzania', *World Development* 3, 5 (May 1975), p. 253; OECD, *Geographical Distribution of Financial Flows to Developing Countries 1969–1975* (Paris, 1977), p. 227.

Table 3.14   *Tanzania's Debt, 1969–75 (US $ millions)*

	1969	1972	1975
External debt	232	311	866
Gross National Product	1,150	1,560	3,060
Exports	245	324	370
Debt as % of GNP	20	20	28
Debt as % of exports	95	96	234

Source: OECD, *Geographical Distribution of Financial Flows to Developing Countries 1969–1975* (Paris, 1977), p. 227.

cellation or rescheduling, Tanzania's growing indebtedness may be a source of difficulty and of renewed subordination in the years ahead, although its stock of foreign direct investment remains low. (This was only $60 million in 1967, with no country controlling more than 50 percent.) Britain was the largest owner (46 percent), followed by Italy (18 percent), Denmark (12 percent) and West Germany (5 percent).[42] In line with, and serving to exacerbate, Tanzania's national debt is its (im)balance of trade, which has gone consistently into the red since 1970. Throughout the 1960s it was usually in a positive balance, averaging between 50 and 320 shs million per annum; in 1967, for instance, it was +90 shs million. From 1970 onwards, however, it was always below −300 shs million, reaching almost −900 shs million.[43]

In his own critical review of Tanzania's attempts at diversification, Bienefeld argues that the post-Arusha pattern 'gives little indication of any fundamental restructuring of the economy, nor even of far-reaching risk-reducing diversification'. He also indicates that the percentage of processed exports has hardly risen since independence. Moreover, alternative trade relations with the socialist states have been limited, unstable and based on a center–periphery exchange of primary products for manufactured goods: 'Whatever the optimal pattern of export diversification may be for Tanzania it is clear that trade with the socialist countries is not making any special contribution to its achievement.'[44] Bienefeld goes on to question whether this is a function of Tanzania's nonalignment and its rather ambiguous policy of 'socialism', arguing that disengagement *per se* is dysfunctional in terms of logic of integration into either the socialist or capitalist world systems.

Our figures reveal that the strategy of diversification has had, overall, a mixed record. Tanzania operates internationally in a much wider network than it did in the 1960s. Its diplomatic, aid and military contacts have been significantly dispersed, breaking down the pattern of dependence on Britain. In the area of trade, however, the record is more spotty. Trade is a less important component of Tanzania's total economic activity, but the typical Third World profile of exporting primary commodities and importing manufactured goods has not been altered significantly. At t_2, then, self-reliance and diversification appear just to be beginning, not ending.

External Penetration

At independence, Tanzania inherited not only a colonial economy, but also all the trappings of British colonial and administrative rule. The major civil service positions were held by British subjects or expatriates. The universities were staffed by foreigners, as were all the leading economic positions in the country. Publications, entertainment and popular tastes received their cues from, or were distinctly modeled upon, foreign counterparts. And perhaps most significant from the political point of view, the modern sector of the economy was owned predominantly by foreigners. The main thrust of the Arusha Declaration was not only to reduce external reliance and dependence, but also to establish full Tanzanian control over the domestic economy and to reduce external penetration.

The Declaration did not initially affect the inflow of foreign private investment. It did, however, alter the balance between private and governmental investment, with the parastatal firms' proportion increasing significantly in the 1970s. In the mid-1960s private investment constituted about half the total investment in manufacturing; as the impact of Arusha became apparent this decreased to a quarter or less of the total.[45] However, foreign investment is important as well because of its impact on technology,[46] imports and employment. And the decline of foreign private capital flows, especially private foreign capital, has not been equaled by the demise of foreign techniques and consultants. Dependence on foreign managers, technicians, supplies and methods continues despite criticism.[47] However, the vulnerability of Tanzania to such factors has been reduced because of changes in ownership patterns and because of the development of an indigenous managerial and technical cadre. And foreign ownership with parastatals goes increasingly into tourism and agriculture and so is less concentrated in manufacturing.[48] The other area in which financial penetration has been transformed is in the area of banking. Foreign, mainly British, banks were nationalized following the Arusha Declaration, along with insurance, brokerage and other financial institutions. Despite initial problems with the National Commercial Bank,[49] Tanzania has reduced financial penetration significantly since Arusha. Indeed, the primary source of foreign economic leverage now is official foreign assistance from bilateral and multilateral agencies rather than private capital. Such foreign aid still constitutes about 50 percent of the government's development budget and may affect the nature and orientation of development projects.

Table 3.15   *Foreign Private Investment in Parastatals (shs millions)*

	1964–5	1966–7	1968–9	1970–1	1972–3	1973–4
Foreign private finance	34	149	110	166	14	32
Local finance	36	33	125	239	208	501

Source: W. Edmund Clark, *Socialist Development and Public Investment in Tanzania 1964–1973* (Toronto: University of Toronto Press, 1978), p. 180.

Table 3.16 *Composition of the Middle and Senior Ranks of the Tanzanian Civil Service, 1961–9*

Citizenship	1961	1964	1967	1969
Tanzanian	1,170	3,083	4,937	6,145
Non-Tanzanian	3,282	2,306	1,817	1,509
Percentage Tanzanians	26	57	73	80

Source: Cranford Pratt, *The Critical Phase in Tanzania, 1945–1968: Nyerere and the Emergence of a Socialist Strategy* (Cambridge: Cambridge University Press, 1976), p. 130.

In the *socio-cultural* area, Tanzania has controlled the impact of taste-transfer and copying of foreign life-styles more successfully than many African states. In part this is a function of poverty; but it is also the result of a self-conscious political culture and continuing efforts at political education. The importation of foreign luxuries and values is limited both fiscally and ideologically. The development of a national 'Swahili' culture has been facilitated by the reorientation of Tanzania's educational system as well as by careful control of the media. Tanzania's educational system has been revolutionized since independence, with the emphasis placed on egalitarian and relevant ideas and skills. The number of foreign teachers and other government officers (see Table 3.16) has fallen dramatically since the 1960s so that now only specialised educationalists are recruited abroad. And these have to conform to a distinctive curriculum based on Tanzanian needs. The media have always been state-regulated and the remaining privately owned newspaper, *The Standard* (now the *Daily News*), was nationalised in 1972. While these measures do not necessarily indicate significant realignment, they are certainly initial measures of regulating foreign cultural penetration.

Finally, external *military* links have been of symbolic rather than direct importance in terms of penetration. At independence and until the mutiny in 1964, Tanzania relied almost exclusively on British military leadership, training and equipment. After the mutiny and the decision to 'politicize' the armed forces, the British presence was rapidly reduced and replaced initially by Canadian and then by Chinese instructors. In the early 1970s the Chinese had almost a monopoly on military assistance but since then Tanzania has once again diversified, receiving training and equipment from East Europe and Cuba as well. But as the military has grown, the foreign assistance component has become proportionately smaller. Tanzania has also established its own military schools for officer cadets. The party remains very resistant to external interference, as does the regime and government in general. In all these efforts and in the absence of a coup, military assistance has been an impotent weapon for the penetration of the local political economy.

Explanations: the Process of the Arusha Declaration

The factors leading to the Arusha Declaration of 1967 can be divided into two sets: long- and short-term in *nature*, and external and internal in *origin*. These four types of factors – almost impossible to weigh in terms of relative potency – come together in the perceptions and decision-making processes of the President, both as an individual and as an institution. In 1967 Nyerere responded to long-term structural dependence and underdevelopment, as well as to shorter-term results of this inheritance, particularly the mutiny and growing opposition; he was also reacting to a series of diplomatic crises with the Western world and to the emergence of internal forces threatening Tanzania's goals of development. As Cranford Pratt suggests, all of these pressures played upon the President so that in 1967, as in 1961 when he resigned temporarily from the post of Prime Minister, Nyerere had to act to reinforce his intellectual, personal and political leadership.[50] Nyerere's reassertion of leadership and control did not take place in a vacuum; neither, however, was he under immense, immediate and irresistible pressure to act. He did so because of his own preferences, policies and perceptions.[51]

The catalyst to the Declaration was, then, the President's perceptions of the need for change if Tanzania was to escape from the inheritance of dependence and underdevelopment. These perceptions were reinforced, of course, by particular long- and short-term factors. The President recognized the contradiction of striving for development through an elite-dominated structure:

> Tanzania had created a modern elite, rewarded its members at levels far above the incomes of ordinary citizens and then relied upon that elite to promote further development of the country and to ensure that more and more of the citizens benefited from that development. An alternative to this pattern existed in theory alone.[52]

Arusha was concerned with translating this theory into practice. This meant confronting long- and short-term features of dependence and underdevelopment such as unequal terms of trade and internal criticism.

In the external arena, major long-term factors leading to the Declaration, in addition to dependence and 'unequal exchange', were overreliance on foreign aid and increasing indebtedness, and powerlessness to deal with the problems of racist regimes in southern Africa. In the short term, these factors were incorporated in a series of diplomatic crises with several Western states. This visible issue of whether to accept Western penetration over, say, diplomatic representation in Zanzibar or Britain's response to UDI or Belgo-American involvement in the Congo, was symbolic of broader and deeper questions of dependence. By opting for Arusha, nationalisation and self-reliance, the Tanzanian leadership was indicating that it was going to limit external penetration in the national political economy.

The historical conjuncture of Arusha was also the result of related external–internal linkages, particularly the association between national and international elites. The Tanzanian leadership had been quite permissive toward external aid, tastes, technology and methods, and was less sensitive about the internal implications of embourgeoisement. By 1967 class-formation and -consciousness were beginning to develop in the various areas of Tanzanian society.[53] To deal with the growing prospect of inequalities, both external and internal, as well as to reassert his own control and to establish a socialist orientation, Nyerere insisted upon a thorough re-evaluation of development policy. He then won the support of TANU's National Executive Committee for the socialist statement now known as the Arusha Declaration. Nyerere was responding, then, to growing alienation and disorientation in the party, Cabinet and government in the short term as well as to the longer-term issues of uneven development, unemployment, urbanization and the intensification of inequalities.

Arusha was successful, according to Pratt, because (i) it was related to traditional communal values, (ii) ministers and media championed it instantly, (iii) classes were embryonic, not strong, so societal resistance was minimal, (iv) senior civil servants were increasingly ready for structural change, given the elusiveness of development, (v) 'reception of the Declaration was also aided by that general radicalization of opinion which had followed the foreign policy crises of late 1964 and early 1965',[54] and (vi) the proposals were well received by the bureaucracy because of the appearance of political discontent on a fairly widespread basis.[55]

The Problematics of Realignment

However, realignment is a difficult and dangerous exercise for most regimes precisely because it involves a simultaneous confrontation of established external and internal interests and of the transnational associations between the two. The difficulties and dangers are particularly acute for poor, weak states because of their vulnerability and because they have minimal reserves on which to rely in case of setbacks and failures. Yet, given their dependence on external forces and the associated underdevelopment of their own political economies, they have every reason to redefine their world politics and reassert their national independence. Such self-reliance is not just a diplomatic gesture; rather, it represents an attempt to capture and maximise national resources to enhance resistance to external penetration and to improve the prospects for development.

Despite the difficulties and slowness of escaping from dependence and achieving a degree of self-reliance,[56] Tanzania's first post-Arusha decade represents a considerable achievement in terms of persistence, program and mobilization, with important external as well as internal effects. Moreover, its ability to deal with transnational dependence and vulnerability in the future has been enhanced between t_1 and t_2, not only because of tangible changes but also because of shifts in other actors' perceptions of Tanzania. As Nnoli suggests, its bargaining power vis-à-vis the industrialized states has improved because of

(a) less reliance on the superpowers and the other big powers for external resources, and less involvement with them in diplomatic life in general; (b) greater reliance on, and interaction with, the middle powers whose political interests in the world community are not as extensive as those of the major powers, and with whom therefore a clash of interests is likely to be less frequent; (c) a more extensive and intensive interaction in economic matters with the predominantly agricultural but advanced states, whose attitudes towards problems of economic development are less divergent from those of Tanzania than perspectives of the industrialized countries; (d) a greater reliance on the socialist states for the achievement of the goals of antiracism and anticolonialism; (e) and a greater degree of coordination of activities with countries of the Third World in relations with advanced countries.[57]

Moreover, other African states may come to learn from the Tanzanian experience and so enhance the prospects for all other efforts at disengagement. Most attempts to follow an egalitarian path in Africa have been short-lived and quite turbulent, whereas in the Tanzanian case there has been a remarkable degree of direction and continuity. Clearly, further attempts to disengage in Africa will tend to be somewhat different, given diverse inheritance, modes of production and global position. To date Tanzania remains one of the very few relatively successful and sustained examples of self-reliance and socialism on the continent. As Pratt notes, one

> reason for the widespread interest in Tanzanian socialism is that Tanzania is a poor and predominantly peasant society which is attempting to find an egalitarian, socialist and democratic way to develop. With so many examples throughout the Third World of the fact that a capitalist pattern of development results in severe class differentials, repressive regimes and actual impoverishment for a sizeable proportion of the population, the Tanzanian endeavour is of global significance.[58]

The failures and limitations of Tanzania's policy of disengagement and diversification have tended to be emphasized rather than the considerable achievements, in part because of the high goals set by the President and party in Arusha and *mwongozo*, and in part because of radical attention to Tanzania's political economy. This chapter does not address itself to the set of salient issues centered on the role of the state, the nature of class conflict and other contradictions in Tanzania. Neither have we gone beyond 1977 and the subsequent suggestions that Tanzania is moving 'backwards' toward a more orthodox development strategy involving greater freedom for local and global 'capitalisms'.[59] Nor have we dealt in detail with Tanzania's foreign policy, conventionally defined, such as its support of the liberation movements in southern Africa and Uganda or its opposition to Western interference in Shaba. Rather, we have limited ourselves to an assessment of Tanzania's development strategy in the decade since 1967.

The period since Arusha has been a fundamental and continuing series of changes–in both policy and practice–in Tanzania's political economy in the direction of self-reliance. First, Nyerere noted in his commemorative survey, 'The measure of our success is that . . . fundamental achievements are generally taken for granted. We are now much more conscious of the difficulties in our daily lives than of fundamental exploitation. And that is as it should be.'[60] The President listed a series of achievements scored in the first decade. These included:

> First and foremost, we . . . have stopped, and reversed, a national drift towards the growth of a class society, based on ever-increasing inequality and the exploitation of the majority for the benefit of the few. We have changed the direction of our national development, so that our national resources are now being deliberately directed towards the needs of this nation and its people.[61]

Second, a positive attitude toward socialism has developed. Third, many socialist institutions have been developed. Fourth, basic human needs and a basic physical infrastructure have been provided. Finally, Tanzania has made a continuing contribution toward the liberation of Africa.

Clearly, the future of self-reliance in Tanzania is by no means assured because of Tanzania's inheritance of underdevelopment, the difficulties of escaping from dependence, the problems of diversification, the persistence of transnational linkages and the possibility of recurrent ecological crises. Moreover, the articulation and implementation of Tanzania's policy of disengagement, diversification and realignment remains essentially a function of Mwalimu Nyerere as President and Chairman of CCM, the ruling party.

So, despite some reduction in vulnerability and penetration between t_1 and t_2 Tanzania remains a very poor and peripheral political economy, still essentially incorporated within the world system. Yet some transnational linkages have been reduced or contained and opposition to self-reliance limited. Moreover, in the decade since Arusha, notions of *ujamaa*, *kujitegemea* and *mwongozo* have been popularized, so making any major overt retreat from socialism highly problematic. Kaduma captures the rather resilient spirit of Tanzania as the country continues to diversify and realign.

> Tanzania believes in Self-Reliance not so much because she is isolationist or inward looking. But she puts emphasis on Self-Reliance because freedom of action—be it individual or national—is impossible in state of dependency . . .
>
> Development to Tanzania, therefore, means liberation. Liberation of man from domination by another man, liberation of man from fear of want, and liberation of man from dependence. The Tanzania citizen which Tanzania wishes to bring up is one who will be self-confident and capable of shaping his own destiny. This is what self-reliance means.[62]

Notes: Chapter 3

1 Julius K. Nyerere, *The Arusha Declaration* (Dar es Salaam: Government Printer, 1967), p. 8.
2 Julius K. Nyerere, *The Arusha Declaration: Ten Years After* (Dar es Salaam: Government Printer, 1977), p. 33.

3 ibid., p. 4.
4 See Cranford Pratt, *The Critical Phase in Tanzania, 1945–1968: Nyerere and the Emergence of a Socialist Strategy* (Cambridge: Cambridge University Press, 1976), pp. 127, 134, 161.
5 See 'Tanzania: New African survey', *New African*, 139 (March 1979), and *Tanzania: Basic Economic Report, Main Report* (Washington: World Bank, December 1977), Report number 1616-TA, pp. viii–x.
6 W. Edmund Clark, *Socialist Development and Public Investment in Tanzania 1964–73* (Toronto: University of Toronto Press, 1978), p. 28.
7 See J. F. Rweyemamu, *Underdevelopment and Industrialization in Tanzania* (Nairobi: Oxford University Press, 1973); S. M. Mbilinyi, R. Mabele and M. L. Kyomo, 'Economic struggle of TANU government', in Gabriel Ruhumbika (ed.), *Towards Ujamaa: Twenty Years of TANU Leadership – A Contribution of the University of Dar es Salaam to the 20th Anniversary of TANU* (Nairobi: East African Literature Bureau, 1974), p. 68; Thomas J. Biersteker, 'Self-reliance in theory and practice in international trade relations', *International Organization*, 34, 2 (Spring 1980), pp. 229–64.
8 Okwudiba Nnoli, *Self Reliance and Foreign Policy in Tanzania: The Dynamics of the Diplomacy of a New State, 1961 to 1971* (New York: NOK, 1978), p. 7.
9 See Pratt, *The Critical Phase in Tanzania*, pp. 1–8.
10 See John Nellis, *A Theory of Ideology: The Tanzanian Example* (Nairobi: Oxford University Press, 1972).
11 See Pratt, *The Critical Phase in Tanzania*, p. 134.
12 See Andrew Coulson (ed.), *African Socialism in Practice? Case Studies from Tanzania* (London: Review of African Political Economy with Spokesman Books, 1979); Biersteker, 'Self-reliance in theory and practice'; *Tanzania: Basic Economic Report*.
13 Nyerere, *The Arusha Declaration*, p. 3.
14 ibid., p. 8. See also G. K. Helleiner, 'Socialism and economic development in Tanzania', *Journal of Development Studies*, 8, 2 (January 1972), pp. 183–204.
15 Mbilinyi, Mabele and Kyomo, 'Economic struggle of TANU government', p. 75. See also Frances Hill, 'Ujamaa: African socialist productionism in Tanzania', in Helen Desfosses and Jacques Levesque (eds), *Socialism in the Third World* (New York: Praeger, 1975), pp. 216–51.
16 See Nnoli, *Self Reliance and Foreign Policy in Tanzania*, p. 202.
17 On this series of policies and acts see Bismark U. Mwansasu and Cranford Pratt (eds), *Towards Socialism in Tanzania* (Toronto: University of Toronto Press, 1979); Pratt, *The Critical Phase*; Biersteker, 'Self-reliance in theory and practice'; *Tanzania: Basic Economic Report*, pp. viii–71.
18 'TANU guidelines on guarding, consolidating and advancing the revolution of Tanzania, and of Africa (Mwongozo)', *African Review*, 1, 4 (April 1972), p. 2.
19 ibid., p. 5.
20 ibid., p. 8.
21 Nnoli, *Self Reliance and Foreign Policy in Tanzania*, p. 236.
22 Clark, *Socialist Development and Public Investment in Tanzania*, pp. 6–24.
23 ibid., p. 71. Cf. Justinian Rweyemamu, *Underdevelopment and Industrialization in Tanzania*.
24 For a critique, see, for instance, Jannik Boesen, Birgit Storgard Madsen and Tony Moody, *Ujamaa–Socialism from Above* (Uppsala: Scandinavian Institute of African Studies, 1977). See also Dean E. McHenry, *Tanzania's Ujamaa Villages: The Implementation of a Rural Development Strategy* (Berkeley, Calif.: University of California Institute of International Studies, 1979).
25 Clark, *Socialist Development and Public Investment in Tanzania*, p. 9.
26 ibid., p. 140.
27 See William Tordoff and Ali A. Mazrui, 'The left and the super-left in Tanzania', *Journal of Modern African Studies*, 10, 3 (October 1972), pp. 427–45.
28 See, for instance, Issa G. Shivji, *Class Struggles in Tanzania* (London: Heinemann, 1976), and John S. Saul, 'Tanzania's transition to socialism', *Canadian Journal of African Studies*, 11, 2 (1977), pp. 313–39.
29 Clark, *Socialist Development and Public Investment in Tanzania*, p. 249.
30 On Tazara, see Martin Bailey, *Freedom Railway: China and the Tanzania–Zambia Link* (London: Collings, 1976); Richard Hall and Hugh Peyman, *The Great Uhuru Railway: China's Showplace in Africa* (London: Gollancz, 1976); Kasuka S. Mutukwa, *Politics of*

the *Tanzania-Zambia Railproject: A Study of Tanzania-China-Zambia Relations* (Washington, DC: University Press of America, 1977).

31 See Reginald H. Green, 'Income distribution and the eradication of poverty in Tanzania', in Irving Louis Horowitz (ed.), *Equity, Income and Policy: Comparative Studies in Three Worlds of Development* (New York: Praeger, 1977), pp. 251–6, and 'Petroleum prices and African development: retrenchment or reassessment?', *International Journal*, 20, 3 (Summer 1975), pp. 391–5; Michael F. Lofchie, 'Agrarian crisis and economic liberalization in Tanzania', *Journal of Modern African Studies*, 16, 3 (September 1978), pp. 451–75.

32 Clark, *Socialist Development and Public Investment in Tanzania*, p. 218.

33 See Biersteker, 'Self-reliance in theory and practice'; *Tanzania: Basic Economic Report*, *passim.*

34 See Earle E. Seaton and Sosthenes T. Maliti, *Tanzania Treaty Practice* (Nairobi: Oxford University Press, 1973), esp. pp. 35–94.

35 See Clark, *Socialist Development and Public Investment in Tanzania*, pp. 177–9.

36 Lofchie, 'Agrarian crisis and economic liberalization in Tanzania', p. 456.

37 James H. Mittelman, 'The politics of rural credit in Tanzania', paper delivered at the meetings of the African Studies Association, Baltimore, November 1978, p. 25.

38 See 'The Canadian military training assistance programme to Tanzania, 1965–70', *Wellesley Paper*, Canadian Institute of International Affairs, Toronto, 1973; George T. Yu, *China and Tanzania: A Study in Cooperative Interaction* (Berkeley, Calif.: University of California, 1970, China Research Monograph Number 5), and *China's African Policy: A Study of Tanzania* (New York: Praeger, 1975).

39 On Tanzania's attempts to diversify its foreign relations, including trade, see David H. Johns, 'The foreign policy of Tanzania', in Olajide Aluko (ed.), *The Foreign Policies of African States* (Atlantic City, NJ: Humanities, 1977), pp. 196–219; Martin Bailey, 'Tanzania and China', *African Affairs*, 74, 294 (January 1975), pp. 29–50; H. M. Othman, 'The Arusha Declaration and the triangle principles of Tanzania's foreign policy', *East African Journal*, 7, 5 (May 1970), pp. 35–42.

40 See Lofchie, 'Agrarian crisis and economic liberalization in Tanzania'; *Tanzania: Basic Economic Report*, pp. 72–81.

41 See Kighoma A. Malima, 'International trade and economic transformation of Tanzania', *African Review*, 1, 2 (September 1971), p. 85.

42 See *Multinational Corporations in World Development* (New York: United Nations Department of Economic and Social Affairs, 1973, E.73. II. 4.11), p. 882.

43 See M. A. Bienefeld, 'Special gains from trade with socialist countries: the case of Tanzania', *World Development*, 2, 5 (May 1975), p. 262.

44 ibid., pp. 256, 265.

45 See Clark, *Socialist Development and Economic Liberalization in Tanzania*, p. 127.

46 See Walter A. Chudson, 'Foreign investment and the acquisition of technology: Kenya and Tanzania', in D. Babatunde Thomas *et al.*, *Importing Technology into Africa* (New York: Praeger, 1976), pp. 83–101.

47 See Peter Neerso, 'Tanzania's policies on private foreign investment', in Carl Widstrand (ed.), *Multinational Firms in Africa* (Stockholm: Almqvist & Wiksell, 1975), pp. 178–85; Issa G. Shivji, 'Capitalism unlimited: public corporations in partnership with multinational corporations', *African Review*, 3, 3 (1973), pp. 359–81.

48 Clark, *Socialist Development and Economic Liberalization in Tanzania*, p. 111.

49 James M. Mittelman, 'Underdevelopment and nationalization: banking in Tanzania', *Journal of Modern African Studies*, 16, 4 (December 1978), pp. 597–617.

50 See Pratt, *The Critical Phase in Tanzania*, pp. 229–30.

51 ibid., p. 228.

52 ibid., p. 225.

53 See Shivji, *Class Struggles in Tanzania*.

54 Pratt, *The Critical Phase in Tanzania*, p. 228.

55 ibid., p. 225.

56 On these, see Timothy M. Shaw and Malcolm J. Grieve, 'Dependence or development: a review article on international and internal inequalities in Africa', *Development and Change*, 8, 3 (July 1977), pp. 377–408; 'Dependence as an explanation of inequalities in Africa', in Larry Gould and Harry Targ (eds), *Global Dominance and Dependence: Readings in Theory and Research* (Brunswick, Ohio: King's Court, 1978); and 'Chronique

bibliographie–the political economy of Africa: internal and international inequalities', *Cultures et Développement*, 10, 4 (1978), pp. 609–748.

57 Nnoli, *Self Reliance and Foreign Policy in Tanzania*, p. 197. See also Ali A. Mazrui, 'Socialism as a mode of international protest: the case of Tanzania', in Robert I. Rotberg and Ali A. Mazrui (eds), *Protest and Power in Black Africa* (New York: Oxford University Press, 1970), pp. 1139–52.

58 Pratt, *The Critical Phase in Tanzania*, pp. 6–7. See also Mwansasu and Pratt (eds), *Towards Socialism in Tanzania*; Lionel Cliffe, 'Tanzania's tricky road ahead', *New Internationalist*, 72 (February 1979), pp. 18–19.

59 On post-1977 Tanzania see, *inter alia*, 'Tanzania: Nyerere backs the little businessman', *New African*, 134 (October 1978), pp. 47–8; John Borrell, 'Tanzania rethinks socialist policies', *Christian Science Monitor*, 8 (August 1978); 'Nyerere supports free enterprise', *Weekly Review*, 142 (31 October 1977), pp. 5–7; Cliffe, 'Tanzania's tricky road ahead'; Lofchie, 'Agrarian crisis and economic liberalization in Tanzania'; 'Tanzania: New African survey'; 'Tanzania' in Colin Legum (ed.), *Africa Contemporary Record – Annual Survey and Documents*, Vol. 10, 1977–8 (New York: Africana, 1979), pp. B401–B432, esp. pp. B404–B405 and B417–B430.

60 Nyerere, *Ten Years After*, p. 21.

61 See Clark, *Socialist Development and Public Investment in Tanzania*, pp. 242–7. For other projections of the mid-term future see Reginald H. Green, *Toward Socialism and Self-Reliance: Tanzania's Striving for Sustained Transition Projected* (Uppsala: Scandinavian Institute of African Studies, 1977, Research Report No. 38); *Tanzania: Basic Economic Report*.

62 I. M. Kaduma, 'Tanzania: a background to the policy of self-reliance', in W. K. Chagula, B. T. Feld and A. Parthasrathi (eds), *Pugwash on Self-Reliance* (New Delhi: Ankur Publishing, 1977), p. 47.

4

From Dependence to Diversification: Canada, 1972–8

K. J. Holsti

In the midst of the 1972 election campaign, the Liberal government of Prime Minister Trudeau announced that it would seek to reduce Canadian vulnerability to American economic might by diversifying its traditional pattern of external relations, particularly in the area of trade. Vulnerability was also seen in the very significant American economic, cultural and communications 'presence' in Canada. To cope with this penetration, steps would have to be taken to strengthen Canada's economic and cultural institutions and to regulate some transaction flows between the two countries. The policy announced in the campaign was not going to be piecemeal, but would affect many of the official and private channels of transactions between the two countries, as well as involve a considerable expansion of Canadian diplomatic and commercial activity in third countries.

The shift in Canadian orientation in the 1970s is one of the few examples of a Western industrialized state seeking fundamentally to alter the profile of transactions with a major neighbor and to revise systematically a set of policies it had adopted in the postwar period. De Gaulle's France, the British loss of empire and decline of defense commitments around the world, its adherence to the EEC, and possibly Willy Brandt's *Ostpolitik* would qualify as important innovations in postwar foreign policy orientations, although all but the first involved only sectoral change and did not take place in a relatively short period of time. Canada is chosen not only because it is a developed industrial country, but also because its shift is fundamental in the sense described in Chapter 1. External diversification and reduction of penetration in the Canadian case resulted in part from a coherent policy philosophy, but also involved some more traditional forms of incremental change. The shift is reflected in multiple policy sectors as well.

Background

During the nineteenth century and until World War II, Canada's relations with Great Britain were typically colonial. Not only did most of Canada's trade in staples – the vast majority of its exports – go to England, promoted and protected by imperial preferential tariffs, but a significant proportion of the capital required to build Canada's transportation system and its industries also came from England. With the significant exception of the Quebec francophones, Canadians were also tied to England psychologically, through education, the churches and other important institutions.

The American presence in Canada nevertheless grew rapidly after the turn of the century. High Canadian tariffs, designed to keep out cheaper American products and to sustain Canada's own industrial development and high employment, prompted American firms to establish subsidiaries north of the 49th parallel. American goods produced in Canada appeared in ever-greater numbers, a significant proportion of which were then exported to England where they enjoyed entry under preferential tariffs. By the 1920s American capital investment in Canada was growing rapidly, while the British stake in the country, relatively speaking, began to decline. Similarly, an ever-increasing amount of Canada's trade became directed toward the United States.

World War II was the great watershed in the structure of Canada's diplomatic and commercial relations. Canada emerged from the war as one of the world's great military powers (the fourth largest fleet, for example), while financially pressed Great Britain was forced to dismantle its empire, and Europe was largely destroyed by war. Canadian–American collaboration during the war was extended into the cold war era, and was reflected in the dramatic growth of intergovernmental consultative and policy-making institutions and, more simply, the bureaucratic interchange. If Britain could claim a 'special relationship' with the United States during the cold war, it never reached the levels of transaction magnitude or diplomatic casualness that were found between Washington and Ottawa.

Few in Canada termed this prolific trade, investment, tourist and intergovernmental relationship one of dependence. Indeed, most Canadians claimed that *they* had a 'special relationship' with Washington. If by that term we mean ease of access, special consideration of requests and informality in conducting intergovernmental business, then this view was correct. Most Canadians also applauded the vast flow of American investment into the country. A few complained that Americans were investing primarily in raw materials, so that Canada's exports were designed to feed America's vast industrial establishment. Yet many industries were developing in Canada as well, and a significant part of that growth was fueled with American dollars. In addition, American firms were buying up Canadian plants at an ever-increasing rate, but few Canadians objected. Already by 1950, 65 percent of Canada's trade was with the United States, and by 1955 American investment in Canada accounted for almost 23 percent of the country's GNP. Canada's imports and exports to the United States accounted for another 22 percent of the GNP. No two other countries in the world were linked so closely, but the benefits to Canada were substantial.

If there was a governmental philosophy about Canadian-American relations at this time, it was one of laissez-faire economics, and quiet and casual diplomacy in the conduct of intergovernmental relations. There were occasional Canadian-American irritations, but nothing that could be termed an 'international conflict'.

Public opinion in Canada overwhelmingly supported the government's general approach to relations with the United States. Respondents to polls indicated strong sentiments in favor of continued American investment in Canada, and support of most American foreign policies and major Canadian-American collaborative enterprises. Only a few critics portrayed the United States as constituting a threat to Canadian economic, cultural, or political interests.

The patterns of Canadian-American collaboration in the 1950s and 1960s are symbolized in three major bilateral arrangements: NORAD (1957), the Defense Production Sharing Agreements (1959) and the Automotive Products Agreement (1965). All these agreements contain integrationist (Canadians call them 'continentalist') features, and for some people they serve as prototypes of other sectors of Canadian-American interchange that should be rationalized.

Under NORAD, North America is carved up into several air defense zones which do not correspond exactly to political boundaries. Most radar installations, such as the DEW line, are financed by the United States, but others are jointly funded, usually in a ratio of one Canadian dollar for every American ten dollars. Within the organization, some Canadian forces are under the effective command of an American officer, and in one zone, American forces operate under a Canadian's command. NORAD headquarters in Colorado Springs are headed by an American, with a Canadian deputy. Under the terms of the treaty establishing NORAD, Canadian contingents in the defense network can be put on alert or into combat operation only with the consent of the Canadian government. But the possibilities of the Canadian government refusing to allow an alert status to become operational, or to allow American fighters to cross over Canadian territory, are theoretical rather than real. Prime Minister Diefenbaker initially refused to activate Canadian forces in NORAD during the 1962 Cuban crisis, but relented within several days under extreme pressure from the Canadian military and other sources. NORAD is classified as a continentalist endeavor because it contains a zonal defense system that is based on military practicality rather than national borders; stationing of American personnel in Canada (to man the DEW line); joint planning for tactical air defense; free access to Canadian air space by American military aircraft, and in some instances, effective American command over some Canadian military units.

Under the Defense Production Sharing Agreements, Canadian arms manufacturers are allowed to bid on American defense contracts on an equal basis with domestic American producers. This arrangement has enabled the Canadian defense industry, which directly employs about 13,000 persons, to survive, whereas it would quickly perish if it had to confine its sales to the small (about 80,000 personnel) Canadian military establishment. Sizable electronics, airframe and munitions industries in Canada are dependent upon sales to the United States. From the American point of view, the DPSA were accepted because they helped disperse the locations of arms sources, particularly in case of nuclear war, and also because many of the Canadian defense firms are really subsidiaries of American companies. Although some voices in the United States have urged the discontinuation of the agreements (because they add to US balance of payments problems and represent job exports from America) the Pentagon has strongly resisted alteration or termination of the agreements. The total military trade between the two countries is not extensive from an American point of view, but for Canada it represents a vital factor in sustaining Canadian military technology, jobs and a more favorable balance of payments situation. For example, between 1959 and 1968, American purchases of Canadian military goods constituted between 26 to 68 percent of all Canadian inedible end product exports to the United States; during the first thirteen years of the agreements, Canada accumulated $500 million surplus in arms trade with the United States.[1]

The Automotive Products Agreement constitutes the final point of the continentalist trinity. Prior to 1965, American automobile plants in Canada produced almost exclusively for the relatively small Canadian market. The result, of course, was high unit costs. The 1965 agreement turned North America into a single production and marketing area. For example, today a Chevrolet plant in Quebec produces all Vega models for the east coast of Canada and the United States. The Ford plant in Ontario produces particular models for sale in central Canada, the east coast of the United States and the midwest. Ford models sold in Vancouver, on the other hand, are built in California. Trade in new automobile parts is also free. An Oldsmobile built in Detroit, for example, may contain numerous parts manufactured in Ontario.

From an economic point of view, the agreement brought substantial economic benefits to Canada until the late 1970s. Automotive output has increased dramatically, and for the first time in history, manufactured goods – mostly cars – have become an important component of Canada's export trade. Thanks to this agreement and the DPSA, Canada is no longer solely a 'hewer of wood and drawer of water' as far as trade with the United States is concerned.

These agreements have also made the defense and automobile industries in Canada dependent upon a single market in the United States, but at the time they were entered into, such dependence did not seem to involve any risks. Indeed, until the energy crisis of 1973, there was much discussion in Ottawa and Washington about developing a continental energy policy, meaning in effect that Americans would pay for the development of Canadian energy resources which would then be distributed according to some formula between the two countries.

These three agreements are important not only because they establish the context within which numerous Canadian-American transactions take place, but also because they reveal the underlying assumptions of Canadian policy-makers of the 1950s and 1960s with regard to Canadian-American relations. The assumptions were that (1) collaborative enterprises and schemes that rationalise production and market conditions bring significant rewards to both parties and minimize costs; (2) there are no notable political consequences involved in continentalist arrangements; (3) Canadian contribution to a healthy American economy or strategic deterrence brings significant benefits to Canada; and (4) there are no other nations with whom Canada could develop relations on a basis similar to those with the United States.

The Pattern of Relations: Time One

Let us now compose the photograph of Canada's externally directed actions, taking data and trends from the postwar period until the election of the Trudeau government in 1968. In trade, as suggested, the trend was toward increasing geographic concentration, although in 1965 there is decreased product concentration thanks largely to the Automotive and Defense Production Sharing Agreements. In 1959, 56 percent of Canada's exports went to the United States. A peak of 71 percent was reached in 1969. Naturally, there was a corresponding decline in trade with Great Britain and Europe. Imports from the United States show a similar trend. In 1960, 67 percent of Canada's imports came from the south, and reached a peak in 1969, when the figure was 73 percent.[2] Such figures are meaningless in themselves, but when we consider that Canada's exports to the United States accounted, on average, for almost 13 percent of Canada's GNP, we can see the extent to which Canada was – and remains – potentially vulnerable to trade fluctuations. In announcing its policy of diversification and vulnerability reduction, the government clearly expected that without its intervention, the trend would continue upward until virtually all of Canada's external commerce was directed to the United States.

In the diplomatic sector, a similar picture emerges. During the first two postwar decades, for example, the voting patterns of Canada and the United States in the General Assembly were virtually identical. We cannot assume, as some have, that the closeness of voting resulted from trade dependence or from American investment in Canada. At most, voting similarity suggests similar outlooks on foreign policy issues, which is not to be unexpected between two countries that share a culture, language and continent. The average score of an index of agreement between Canada and the United States in General Assembly Yes and No votes between 1946 and 1967, the last full year of the Pearson government, is ·951. In 1952, 1956, 1957, 1960, 1963 and 1965–7, there was complete agreement, a pattern more commonly thought as typical of the Soviet bloc countries. Indices of agreement where abstentions are counted as a no vote show similar parallelism, but at a lower level. The average score is ·704 between 1946 and 1967. Without drawing unwarranted inferences from these figures, it is clear that on this single form of diplomatic activity, Canadian and American voting patterns are almost indistinguishable.

In the NORAD bilateral relationship, similarity of purpose and close collaboration were also prominent. The Cuban missile crisis presented an exception to the rule; Diefenbaker's foot-dragging was not typical of the relationship. The Canadian defense bureaucracy, for example, maintained strong informal and formal networks of communication with the Pentagon; if there were important differences on policy questions, they were not made public. In the 1963 Canadian electoral campaign, however, the arming of Canadian NORAD and NATO forces with nuclear weapons became a major issue. Indeed, Diefenbaker's government collapsed because of Cabinet dissension on the problem, although in the former Prime Minister's recollection, it was American pressure on Canada to accept the arms that eventually led to his downfall. Once in office the Pearson government accepted the arms, although by that time some of the weapons designated for NORAD were nearing obsolescence. Through the remainder of the 1960s there was no basic conflict in the Canadian-American defense issue area.

Vietnam represents a more difficult case for identifying parallelism in Canadian and American policies. Critics of the Canadian-American relationship often point to Canada's role in Vietnam as an example of Canadian 'complicity' in American aggression. According to them, Canadian behavior is explained satisfactorily by the American economic domination of Canada. Several well-selected quotes from speeches by Prime Minister Pearson suggest that the government was not as free to criticize American actions as it might have wanted to be. In some cases, indeed, fears of American economic retaliation were expressed. On the other hand, there is little question that during the early years of the war, Canadians defined the situation – and the stakes – in Southeast Asia in virtually the same terms as did the American government. Public opinion polls showed that a large majority of Canadians supported the United States well into 1966 and that a significant minority hoped the United States would escalate the war.[3] With such public sentiments, it is not likely the Canadian government would blithely criticize Washington for its Vietnam venture.

But even during the early stages of the war, Ottawa's position was perceptively different – not perhaps in the assumption of the domino theory or the legal and moral right of the United States to intervene, but rather in its expectations that the conflict could be resolved by diplomacy rather than through the escalation of violence. The Pearson government constantly urged the United States to explore diplomatic solutions and to abandon the strategy of forcing North Vietnam to the conference table by bombing, and on one occasion Pearson personally delivered a speech in Philadelphia urging President Johnson to announce a bombing halt. This démarche led to an undiplomatic rebuff from the White House, but there is no evidence that the American government in general or Johnson in particular ever considered turning economic screws on Canada in order to make it line up 100 percent with American policies in Southeast Asia.

The critics were correct in one respect, however. The Canadian government could not contemplate shutting off the flow of war materiel to the United States because of the negative economic consequences. The defense production agreements tie the Canadian arms industry closely to the American market, but it is a mere trickle in terms of America's total defense production. Whether or not the calculation was ever made in Ottawa remains unknown, but a threat to stop selling arms to the United States during the Vietnam war would have had serious economic consequences on Canada with no probable impact on American policy. This is one result of asymmetrical dependence. On Vietnam, then, Canada appeared to most Canadians as an accomplice, and to others as an overly timid critic.

But the similarities in outlook can be understood more as a function of common values and perceptions of the 'communist threat' than as a result of American economic influence in Canada.

In many other areas of foreign policy, the picture was essentially the same: some disagreements on details and tactics, but no fundamental conflict. Strong parallelism existed, for example, in multilateral GATT negotiations and the development of NATO strategy. The Canadian government continued to be a recipient of select information obtained by American intelligence agencies (which helps explain Canada's agreement with the United States on the fundamental problems involved in the Vietnam war); and on matters of internal security, cooperative arrangements between the FBI and RCMP, established during World War II, continued without significant change.

But there were also some issues where Canada and the United States held distinctive points of view, although they did not lead to bilateral conflict. Canada never broke diplomatic and commercial relations with Cuba and, indeed, took up at least part of the trade the United States had lost from its embargo and boycott of the Caribbean island. Canada also refrained from joining the Organization of American States, despite Kennedy's personal pleas to Diefenbaker and members of the Canadian parliament. The government was reluctant to join an organization in which it might have to choose between supporting Latin American states and Washington, particularly on the Cuba issue.

The Canadian members of the International Control Commission in Vietnam, despite being selected to the Commission as the 'Western' representative, occasionally criticized the United States for its violation of the 1954 Geneva agreements. In general, the Canadian representatives on the ICC were torn between their duty to supervise a hopeless peace, to appear reasonably objective and to represent the 'West' in order to balance off the Polish delegation which, of course, was incapable of seeing any North Vietnamese transgressions. Finally, as a member of the Geneva Disarmament Commission, Canada in the 1960s frequently criticized the United States, particularly on the questions of nuclear testing and on-site inspection. While the American delegation continued to hold out for inspection as a necessary condition for cessation of nuclear testing, the Canadians and Swedes emphasized that the technology necessary for distinguishing nuclear explosions from earthquakes already existed. Canadian delegates generally opposed the more meaningless Soviet proposals, but they did not automatically espouse American positions either.

Our photograph of Canada's externally directed actions in the 1950s and 1960s thus shows strong parallels to American positions, but not unanimity. Collaboration in bilateral relations was flourishing, and the growth of transnational and transgovernmental contacts was in an almost constantly upward direction. Differences on questions such as Cuba, Vietnam and Latin America did not spill over into other sectors of the relationship, or into other foreign policy issues. Indeed, one of the major characteristics of the relationship was the extent to which the various sectors were isolated from each other and how the governments could not – or would not – use bargaining advantages in one sector to extract concessions in another.

There was no American 'policy' toward Canada, nor did Ottawa have a 'policy' toward the United States. Transgovernmental bureaucracies tended to conduct their business with little or no coordination by formal diplomatic mechanisms or by Cabinet-level officials.

The photograph of the relationship is incomplete without a brief outline of the movement of people, as well as goods, money and diplomatic notes. During the 1950s and 1960s, there was a pronounced movement of intellectual and artistic talent from Canada to the United States. Canadian physicians, dentists, theater personalities and some intellectuals went south because of considerably greater career opportunities or, for physicians, higher salaries and less government regulation of medical practice. Oscar Peterson, Paul Anka, Robert Goulet, Lorne Green, Genevieve Bujold, Harry Johnson, Ferguson Jenkins and David Easton, just to name a few from a variety of professions, were among the Canadians who went south after World War II. In a typical year during this period, about 30,000 Canadians emigrated to the United States annually, while only about 9,000 Americans moved north. Except for a few football players who came to play in Canada, there were few American celebrities among those 9,000.[4]

What of American penetration into Canada? What sort of attitudes governed 'foreign influences' in the country? Government policies were of a liberal, laissez-faire nature, although a few sensitive areas such as banking and transportation were regulated to exclude foreign ownership. The other areas of the economy remained wide open for foreign investment or for the purchase of extant Canadian firms by outsiders. At its high point in 1955, American investment in Canada represented 84 percent of all foreign investment in the country, although in terms of investment as a proportion of GNP, the peak was not reached until 1960, when American investment or takeovers accounted for 27·5 percent of Canada's GNP.[5] In various industries such as oil, chemicals, auto manufacturing, electronics and telephone communications, the vast majority of Canadian enterprises were owned or controlled by Americans. A general figure is that in the 1950s and 1960s, 55 percent of Canada's manufacturing sector was owned or controlled by Americans. No other country in the world had – or has – such a magnitude of its economic activity accounted for by foreign investors. If British capital launched Canadian modernization in the nineteenth century, American capital completed the job in the twentieth century. The difference is that British capital took the form of portfolio investment, while America's contribution to Canada's growth has been in the form of direct investment and purchase of existing Canadian enterprises. This form of investment is permanent and, as will be suggested below, may have an impact far beyond the economic realm. It is because of its actual or potential influence on consumption habits, cultural patterns, employment levels, research and development, and politics that investment from abroad can be conceived as a form of external penetration.

In the realm of communications, the American presence in Canada was no less pervasive. By the mid-1960s American publications accounted for about 53 percent of the magazine circulation in Canada; nearly 50 percent of Canadian advertising spent in magazines went to two American publications, *Time* and *Reader's Digest*.[6] Most pocket books sold on Canadian newsstands were American, since it was American firms in Canada that controlled the trade. Even though there is no lack of paperback publications in Canada, they were seldom sold outside traditional bookstores.

The situation in the film industry was similar. In the rough time-span of our first photograph, about 40 percent of the films shown in Canada originated in the United States. The remainder came from Europe, with only a miniscule showing of Canadian films.[7] High production costs made Canada an unlikely country for developing a film industry for the small Canadian market. Yet a large majority of theaters in Canada were and continue to be owned by American firms – particularly United Artists – whose tie-ins with the motion picture industry in the United States prevented them from showing Canadian films, even when good ones were available. As a result, Canadian writers and actors (with some important exceptions in Quebec) went abroad to make their careers, and the Canadian film industry remained centered around a quasi-government agency, the National Film Board, which produced speciality films and shorts.

Although Americans do not own the television industry in Canada, the viewing habits of Canadians in the 1950s and 1960s resembled their habits in publications and films. Canada has two nationwide television networks, but most viewers were watching American television most of the time. In part, this was because most of the country's population lives within 100 miles of the American border and could thus pick up television signals from American border towns, and in part because a large proportion of the programs broadcast on the CBC and CTV were originally produced in the United States. Thus, even before the advent of cablevision, there were more American channels available to most Canadians than Canadian channels, and if we multiply this by the total hours of American programming available in Canada, on whichever network, then perhaps as much as 80 percent of the total television viewing possibilities originated south of the border. If the public viewing habits are any indication of quality, then during the 1950s and 1960s Canadians preferred American to Canadian programs.[8] The exception, again, was Quebec, where much heavier reliance upon Canadian-produced shows was the rule. It is possible to argue, then, that with the exception of a few ritual offerings such as 'Hockey Night in Canada', Canadian viewers were tuned into programs with American style, content and advertising. Although some American border communities could easily pick up Canadian television signals, there is no indication that Canadian programs were watched extensively in the United States; indeed, for most of them, the shows they could pick up from the CBC or CTV were the same ones available to them from ABC, NBC and CBS. Thus, in terms of the flow of messages between the two countries it was almost exclusively a movement from south to north.

The impact of television on viewers has long been debated. While there have been strong critics of American investment in Canada, few Canadians argued vigorously that American programs should be curtailed or that the CBC should try to produce shows with unique Canadian content. Partly this was because such actions might smack of censorship, but perhaps it was also because American television had been genuinely popular in

Canada. Yet studies have demonstrated that Canadian children know a great deal more about American politics and celebrities than they do of the politics of their own country or province.[9] In part this may be attributed to the relatively greater excitement of American politics, but the information must be conveyed through television, since the Canadian press gives much more coverage to Canadian politics than it does to the United States. No particular judgement can be made from these knowledge differentials, but they do allow the observer to infer that television constituted an important medium of foreign penetration (or perhaps 'spill-over' is a better word) into Canada.

One final area of penetration needs to be outlined to complete the photograph. During the 1960s Canadian universities expanded rapidly. Institutions which were really liberal arts colleges in the 1950s began graduate programs; new universities were planned and built by the dozens; older institutions vastly increased the breadth of the course offerings, and organized new departments. Clearly there were not enough qualified Canadians to man all the new positions. Canadian universities had traditionally recruited staff from all over the world (and are better because of it), a practice that was almost unique among the developed countries. The Canadian government, thanks to its liberal immigration policies and provision of a two-year income tax holiday to incoming academics, helped in its own way to support the needs of the universities.

In these circumstances – and perhaps propelled by disillusionment over Vietnam and civil disturbances in the United States – American academics flocked to Canada throughout the decade. By 1970, more than 15 percent of all academic positions in Canada were held by American citizens.[10] There were, of course, many more who had been born, raised and educated in the United States, who later became Canadian citizens and are thus not included in the figure. Critics of this situation argued that even these persons constituted a type of foreign penetration because they would teach and do research in terms of the intellectual fads and paradigms popular in the United States. Some critics even warned that by the late 1960s or early 1970s, Canadian-born educators were due to become a minority in their own institutions. This situation did prevail in some departments.

As with television, it is difficult to estimate the consequences of foreign teachers in institutions of higher learning. There is no question that non-Canadians have made very impressive contributions to Canadian academic life. The field of anthropology was almost created in Canada by outstanding scholars from New Zealand, England and the United States. There is little doubt, as well, that area studies have profited immensely from foreign scholars. If the typical Canadian student was somewhat parochial in his world outlook, some compensation could be found through educational experience with professors from many different backgrounds.

But there is another side to the issue. Some Americans, as department heads, hired their friends and graduate students from the United States without even inquiring if suitable Canadians were available. Others, taking a universalist (read American) perspective on what is important in scholarship, refused to expand Canadian studies or, in some extreme cases, even to offer *any* courses in subjects such as Canadian literature, politics, social problems or music. These incidents were no justification for the type of academic nationalism which emphasizes national problems to the exclusion of all other subjects, but they did give rise to serious concern. A trend in penetration had started which, if continued, could eventually have led to the atrophy of student knowledge of their own country's history, politics and society. While most academics in Canada could not sympathise with the ardent advances of national seclusion, almost all of them recognized that the pattern of academic staffing in the 1960s should probably not carry on into the 1970s. Even with some exclusionist policies, Canadian academia would still stand unique in the world in terms of the diverse national origins of its staff.

In the areas of investment, communications and higher education, then, Canada by the 1960s was highly penetrated by foreign and particularly American investment, media, messages and teachers.[11] Where Canada differed significantly from some of the other cases in this book is in the area of government penetration. Unlike Tanzania, Bhutan and Burma, whose capitals were flooded with military, educational, technical, agricultural and government advisers from abroad, Ottawa's policies were made by Canadians without the benefit or cost of external advice. The forms of penetration we have discussed in this chapter all resulted from the free flow of goods, ideas and people between Canada and the United States, a flow that continues to be unique in terms of its size, ease of movement and multiplicity of dimensions. But as our picture demonstrates, it was predominantly a one-way flow from south to north, movement of talent being the sole exception. There was and continues to be substantial Canadian investment in the United States, but until recently most of it was portfolio investment, and as a proportion of total American investment it was puny indeed. Few Americans watch Canadian television programs since further south than Seattle, Detroit, and Burlington, Vermont, Americans are not even aware that the CBC exists. Similarly, while some Canadian academics have gone to institutions in the United States, no American faculty need fear that soon its membership will be outnumbered by professors of foreign origin. Given, then, that the flow was basically in one direction, taking place within a bilateral relationship that is inherently asymmetrical, it is not surprising that some exclusionist responses would arise in Canada. We turn, then, to the government and grass-roots actions which were designed to halt or reverse the trends established in the first two-and-one-half decades after World War II.

The 'Third Option': Strategies for Reducing Vulnerability

The election of 1968 which brought Pierre Trudeau to the Prime Minister's office was not organized around the issue of American influence in Canada, although by that time it had already become a matter of some public debate. Trudeau's campaign rhetoric did not suggest that relations with the United States constituted a problem for Canada. Yet shortly after his election, a few steps were taken by the government suggesting that there would be at least some change from the policies of Pearson and his predecessors. For one thing, the government's defense review recommended that 'protection of Canadian sovereignty' become the first priority in defense planning and allocations, while commitments to NORAD, NATO and international peace-keeping would assume lower priority. Moreover, the Canadian Radio and Television Commission (CRTC) placed a minimum requirement of 30 percent Canadian content on all AM radio stations. The objective was, presumably, to promote Canadian musical talent which hitherto found career possibilities only in the United States. This policy was also designed in part to give effect to the argument that

> An adequate Canadian content in television [and radio] is unlikely to be achieved by a laissez-faire policy of minimum regulations, governing advertising volume, morality, and the like. Economic forces in North America are such that any substantial amount of Canadian programs will not appear on television schedules unless room is reserved for them by regulation. The plea of private stations that they would produce better Canadian programs if they were allowed to concentrate the available money on fewer productions is not supported by the experience of radio, for which there is no specific Canadian content requirement.[12]

The CRTC's Canadian content minimum requirement was the first systematic attempt to regulate the market forces operating between Canada and the United States.[13] But the regulation was imposed by an independent government agency operating under the 1968 Broadcasting Act, and was not the result of a comprehensive Cabinet-level change in policy vis-à-vis the United States. Indeed, in its 1970 major foreign policy review, 'A Foreign Policy for Canadians', the government did not include a section on relations with the United States–even though it acknowledged that those relations were the most important single fact in Canada's external activities. In October 1972 the Secretary of State for External Affairs, Mitchell Sharp, published a special issue of his department's journal, entitled 'Canada–US Relations: Options for the Future'.[14] Sharp outlined three possible strategies for conducting future diplomatic and commercial relations with the United States. The first alternative was to seek more integration with the United States, through further continentalist agreements. This alternative was rejected on the grounds that it would lead to the loss of Canadian political sovereignty and would not be consistent with the views of a majority of Canadians. The second option (Sharp's essay has come to be known as the 'Three Options Paper') was to let present trends continue, that is, to reaffirm the desirability of the free flow of people, goods, money and ideas between the two countries, and to leave most transaction flows unregulated. Sharp predicted that the ultimate result of this option would be similar to that of formal integration: Canada's capacity to act independently in economic and foreign affairs would become increasingly circumscribed. The 'third option', then, was to adopt a 'comprehensive long-range strategy to develop and strengthen the Canadian economy and other aspects of its internal life and in the process to reduce the present vulnerability [to the United States]'. He indicated that henceforth the Canadian government would seek to establish counterweights in its foreign relations and build up domestic Canadian institutions to the point where American penetration would no longer be seen as a threat to the survival of those institutions.

The paper was not without its ambiguities, as critics were quick to point out. Nor did the paper launch all of the policies designed to reduce vulnerability. As suggested, there had already been incremental policies, particularly by the CRTC, which sought to regulate broadcasting, and Trudeau had often spoken of the need for creating counterweights to Canada's relations with the United States.

Various government agencies interpreted Sharp's document in different ways, but between the publication of the overall foreign policy review in 1970 and the 'three options' essay, four distinct strategies for dealing with the United States were outlined: (1) establishing various 'border-screening devices' to monitor and regulate the flow of people, goods and information between the two countries; (2) building up Canadian institutions by providing subsidies or special protection; (3) creating bureaucratic mechanisms for establishing some degree of central control over the full range of Canada's official transactions with the United States – what John Kirton has called an 'arms-length' approach to diplomacy rather than the loose and casual contacts maintained in an era of 'good partnership'; and (4) diversifying diplomatic and especially commercial relations with various countries.[15]

Monitoring and Regulating Bilateral Transactions: 'Border-Screening' Devices

The CRTC, after its initial regulatory ruling on Canadian content on AM radio, continued to extend these regulations into television broadcasting and advertising, despite criticism from the private broadcasting industry and, in some cases, from segments of the Canadian public. In its own words, the CRTC stated:

> The year 1970–71 may be considered a turning point in the history of Canadian broadcasting in the light of major transactions occurring in the system at all levels . . . Only a decided effort to integrate production resources to provide Canadian programming will allow the system to remain Canadian and serve the social, cultural, political, and economic goals required of it by the Broadcasting Act.[16]

By 1971 Canadian television broadcasters were required to devote 60 percent of air time to Canadian material. A certain proportion of the 60 percent also had to appear on 'prime time'. Of the remaining 40 percent, only three-fourths of the material could originate from any single country, an obvious limitation on the showing of American-produced programs.[17] By 1975 the CRTC had also ruled that FM radio stations would have to 'give highest consideration and encouragement to the broadcast of extended works written, performed, and produced by Canadians in

Canada'.[18] The following year the CRTC announced the guidelines it would use in granting cable TV licenses. In practice, the policy has been to grant licenses to community-oriented stations rather than to allow new American stations to be carried on cable. In one case in Vancouver, the CRTC allocated a prime channel to a new Canadian station and moved a Seattle-based cable station to a channel which offered poorer reception. The total number of American-based channels available in Canada has not been reduced, but the CRTC has openly encouraged and favored Canadian licenses for new channels.

The CRTC also moved to control broadcast advertising. In 1975 it required that all licensees 'be willing to delete commercial messages from signals received from broadcasters not licensed to serve Canada, and their replacement by suitable Canadian material'.[19] In effect this ruling eliminated the 'spill-over' of American commercials into Canada. At the same time the CRTC moved to increase Canadian participation in commercials broadcast in Canada. By the end of 1979, because of new regulations, 80 percent of the commercials shown on Canadian television channels were made in Canada, by Canadian musicians, singers, announcers, technicians and production facilities. The move has not only stopped most Canadian advertising dollars going to the south, but has become a great boon for the advertising industry. Finally, in its attempt to regulate American communications penetration into Canada, the CRTC in 1969 restricted foreign ownership of broadcasting companies to a maximum of 20 percent of the shares. In 1970–1 alone, forty-eight companies were required by the Commission to divest themselves of non-Canadian interests.

By the end of 1979, then, the CRTC achieved what was proposed in the 1966 Fowler Report, namely, the establishment of a strong Canadian broadcasting industry, designed to provide as much employment and support of Canadian talent and production facilities as is consistent with a reasonably free flow of communication between the United States and Canada. The CRTC has not attempted to influence program content other than to insist that a certain percentage of it be of Canadian origin.

The government also took measures to prop up the Canadian publishing industry prior to the publication of Sharp's paper. In 1965 the Pearson government terminated the tax exemption Canadian advertisers received for publishing their materials in magazines originating in foreign countries. Under strong pressure from Washington, however, *Time* and *Reader's Digest* were exempted from the legislation. Bill C-58, which became law on 1 January 1976, effectively ended this special status, at least for *Time* magazine. The law stated that henceforth advertisers would receive tax exemptions only for material published in magazines which were at least 80 percent different in content from American publications. Since the Canadian edition of *Time* was basically the American edition with a few pages of Canadian material tacked on at the front, advertisers using its pages would no longer be able to deduct their costs. *Time* therefore ended the publication of its Canadian edition. Because *Reader's Digest* in the Canadian edition is totally produced in Montreal, its advertisers continue to enjoy the tax exemption.

The secretary of state, Hugh Falkner, under whose jurisdiction matters of culture and communications lay, followed somewhat different tactics in the area of films. He offered heavy subsidies to the Canadian Film Development Corporation, while arm twisting major theater chain owners into showing Canadian films. His ultimate goal was for the theaters to show Canadian films up to two weeks of each quarter and return some of their profits to the Canadian film industry.[20] The tactics have differed, but the overall strategy of 'Canadianization' was similar to other areas: do not restrict American penetration, but build up Canadian institutions, through government assistance, to the point where they can compete on a more equitable basis.

American investment in Canada was probably the most contentious issue in the debate about American penetration. The critics of the 'free market' approach singled out the American ownership of economic enterprise in Canada and the increasing rate of takeovers of Canadian companies by foreign firms, as the single most important form of penetration. The consequences ran all the way, it was claimed, from distortion of the Canadian economy to meet American needs, to secret manipulation and pressures on Canadian governments by American subsidiaries and their allies in Washington.

Though foreign investment had aroused debate as early as 1965, the government did not move to alter its position of being one of the most liberal countries in the world in its treatment of foreign capital. Finally, in 1974, Parliament passed the Foreign Investment Review Act, which established an agency to screen all new investments worth more than $2 million and to review takeover bids of Canadian firms by foreigners. To obtain approval, an application must indicate that the investment or takeover will bring a 'significant benefit' to Canada in the form of increased employment, transfer of technology, creation of export markets, and the like. While the Review Board has exercised its mandate in a very liberal manner (see below), the government at least has the potential capacity to regulate new investment and takeover bids. In short it can halt the trend of the 1950s and 1960s, but to the disappointment of some, it cannot undo what took place after World War II.[21]

These policies represent a substantial change from the practices of the 1950s and 1960s. They were a response to a set of trends which came to be seen by many Canadians as threatening to certain types of institutions and perhaps ultimately to Canadian political independence. Not all Canadians agreed on the nature or severity of the threat and, as will be discussed below, the government's response to the situation was both slow in coming and, according to some, not sufficiently restrictive. As in other cases in our study, then, a fundamental change in attitudes and policies toward other states may result not from a military threat, but from the seemingly inexorable growth of the flow of money, goods and messages between societies. What to most Americans and some Canadians looked like a classical relationship of interdependence, by the late 1960s came to be regarded by an increasing number of Canadians as a system typified by dependence, vulnerability and penetration, with absorption as the ultimate consequence of these. Faced with a basically asymmetrical structure of transactions, the smaller party will likely respond with measures that go far beyond the classical demands for tariff protection. In the Canadian case, several important 'border-screening' devices were used to regulate and, in some cases, to reduce the amount of foreign penetration. Such actions were not confined to central government policy either.

Both labor unions and universities acted to alter situations they conceived to be inimical to certain national values. Canadian unions have traditionally been locals of American-based 'international' unions, a situation having many historical roots, including the aspiration of Canadian labor to obtain parity with American wage rates. Since the mid-1960s, however, the Canadian labor movement has systematically broken its formal relationships with American unions and has created a large number of Canadian-based organizations. As the last section of this chapter demonstrates, this movement constitutes a very dramatic form of disintegration in one social sector.

The universities instituted policies requiring all vacant positions to be advertised throughout Canada. Beyond this formal regulation, most university departments unofficially gave preference to Canadian candidates, all other things being equal. A few departments, particularly in the social sciences, adopted informal rules which in effect excluded American applicants from positions. In other sectors, there has been considerable support directed toward the arts and entertainment that was not previously available. This is not the place to evaluate the arts in Canada today, but compared to the 1960s most people would agree that at least it is not mandatory for Canadian talent to move abroad to receive adequate training and possibilities for making a career.

Finally, several provincial governments passed legislation to regulate the sale of recreational and other properties to foreigners, halting a trend in the 1960s which saw an increasing amount of prime waterfront and agricultural land being sold to Americans. This high American demand for such land had, of course, driven up values substantially, thereby increasing profits for speculators, but decreasing the accessibility of such land to Canadian citizens.

Institution-Building and Canadian-American Relations

The practice of using government funds to establish and sustain institutions which would tie the diverse regions and ethnic groups of Canada into a united whole was not invented by the Trudeau government. Air Canada, the CBC and other undertakings of the 1920s and 1930s were designed in part to overcome the divisive effects of Canada's vast geographic expanse. Crown corporations and other bureaucratic devices have played a prominent role in molding Canada into a coherent, if not totally cohesive, society. Under the pressure of the American problem, new initiatives to support Canadian institutions were launched by the Trudeau government. The Canada Development Corporation emerged as an institution designed, in part, to buy back American-owned subsidiaries in Canada, to provide Canadians with a vehicle for investing in Canada rather than in the United States, and to undertake new industrial projects. Petro-Canada, another crown corporation, was launched to ensure that national priorities rather than the profits of American-owned oil corporations would figure prominently in the development of Canadian oil and gas resources as well as energy policy. Government grants to the Canada Council, which funds numerous artistic and academic enterprises, grew substantially in the late 1960s and early 1970s. Finally, the CBC – perhaps the prime instrument for helping to create or sustain an identifiable culture – vastly expanded its broadcast facilities and its range of locally originating programs. This list of government-sponsored undertakings is not exhaustive, but it does indicate the importance of using public revenues for purposes of subsidizing local undertakings as a method of adjusting relations with a dominant state. Institution-building was a major element in the strategy of reducing vulnerability to, and penetration by, the United States.

Establishing Central Control over Policy and Diplomacy toward the United States

Throughout most of the postwar period, Canada's relations toward the United States were neither conducted with coordination nor guided by any sense of an overall strategy or set of objectives to be achieved. The relationship featured loose transgovernmental contacts, with each of the policy sectors more or less isolated from the other. Diplomacy was characterized by ease of access between the two capitals, non-linkage of issues during bargaining, low conflict levels and overall lack of direction or control at the Cabinet level. Arrangements and agreements were made directly between the two national bureaucracies concerned, without necessary reference to either the Department of External Affairs or to the State Department.[22]

Since publication of the 'Three Options Paper', the Department of External Affairs, and particularly its USA division, sought to 'manage' the entirety of the Canadian-American relationship. According to Kirton, the idea that the relationship can be managed rests on several new conceptions about the future: (1) a new era in the bilateral field has begun; (2) divergent interests rather than common interests predominate; (3) while not eschewing mutually beneficial solutions to problems, more issues than previously contain seeds of conflict; (4) whatever advantages may have been gained through 'special relationships', 'exemptionalism', 'good partnership' or client state status, the appropriate strategy for new conditions should be one of 'arms-length' diplomacy. With an increasing volume of issues to be resolved, and higher friction levels between Washington and Ottawa, the government sought to create 'a coordinative center to maintain a continuous overview of the entire relationship, identify interrelationships among its components and prepare a strategy for conducting it in an orchestrated manner'.[23]

In giving effect to these views, External Affairs achieved some success in eradicating the 'no border' syndrome that prevailed in Ottawa's officialdom prior to the Sharp paper. There has been, then, some decline in the level of transgovernmental relations between Ottawa and Washington, and a growing role for the DEA in handling all those aspects of the relationship that previously were dealt with directly between the two countries' bureaucracies. The Cabinet, too, became involved in American-related issues 'in a more detailed, regular and systematic manner than was the case before'.[24] Finally, in conducting negotiations, Canadian diplomats unlike their predecessors became willing to tolerate increased levels of conflict, and more frequently initiated discussions, even on controversial matters, rather than reacting to American initiatives. The effects on Canadian interests in terms of gains and losses are not possible to measure, but it is important to point out that in Canada's case, at least, the attempt to restructure foreign policy was accompanied by significant changes in patterns of decision-making and control over transgovernmental relations, as well as changes in the types and directions of actions.

Diversifying External Relations

The strategy of external diversification was pursued primarily through three sectors – trade, diplomatic communication and cultural relations. The attempt to expand trade relations with other countries was argued on the grounds that diversification is the best way to reduce Canada's vulnerability both to fluctuations in the American market and to decisions made in Washington which have a harmful impact on the Canadian economy. In addition, Canada should seek to get other countries to appreciate that Canadian economic interests are often distinct from those of the United States, so that in multilateral negotiations in particular there would be some recognition of Canada's special needs. The effort to arrange some special relationship between Canada and the EEC, for example, was based in part on the fear of developing trade blocs, in which Canada would obviously remain simply an integral part of 'North America'.

After several years of diplomatic work, including several visits by Trudeau to Europe, the EEC and Canada signed a 'Framework Agreement' in 1976. This was the first treaty between the Europe of the Nine and another industrial country. The agreement established no special trade advantages for Canada nor, indeed, did it elaborate any new ground rules for cooperation. However, the treaty did achieve the Canadian objective of obtaining European recognition of Canada as a country with economic interests distinct from those of the United States. The agreement established a Joint Cooperation Committee which was designed to identify areas where trade and investment could be increased. The Canadians apparently hoped within a decade to double trade with the EEC from the 7 percent of the early 1970s.

A similar increase in trade was also sought with Japan. In October 1976 Prime Minister Trudeau visited Tokyo and signed a 'framework for economic cooperation' between the two countries. The agreement contained no specific obligations. It was designed primarily as a 'consciousness-raising' exercise, to exploit the close government–business links in Japan and to create increased awareness of Canada's desire to expand trade – particularly in finished goods – with Japan. Implementation of the agreement was to depend almost entirely on private decisions, but in an optimistic note, Trudeau characterized the agreement as 'the final piece in the balancing act we tried to establish when we went into the third option'.[25]

During his visit to Japan, Trudeau also held out for establishing procedures for more formal consultations between the Japanese and Canadian governments on issues other than trade. Although the 'Three Options Paper' did not mention such consultative arrangements as part of the diversification strategy, it had been apparent for some time that Trudeau's version of diversification included an information dimension. In Japan, he mentioned that Canada needed 'more windows on the world', an admission, perhaps, that hitherto Ottawa had taken its cues about world developments too much from the United States, and that in order to pursue a genuinely independent foreign policy, multiple channels of information to the other world powers would have to be developed. The request to the Japanese had an important precedent. In May 1971 – about one year before President Nixon's visit to Moscow – Trudeau concluded a protocol with the Soviet government which required the two parties to consult during any international crisis. The prototype of this treaty was an earlier agreement between the Soviet Union and France. While the protocol is more of symbolic than practical consequence (during the 1973 Middle East war the Soviet and Canadian governments did not consult officially), it reflects not only a desire to have an arrangement with the Soviet Union which is distinct from any Soviet-American agreement, but also to establish a framework through which the Canadian government can obtain first-hand official information from the highest Soviet level, rather than through lower-level diplomatic, or American, sources.

The third dimension of the diversification strategy was in the area of cultural affairs. After the publication of the Sharp paper, the Department of External Affairs launched reasonably ambitious cultural exchange programs with Great Britain, France, Italy, Japan and Israel. All the activities under these programs – exchange of scholars, building library collections on Canadiana abroad, the organization of lecture tours and seminars on Canadian subjects, and attempts to include Canadian materials in foreign university courses – were designed to emphasize Canada's distinctiveness from the United States and to develop a core of foreign academics and scientists who would focus their own work toward Canadian subjects (for example, to create a group of Japanese experts on Canadian economics and politics).

At the symbolic level, at least two decisions might also be mentioned as having the objective of emphasizing Canada's distinctness from the United States. Both can be explained partly in terms of the concrete benefits they brought to Canada, but the symbolic dimension appears important as well. The establishment of diplomatic relations with Peking in 1970 gave effect to a campaign promise by Trudeau in 1968. It also reflected his views of China, which he had visited in 1955, and which were not so hostile as those commonly found among American government officials during the Vietnam war. But the decision was probably taken also for reasons of domestic and external publicity, to make a diplomatic move that distinctly preceded any American thoughts in that direction. The critics of Canadian foreign policy, those who liked to characterize Canada as a 'satellite' of the United States, were hard pressed to explain how this decision (and the Canadian vote to seat Communist China in the United Nations) squared with their view that Canada was dominated by American investment and must therefore follow the desires of American capital and Washington.

The second relationship containing symbolic content was with Cuba. Throughout the Caribbean cold war, Canada maintained relations with Havana and a reasonably impressive trade and tourist flow developed over the years. This interaction has not been publicized much by Ottawa, but in 1976 Trudeau included a visit to Cuba as part of a larger trip through Latin America. That visit – taken during Cuba's intervention in Angola – raised much criticism in the United States and in Canada, but did not dampen Trudeau's enthusiasm for looking at novel social experiments and emphasizing Canada's continued interest in expanding relations with Cuba.

Overall, then, the thrust of Canada's externally directed actions since – and sometimes prior to – the 'third option' was to expand Canada's trade with other partners, particularly the EEC and Japan, to raise Canada's international 'visibility' – particularly its distinctiveness from the United States – and to cultivate more diverse sources of information about global problems.

Explanations

The origins of the border-screening devices, 'arms-length' conduct of relations with the United States and external diversification lie in many sources, but in general the policies described in the previous section were a slow government response to a considerable build-up of public concern about the extent of American investment in Canada and the anticipated political and cultural consequences this would have on the country.

The New Democratic Party, a small, mildly socialist group in Parliament (but often successful electorally in some Canadian provinces), persistently raised the issue of American investment in Canada as a threat to Canadian political independence, but its appeals made little impact on the two governing parties of the 1950s and 1960s, the Liberals and Progressive-Conservatives. The business community, with which both parties have strong connections, was firmly wedded to the laissez-faire approach to relations with the United States.

By the mid-1960s, however, this consensus began to dissolve. The Liberal Minister of Finance, Walter Gordon, was among the first Cabinet-level politicians to warn of the possible economic consequences of continued American takeover of Canadian firms, but his attempts within the government to impose restrictions or regulations on foreign investment came to naught and he eventually resigned from the Cabinet. Kari Levitt, an economist at McGill University, subsequently published a book which was to become standard reading in university and government circles.[26]

The study sought to document that many of the acknowledged benefits of foreign investment were offset by economic costs. These included the creation of Canadian dependence upon American technology, thus impeding the growth of an indigenous research and development capacity, the displacement of Canadian enterprises by American-based firms, vast increase in Canadian-American trade accounted for by intra-company transfers, and the perpetuation of a 'miniature replica' economy in Canada which prevented economic rationalization in the form of consolidating product lines and thus reducing prices to Canadian consumers. In her opinion, it made no sense to have firms produce forty-three types of refrigerators for a market as small as Canada's. Professor Levitt also sought to demonstrate the political costs to Canada for its economic dependence on the United States, citing the well-known cases of the American application, extraterritorially, of its Trading with the Enemy Act, to prevent American subsidiaries from exporting to communist countries, occasional interventions in Ottawa by American officials to protect the interests of American firms, and the like.

Uneasiness about the state of Canadian-American relations was also demonstrated in several official studies. The Watkins Report[27] meticulously studied the costs and benefits of continued American investment in Canada and concluded that regulation of foreign investment was justified and desirable. But the Trudeau Cabinet made no official response to the study and no legislation resulted from it. Next came a voluminous study on the full range of Canadian-American relations authored by the Parliamentary Committee on External Affairs and Defense (the Wahn Report).[28] The lengthy hearings preceding the report included testimony from government officials, businessmen, academics and members of the media. While most of the government and business representatives saw little cause for concern, others argued that the American presence in Canada had reached alarming proportions and that government regulative activities would have to be instituted to protect Canada from some of the undesirable consequences of the asymmetrical relationship. The Committee's final report steered a middle course, but urged the government to introduce legislation to screen foreign takeovers and new investment. Again, no policy changes resulted from these recommendations.

Apparently responding to the growing public concern over American ownership of the Canadian economy, Trudeau appointed his Minister of Consumer and Corporate Affairs, Herb Grey, to undertake yet another study of the investment and takeover problem. The 'Grey Report'[29] confined itself solely to the investment issue and noted that the political impact of takeovers and new investment was minimal and that there was no evidence of undue American interference in Canadian domestic politics. However, the constraints on policy-making in Canada, due to economic ties with the United States, were considerable. The report urged the government to introduce legislation to regulate foreign investment and to require that all incoming funds or takeovers bring notable economic benefits to Canada.

These reports clearly revealed a growing uneasiness with the extent of American investment in Canada, but by no means did they reflect the very strongly expressed opinions of the NDP and academic nationalists. To most Liberals, it was more a potential than actual threat, and many argued that Canada needed more foreign capital, not less.

Public opinion polls of the period document the growing concern of the population as well. Attitudes toward American investment became increasingly critical, and by 1972, 53 percent of the respondents to a poll indicated that they thought Canadian dependence upon the United States was 'not a good thing'. Another study indicated a strong correlation between anti-American feelings in Canada and the size of the American economic presence in the country.[30]

Part of the public's concern about the issue of Canadian independence in general and American investment in particular no doubt derived from a lack of enthusiasm for some American foreign policies during the 1960s. While President Kennedy had been very popular in Canada, the same could not be said of his successor. The Dominican intervention raised considerable condemnation, and by 1968 Canadian public support for the Vietnam war had largely eroded; the primary opinion leaders now were found in the universities, and they almost unanimously condemned the United States. The Trudeau government, focusing its attention on the Quebec problem, was virtually mute on Vietnam.

There is little evidence to suggest that prior to 1970 the government – a few Cabinet ministers excepted – seriously considered a re-evaluation of the relationship with the United States. Indeed, until 1973 there was even talk by the Energy Minister of concluding some sort of 'continental' energy policy. Nor is there any evidence that prior to 1970 strong voices within the bureaucracy were pushing for alterations of the traditional pattern of conducting relations with the United States. The exception, of course, was the CRTC which by virtue of its relative autonomy went ahead to rescue the Canadian broadcasting industry.

In the Cabinet, Herb Grey obviously favored instituting regulatory devices to control foreign investment and takeovers. The Postmaster-General, Eric Kierans, a former colleague of Kari Levitt, was known to be concerned with the extent of American economic presence in Canada. But if there were other Cabinet members who paid much attention to the problem, they did not speak publicly about the issue.

What of the Prime Minister? Here the evidence is contradictory, for his comments and policy choices between 1968 and 1972 point to no clear direction as far as relations with the United States are concerned. As early as May 1968, Trudeau had mentioned Europe as a counterweight to the preponderant American relationship. And during his 1971 visit to the Soviet Union, the Prime Minister had commented that Canada needed closer ties with the Russians in order to protect itself from American political, economic and even military domination.[31] As noted earlier, Trudeau also seems to have been concerned that Canada should develop independent sources of information abroad and rely less upon American interpretations of world developments. The foreign policy review of 1970,[32] which strongly reflected Trudeau's intellectual imprint, made no mention of a 'special relationship' with the United States but did emphasize Canada's desire to diversify economic and cultural relations with

Europe, Latin America and Asia. The primary theme of that review was the importance of establishing Canada's identity abroad, protecting sovereignty and basing policy on calculated national interest. Finally, Trudeau's defense policies, announced in 1969, placed highest priority to protection of sovereignty and increased capability for coastal surveillance, followed by North American air defense, NATO and international peacekeeping.[33] A statement in 1968 even revealed Trudeau's apprehensions about the spill-over of American radical activity into Canada and the possibility of having to use Canadian armed forces for purposes of quelling insurrection inspired, if not organized, from the United States.[34] In brief, one can locate numerous statements that reflect a perception of threat to Canada's identity, independence and sovereignty emanating from the United States. But there was no simple statement by Trudeau which outlined the forthcoming long-range strategy of employing border-screening devices, 'arms-length' diplomacy and external diversification to reduce Canada's vulnerability to the United States. It appears that the CRTC's policies between 1968 and 1971 reflected bureaucratic nationalism more than the Prime Minister's or Cabinet's direction.

Trudeau, of course, had enunciated nationalist sentiments in his speeches and philosophical writings. But his understanding of the term involved a commitment to the promotion of Canadian national unity and maintenance of a viable multi-ethnic society, and not the promotion of Canadian grandeur or national chauvinism. His nationalism was not inconsistent with the traditional Liberal belief in free trade and the free circulation of ideas and people.[35] Trudeau had often portrayed the United States as Canada's natural ally, a generally benevolent society sharing common values and a continent with Canada. Moreover, he had long believed that a certain amount of economic integration in North America brought significant benefits to Canada, and that Canada's dependence upon American technology and industry was a fact that could not be ignored, much less changed significantly.[36] Certainly, Trudeau did not share the concern of the economic nationalists who claimed that American investment constituted a serious threat to Canada's economic and political independence. Although the Prime Minister had raised economic growth and national identity as important priorities in foreign policy, he did not conclude that growth, aided by foreign investment, was inconsistent with the promotion of Canada's separate identity from the United States. In brief, there is no strong evidence either in Trudeau's philosophical positions or in his general attitude toward the United States that would lead one to predict that a major purpose of his government in foreign policy would be to reduce ties with the United States.

What of bureaucratic factors? The 1970 foreign policy review, while it did emphasize a necessity for diversifying Canada's external contacts, did not include a section on Canadian-American relations, a lacuna that was roundly criticized by the Canadian media, academics and some members of the Department of External Affairs. In late 1970 the Western Hemisphere Bureau of the Department, supported by the small Policy Analysis Group (PAG), began drafting a report on Canada and the United States. At this time the Cabinet was preoccupied with domestic concerns, so the main lines of the work emphasizing vulnerability reduction and more 'arms-length' formal diplomacy toward the United States was being developed without Cabinet supervision. The DEA circulated drafts of the paper to other departments for comment, but amendments were not accepted. The USA division of the Department of Industry, Trade and Commerce vigorously opposed the document on the grounds that, if implemented, the recommended policies would jeopardize Canada's trade expansion policies. It was due in part to the opposition by ITC that the 'Three Options Paper' was published under the imprimatur of the Secretary of State for External Affairs, rather than as a government document. This was subsequently to raise the issue whether the ideas in the paper were official government policy, or merely an expression of hope by one government department.

The document, in any event, reached the Cabinet in the summer or autumn of 1971, where it was given high priority and strong support for continued development.[37] Initiation of the review of Canadian-American relations and suggestions for a reordering of those relations lay with certain sectors of the External Affairs Department. The strategy of diversification had already been formulated in 'A Foreign Policy for Canadians' in 1970, but it was not hitched on to a more comprehensive strategy for restructuring important parts of Canada's orientation to the outside world.

Despite the important bureaucratic advocacy of altering relations with the United States, a series of decisions in Washington in 1971 finally prompted the Cabinet to accept the major lines of the Western Hemisphere–PAG initiative.

On 15 August 1971 President Nixon, attempting to cope with an unprecedented trade deficit and pressure against the dollar, devalued the dollar and imposed a 10 percent surcharge on all imports into the United States. No foreign government was forewarned of these decisions. For Canada, which at that time sent 70 percent of its exports to the United States, the surcharge created the possibility of major economic dislocation, including the reversal of a favorable balance of trade (a generally rare occurrence in postwar years) and increased unemployment. Faced with these prospects, the government did exactly what it had done throughout the 1950s and 1960s when faced with adverse American economic policies: it immediately sent a delegation to Washington pleading exemption from the American regulations. The delegation met with John Connally, the Secretary of the Treasury, who, in a reportedly undiplomatic manner, rejected the Canadian request and, indeed, blamed Canada for being a major cause of the United States' economic plight. Nixon's economic decisions, combined with the tough stance of Connally, must have driven home the point to Trudeau and his Cabinet that Canada could no longer rely on quiet diplomacy or a mythical 'special relationship' to protect itself against market or governmentally sponsored fluctuations in Canada's major export market. Two months after the interview with Connally, the Cabinet decided in principle to reduce Canada's economic vulnerability by diversifying its trade patterns and launching programs to strengthen Canadian institutions.[38]

The decisions taken at that meeting were not announced publicly until the appearance of Sharp's paper one year later. The delay is accounted for by continued bargaining by bureaucratic elements over the final shape of the paper, and possibly by Trudeau's knowledge that he would soon face an election. He wanted to use the new diversification policy to appeal to Canadian nationalist sentiment which was in danger of being mobilized by the New Democratic Party. Shortly after the election of 1972 (in which the Liberals were returned with only a minority and had to rely on the NDP to remain in office) contacts with the EEC were established, and much was made of the fast-growing trade between Canada and Japan. But by that time, the Canadian trade union movement was well along the road of establishing independent organizations, the universities had instituted procedures for ensuring that all positions were advertised in Canada, and the CRTC had already established minimum amounts of Canadian content on both television and radio. The change in foreign policy orientation – particularly its external dimension – was thus the last and not the first act. It can be understood as a policy taken somewhat grudgingly in the face of considerable public concern in Canada about the size of foreign investment in the country, the growing popularity of the NDP for its stand on the investment issue and the shock of Nixon's economic decisions of 1971. There is no way to assess quantitatively the relative influence of these factors or to establish concretely that event A or B had a larger impact in bringing about response X. But it is clear that initiative lay with two subdivisions of the Department of External Affairs and that the Cabinet basically *responded* to domestic opinion and a major external event in formulating its policies. It did not act in a leadership capacity, for the border-screening devices and trade diversification components of the new strategy policies were basically antithetical to the traditions of the Liberal Party, to its business support, to many of the personal political preferences of the Prime Minister and to some bureaucratic interests, particularly the Ministry of Industry, Trade and Commerce.

Foreign Policy Restructured?

It is clear that an important change took place in Canadian attitudes about the American 'presence' in the country and that a variety of policies were implemented to monitor, regulate and even reduce American access and penetration, as well as to bolster Canadian institutions to make them less vulnerable to American competition. On the access side of foreign policy, fundamental change did occur. Let us examine, then, our photograph at t_2, which is approximately a dozen years after the first expressions of concern began to arise among politicians and the public.

At the level of private interactions and organizations, important modifications from the practice of the 1950s and 1960s can be noted. Throughout the 1970s Canadian labor unions increasingly divorced themselves from the internationals, that is, from American unions. In 1966, 70 percent of Canadian labor union members belonged to internationals with American headquarters. Eleven years later this figure had shrunk to 49 percent.[39] As an increasing proportion of the Canadian labor force became unionized, and as Canadian wage scales surpassed those paid in the United States, the necessity of depending upon the strength of the American labor organizations declined. Thus, the change to Canadian autonomous unions was not based solely on nationalist considerations. The rate of defection from American-based unions would probably have been slower in the absence of rising nationalism in Canada during the period, however.

In the universities, the ingress of foreign professors declined, but not dramatically. In 1970–1, 15·2 percent of the Canadian professoriat were American citizens. The figure declined slightly to 14·4 percent for 1974–5[40] and has continued to decline as the availability of academic positions in Canada has become highly restricted. While some continued to decry the inadequacy of 'Canadian studies' in the universities, the problem of foreign academics was largely resolved by a combination of reformed university hiring procedures and enrolment declines which significantly reduced public funds available for higher education.

Migration patterns changed as well. Whereas in the 1960s an average of 30,000 Canadians emigrated to the United States annually, by 1974 this number had decreased to 7,300. American immigration into Canada grew significantly to an average of 24,000 in the same period.[41] The changes can be attributed to a number of factors, including new American immigration regulations, higher wage scales in Canada and the much greater number of economic and artistic career opportunities available in Canada compared to earlier years. The political climate in the United States during the Vietnam war and the Watergate years may have influenced migration patterns as well.

Changes resulting from government policy were mixed. In the area of communications, the arts, publication and culture, the trends of the 1950s and 1960s were dramatically reversed. The actions of the CRTC, the secretary of state and Bill C-58 gave a new lease on life to the Canadian media and arts. Budgets for the CBC more than tripled in the 1970s and the viewing of Canadian-originated television also increased. It is impossible to say, however, whether the change resulted from the minimum Canadian-content regulations or from the choice of viewers. While the Canadian film industry concluded that it might best survive by undertaking joint ventures, in the field of music production and recording a viable industry and pool of talent developed. Bill C-58 effectively removed *Time* as Canada's major news magazine. Ten months after the legislation was approved in Parliament, *Time* had ended its operations in Canada and its circulation declined by 37,000 subscribers; in the meantime, its major competitor's circulation climbed by 12,000. As *Time* subscriptions ran out, its share of the total newsmagazine market (24 percent as of October 1976) declined further.[42]

The foreign investment sector, which above all symbolized the concern of Canadians about growing American influence in Canada, also showed significant change; but the change resulted from the operation of market forces, and not because of restrictive practices by the Foreign Investment Review Board. By 1979 FIRA had examined 2,089 applications from foreign businessmen to move into Canada or to take over Canadian firms and had disallowed only 136. However, during its first five years, FIRA managed to persuade thirty foreign applicants to revise their proposals, making them more beneficial to Canada. It also helped convince 161 potential investors to cancel plans to move into the country.[43]

By 1977, when American investment in Canada had come to a virtual trickle, and as an increasing number of Canadian firms were establishing plants in the United States (due to more favorable tax laws and higher Canadian wage rates), the government began to urge foreigners to invest in the country. The Minister of Industry, Trade and Commerce, under whose jurisdiction FIRA operates, declared that year that his function would be not so much to reduce foreign investment as to attract it! As with the problem of the universities, the foreign investment issue was re-solved – at least temporarily – through market mechanisms rather than by vigorous government action. It has largely ceased to be a political issue in Canada. If present trends continue, then, the amount of foreign ownership as a percentage of total Canadian economic activity should begin to decline.

What of externally directed actions? Here, the short period of time since most of the diplomatic steps were completed has not allowed any signifi-cant trends to be noted – particularly in the area of trade. However, there are a few indicators that show some change from the pattern of the 1950s and 1960s. For example, the average index score of agreement between Canada and the United States in General Assembly votes between 1946 and the last year of the Pearson Cabinet was ·951. Between 1968 and 1976 the figure declined to an average of ·888, not a dramatic change but perhaps the beginning of a longer-range trend. The average score on an Index of Agreement on Yes, No and Abstentions in the earlier period was ·794; for the Trudeau era, this figure declined to ·640. Despite these changes it is difficult to make any strong inferences, for the United Nations was not the arena in which the 'third option' was being played out. Also, some votes were much more significant than others; Canada's vote to seat the Peking government as the Chinese representative in the United Nations was of greater significance than, say, a vote on apartheid might be. All we can say is that Canadian-American agreement within the United Nations on a host of global issues appeared to decline slightly, but the explanation probably is found in the substance of each issue rather than in a deliberate policy of voting independently from the United States.

There have been, however, significant changes in the defense issue area which should be noted. When Canada renewed its NORAD obligations in 1975, the government insisted on insertion of a proviso that the agreement could be terminated on one year's notice and demanded the transfer of responsibility for control of Canadian airspace to a Canadian command centre.[44] This was a significant assertion of Canadian sovereignty, a step designed to ensure that the theoretical statement of sovereignty in the defense agreement (Canadian consent) is given practical effect. The con-sequence of this provision also dilutes some of the integrationist features of NORAD.

It may be too early to gauge any effects of Canada's two agreements with Japan and the EEC. Although both documents established ministerial-level working committees, the Canadian government emphasized that the initiative of businessmen would be necessary to expand Canada's exports to these two markets. In any case Canadian trade with Japan increased rapidly. By 1972 Canada was Japan's fourth largest trading partner, although by 1977 it had slipped to fourteenth. The dollar sums, however, continued to increase much faster than the average rate of increase for all Canadian exports and imports.

While trade with third countries grew steadily, it apparently was not at the expense of Canadian-American trade. The strategy of diversification, if it was intended to reduce North American trade, was a notable failure. During the mid-1970s, Canadian exports and imports with the United States declined slightly from the peaks reached in 1968 (73 and 71 percent respectively), but by the end of the decade the figures were again over 70 percent. The rapid decline in the value of the Canadian dollar, combined with new oil and gas discoveries, should actually increase Canadian exports to the United States for the next several years.

Forecasts about the possibilities of dramatically accelerating trade with Japan and the EEC are not optimistic. For a variety of reasons, including official and unofficial protectionist measures, Japan holds out few possibilities of becoming a market for Canadian manufactured goods – which is exactly what the Canadian government would like to export. Today, approximately 97 percent of Canada's exports across the Pacific remain raw materials and semi-finished goods. The same problem arises with European trade. The Europeans are interested in Canada primarily as a source of raw materials, rather than as a competitor in manufactured items. The Trudeau government thus faced a dilemma: while it wished to diversify its trade contacts, the markets in Japan and the EEC were open primarily to commodities and semi-finished products. The United States offers a much more important market for Canadian manufactured goods. Hence, the diversification policy clashed with another Canadian priority, the emphasis on industrialization and industrial exports.

Did Canada, then, represent a country which reoriented its foreign policy? Here we face the problem of intent versus action. The intent was clearly enunciated in the 'Three Options Paper' and many subsequent government statements. For the dimension of external penetration fundamental change did occur, since in virtually all the sectors of penetration the trends of the 1950s and 1960s were reversed – in some cases dramatically – by government and private action. In the dimension of externally directed actions the change was much more modest, perhaps fundamental only in the sense that it involved planned diversification rather than slow adaptation to market forces, and because it touched upon two of the most important sectors in Canadian-American relations, trade and defense. It must be understood clearly, as well, that the 'third option' did not require total disengagement from the United States. The objective was to reduce vulnerability by diversifying trade, while maintaining friendly relations with the United States. There was never any intention to alter the relationship to the extent that, for example, Burma changed its contacts with the outside world in the 1960s. But how much diversification is required to reduce vulnerability? The government never published a stated target for trade so we have no benchmark against which to measure success or failure. But if it was the intention of Ottawa to double its trade with the EEC by 1981,[45] as well as with Japan, then these two targets should make up approximately 26 percent of Canada's trade by the early 1980s. Trade with the rest of the world might amount to approximately 22 percent of the total, which means that a rough target for trade with the United States by 1981 might have been in the vicinity of 50 percent. Whether or not this amount would actually decrease Canadian vulnerability to economic changes in the United States is difficult to judge. It is clear that such target figures will not be reached by the early 1980s or even later in the decade. Even with growing commercial opportunities in the Middle East and China, the comforts and convenience of conducting trade within North America render trade diversification almost impossible to achieve. Canada is one of the world's foremost trade nations, but despite significant increases in commercial contacts with other regions of the world, Canada remains and will remain vulnerable to policies such as those taken by the United States in 1971.

The attempt to diversify external contacts is not an entirely new policy for Canada. Canadians have traditionally envisaged their relationship with Great Britain as some sort of counterweight to the preponderant Canadian-American connection. The actions and policies outlined above do represent a new departure in their comprehensiveness and degree of intent, however. Many of the domestic policies employed to counterbalance American penetration were also unique for Canada; they went far beyond the traditional tariff devices used to protect Canadian industries. The sum total of governmental and private action in dealing with penetration largely succeeded in fulfilling the strategy of 'developing and strengthening the Canadian economy and other aspects of its internal life'. The perception of threat, or asymmetrical competition, has significantly declined (partly due to market forces) and Canadian nationalist measures have operated in a manner that has been reasonably liberal.

The American Response

Our first chapter indicated that attempts to alter foreign policy fundamentally often generate intense international conflict. Mentors are seldom pleased to see their wards break away, particularly if the break involves significant new relationships with the enemies of the mentor. In the case of Canada the diversification strategy was never seen as an anti-American policy, nor was the focus of diversification either the Soviet Union or China. While some American economic interests were affected by diversification (in fact, very few have), security issues were never involved beyond the alteration of the NORAD agreement. Given the Nixon administration's own emphasis on national interest, it was hardly in a position to oppose similar claims of priority by the Canadian government. When President Nixon visited Ottawa in 1972, he emphasized that Americans understood that not all Canadian interests were identical with those of the United States and that divergences should be honestly recognized and discussed. Hence, there was never any American disparagement of the overall diversification strategy. There were some fears expressed that the FIRA would discriminate against American investment, but they were not borne out by the FIRA's actions. The American government also expressed misgivings about nationalization of American firms in some Canadian provinces (such actions create a 'bad climate for investment'), but since these actions do not fall under Ottawa's jurisdiction, there was little that the Canadian government could do. Finally, some American broadcasting interests and senators deplored some of the CRTC regulations – and threatened retaliation – but the State Department did not press their cause vigorously. In other areas of policy, both domestic and external, Washington remained publicly silent. All this means that the reorientation of Canadian policies was achieved at virtually no cost to Canada. It did not face any form of American retaliation, much less threats by the United States to undertake its own 'agonizing reappraisal' of relations with Canada. There is no indication that trade diversification, alteration of NORAD, or CRTC regulations had any impact at all on other sectors of the bilateral relationship. Our conclusion must be, then, the partially successful restructuring was achieved without generating bilateral conflict, and without the expenditure of significant economic, political, or social costs.

Notes: Chapter 4

1 Cf. John J. Kirton, 'The consequences of integration: the case of the defense production sharing agreements', in Andrew Axline *et al*. (eds), *Continental Community? Independence and Integration in North America* (Toronto: McClelland & Stewart, 1974), pp. 116–29; *Vancouver Sun*, 29 February 1972.
2 Figures obtained from Statistics Canada, *Exports of Commodity* (65-004), 1961–8; Statistics Canada, *Exports by Country* (65-003), 1969–75; Statistics Canada, *Imports by Country* (65-006) (Ottawa: Statistics Canada).
3 John H. Sigler and Denis Goresky, 'Public opinion on U.S.–Canadian relations', *International Organization*, 28 (Autumn 1974), p. 622.
4 See Canada, Dominion Bureau of Statistics, *Canada Yearbook* (Ottawa: Queen's Printer, 1966) for figures for the late 1950s to mid-1960s, pp. 228, 234.
5 Figures from Canada, Department of Trade, Industry and Commerce, Foreign Investment Division, *Direct Investment in Canada by Non-Residents Since 1945* (Ottawa, n.d.); Statistics Canada, *Quarterly Estimates of the Canadian Balance of International Payments* (Ottawa: Queen's Printer, quarterly).
6 Circulation and advertising figures are available in *Canadian Advertising Rates and Data* (Toronto: Maclean-Hunter, monthly).
7 Figures averaged from data in R. A. Manzer, *Canada: A Sociological and Political Report* (Toronto: McGraw-Hill Ryerson, 1974), p. 111.
8 Sigler and Goresky, 'Public opinion on U.S.–Canadian relations', p. 659.
9 Gordon S. Galbraith, 'The theory of the partial political system', MA thesis, University of British Columbia, 1964, ch. 4. To my knowledge, no studies have been conducted to see if Canadian children also know more about British or French or Russian politics.
10 Statistics Canada, *Salaries and Qualifications of Teachers in Universities and Colleges* (Ottawa: Queen's Printer, 1971), pub. #81-203.
11 The problem of American academics in Canada, if it was a problem, was confined primarily to the humanities and social sciences.
12 Canada, Secretary of State, *Report of the Committee on Broadcasting* (Ottawa: Queen's Printer, 1965), p. 139.
13 Like the United States, Canada has traditionally manipulated tariff rates to protect cer-

tain industries, so perhaps it would be more appropriate to argue that the CRTC regulations are among the first in the non-economic realm. In the 1930s the Canadian government imposed tariffs on American publications in order to protect Canadian magazines.

14 Mitchell Sharp, 'Canada-US relations: options for the future', *International Perspectives* (bimonthly publication of the Department of External Affairs), special issue (Autumn 1972).

15 John Kirton has emphasized that although not all government officials read the paper in the same way, it did provide a three-pronged strategy for coping with the American problem. The most thorough analysis of the inception and application (or non-application) of the 'third option' strategy is in John Kirton, 'The conduct and co-ordination of Canadian government decisionmaking towards the United States', unpublished Ph.D. dissertation, The Johns Hopkins University, Baltimore, Maryland, 1977, esp. pp. 217–31.

16 Announcement of the CRTC, April 1971, quoted in CRTC, *Annual Report, 1970–1971* (Ottawa: Canadian Government Publication Centre, 1971).

17 ibid.

18 CRTC, *Annual Report, 1973–1974* (Ottawa: Canadian Government Publication Centre, 1974), p. 14.

19 CRTC, *Annual Report, 1975–1976* (Ottawa: Canadian Government Publication Centre, 1976), p. 18.

20 *Montreal Star*, 8 September 1976, section A, p. 10.

21 Prior to the FIRA, the Canadian government had acted to stop takeover bids of particularly sensitive areas. In 1965 the government, withstanding considerable American pressure, prevented the sale of the Mercantile Bank to Chase Manhattan, and several years later the Prime Minister stopped an American bid to buy out Denison Mines Ltd, a major Canadian uranium producer.

22 K. J. Holsti, 'Canada and the United States', in Steven Spiegel and Kenneth Waltz (eds), *Conflict in World Politics* (Boston: Winthrop Publishers, 1971).

23 Kirton, 'The conduct and co-ordination of Canadian government decisionmaking towards the United States', pp. 226–7.

24 Harald von Riekhoff, 'The third option in Canadian foreign policy', in Brian Tomlin (ed.), *Canada's Foreign Policy: Analysis and Trends* (Toronto: Methuen, 1978), p. 97.

25 Quoted in *Vancouver Sun*, 22 October 1976, p. 12.

26 *Silent Surrender: The Multinational Corporation in Canada* (Toronto: Macmillan of Canada, 1970).

27 Canada, Task Force on the Structure of Canadian Industry, *Foreign Ownership and the Structure of Canadian Industry* (Ottawa: Queen's Printer, 1968).

28 Canada, House of Commons, 2nd sess., 28th Parl., *Eleventh Report of the Standing Committee on External Affairs and National Defense Respecting Canadian–U.S. Relations* (Ottawa: Queen's Printer, 1970).

29 Canada, Grey Task Force, *Foreign Direct Investment in Canada* (Ottawa: Information Canada, 1972).

30 Sigler and Goresky, 'Public opinion on U.S.–Canadian relations', p. 659; poll results reported in *Montreal Star*, 12 September 1972; Cong-soo Tai, Erick J. Peterson and Ted Robert Gurr, 'Internal versus external sources of anti-Americanism: two comparative studies', *Journal of Conflict Resolution*, 17 (September 1973), pp. 455–88.

31 See Bruce Thordarson, *Trudeau and Foreign Policy: A Study in Decision-Making* (Toronto: Oxford University Press), p. 208.

32 Canada, Secretary of State for External Affairs, *Foreign Policy for Canadians* (Ottawa: Queen's Printer, 1970).

33 Canada, Department of National Defense, *White Paper on Defence: Defence in the 1970s* (Ottawa: Information Canada, 1971). Until 1971 the air defence of Canada's prairie provinces and Newfoundland was provided by American interceptors. The defence White Paper announced that henceforth this task would be assumed by Canadian planes.

34 Thordarson, *Trudeau and Foreign Policy*, p. 74.

35 ibid., ch. 3 for a discussion of Trudeau's philosophical positions as they relate to foreign policy.

36 ibid., p. 188.

37 Kirton, 'The conduct and co-ordination of Canadian government decisionmaking towards the United States', p. 219.

38 Von Riekhoff, 'The third option in Canadian foreign policy', p. 2.
39 *Financial Times of Canada*, 9 May 1977, p. 8.
40 Statistics Canada, *Teachers in Universities: Part IV: Citizenship* (81–244) (Ottawa: Information Canada, 1975), Tables 1A, 1B, 1C.
41 Statistics Canada, *Canada Yearbook* (Ottawa: Queen's Printer, 1975), p. 189.
42 See *Canadian Advertising Rates and Data* (Toronto: Maclean-Hunter, October 1976). That *Time* had been a highly popular publication is indicated by the redesigning of *Maclean's* shortly after Bill C-58 became law; its format is almost a copy of *Time's*, although the substantive material focuses on Canadian issues. *Time*, of course, is still available in Canada but it must be imported from the United States which has significantly raised the cost to purchasers. In a bid to keep its Canadian readers and advertisers, *Time* drastically reduced its advertising rates to about 30 percent those charged by *Maclean's*. This move was inadequate to restore *Time's* former circulation, however.
43 *Vancouver Sun*, 30 October 1979, p. D-1.
44 Canada, Department of External Affairs, *Annual Review, 1975* (Ottawa: DEA, 1976), p. 31.
45 Based on interview with Canadian officials, cited in Jeff Erndst, 'Nationalism and the "contractual link" ', *Vancouver Sun*, 9 April 1976, p. 5.

5

From Diversification to Isolation: Burma, 1963–7

K. J. Holsti

'We would rather be poor and our own masters than slaves to a foreign power. We have sipped that bitter tea before.'[1] This comment by a Burmese government official in 1968 summarizes a complex set of attitudes which help explain why this Southeast Asian country, a leader of the movement of non-aligned states in the 1950s, should suddenly abandon more than a decade of outward-going diplomacy and adopt an orientation of isolationism, with strict exclusionist policies and a dramatic diminution of involvement in regional and global affairs. Burma, while never an international crossroads, chose to become a hermit nation. Although the motivations of the Ne Win government in Burma are difficult to untangle, the evidence suggests that Burma's turn inward after 1963 was occasioned not by any immediate security threat, as in Bhutan's case, but more by a judgement among the top military leaders and government officials that previous policies of keeping the country open to a flood of foreign aid advisers, missionaries, teachers and businessmen had led to excessive penetration, which was threatening to complete the destruction of a society that had already undergone social disintegration under British colonial rule. The 'bitter tea' in the quote did not refer so much to Britain's physical occupation of a once independent society, as to its inadvertent destruction of a peasant-based social system that had been characterized by harmony and relative plenty. Burma represents a classical case of a state rebelling against excessive foreign penetration. To the Burmese leaders, and particularly to General Ne Win, the 'threat' to the nation lay more in excessive foreign tutelage, and possible spill-over of the cold war into the country, than in a specific military opponent.

Burma's isolation in the 1960s and 1970s was preceded by more than a decade of active diplomacy. From 1947 until 1963 there was little to distinguish Burma from other newly independent countries. Under U Nu's leadership (1948–58, 1960–2), Burma adopted a foreign policy of non-alignment, meaning that the country would make no permanent military arrangements with any major power and would adopt positions on international issues on the merits of the case, and not because of fidelity to a mentor state.[2] Hence the government consistently supported the reversion of China's seat in the United Nations to the Peking government, but also publicly criticized the Soviet Union's invasion of Hungary in 1956. As a non-aligned state, Burma in the 1950s also perceived an obligation to mediate in East–West conflicts.[3] U Nu made at least one abortive attempt during his premiership to promote a Sino-American reconciliation.[4] He was also instrumental in organizing the 1955 Bandung Conference, and took an active interest in the affairs of the so-called Colombo Powers. Burma participated in the fourteen-nation conference on Laos in 1951, and was active in United Nations affairs. In 1955 it was elected to the Trusteeship Council, but its most sustained participation in an important international body came as a representative of the non-aligned states on the Geneva Disarmament Committee.

U Nu's personal interest in international affairs led him to make many visits abroad. During his twelve years as Prime Minister he made state visits to Israel, Yugoslavia, Britain, the Scandinavian countries, the Soviet Union, India, Ceylon, the United States and several neighbors in Southeast Asia. Institutionally, Burma's representation abroad developed rapidly even though it could not afford an extensive diplomatic network.[5] In fifteen years of independence it established twenty-five embassies abroad.

In other respects its diplomacy also resembled the patterns of behavior of most non-aligned states during this period. For example, on peace, disarmament and nuclear energy issues from the third through fourteenth sessions of the General Assembly, it voted 65 percent with the United States and 35 percent with the Soviet Union.[6] Burma received large contributions of foreign aid from all the major powers, as well as from India, the IMF and the World Bank. Thousands of Burmese students went to England and the United States to receive higher education; a few also went to the Eastern countries.[7] On the economic front, U Nu's government appealed to the industrial countries for private investment, although the terms it offered were hardly likely to attract large sums.[8]

Under U Nu, Burma was open to a variety of foreign influences. Numerous foreign aid officials roamed the country; tourism, while not an important industry by any means, was actively encouraged; American and British academic and cultural programs flourished. The Soviet, Chinese and Western embassies conducted a fierce competition trying to win over Burmese loyalty or admiration for their respective societies and policies. Press releases, films, embassy libraries, handouts to Burmese editors (some of which were the fabrications of foreign intelligence services)[9] were all used in the contest. English-language newspapers were widely read in the country, and the literate public had access to a variety of foreign published books, periodicals, magazines and films. Missionaries also had unfettered access to this Buddhist society; for decades they had run schools and hospitals and undertaken proselytizing activities – even among the ethnic minorities whose political relations with Rangoon were seriously strained. Western scholars staffed Rangoon University, and foreign anthropologists, economists, political scientists and orientalists worked freely at their research. In short, there was no sector of Burmese society that was not readily accessible to, and in some cases dominated by, foreigners. They were active from the village level all the way to the top of the national administration, where they advised government ministers on fiscal, trade, agricultural and development policies.

When U Nu appointed General Ne Win in 1958 to a caretaker prime ministership to try to cope with the country's ethnic and communist insurrections, the main directions of foreign policy and open doors to foreigners remained unchanged.[10] Indeed, Ne Win's government extended Burma's relations with non-bloc states, introduced more liberal laws to attract foreign investment, and when Burmese interests sought to reduce the British and Indian minority's hold over Burmese retail trade, it rejected these demands as a 'most impractical form of ultra-nationalism'.[11] When U Nu returned in 1960 as Prime Minister, he introduced a few measures to reduce the foreign presence in the country. His government had already terminated immigration from India and Pakistan[12] and just one month before the 1962 military coup, the government decided to nationalize the foreign trade sector, which was run mostly by foreigners.[13] And finally, upon the prompting of the military, U Nu decided to request the withdrawal of British and American military advisers.[14] In its major outlines, however, Burma's pattern of foreign relations continued to resemble that of many non-aligned states, and its policies with regard to foreign penetration remained decidedly liberal.

Burma's foreign relations in the post-colonial period can be termed 'diversified', not only because the U Nu government maintained diplomatic and cultural relations with a variety of states and received aid from numerous sources, but also because its trade – unlike that of most former colonies – was spread among a large number of export markets and sources of supply. Rice, the major foreign currency earner, went to Europe, the Soviet Union, China, Ceylon, India, Singapore, Indonesia and Japan. Imports came from a similarly broad range of sources, although heavy capital goods came primarily from England and West Europe. Burma's monocrop export sector was of course subject to fluctuations in world rice prices, but at least it had a variety of actual and potential markets for its surplus production. In the economic realm, then, Burma did not exactly fit the classical case of dependence where the underdeveloped country sells and buys primarily from the former colonial power. Despite export product concentration, Burma's economic vulnerability and sensitivity were somewhat less pronounced because of market and source diversification. On the other hand, the typical neo-colonial situation, where the society's most modern institutions were dominated by foreigners, continued to prevail in the first decade-and-one-half after independence.

The Military Takeover and Foreign Penetration

General Ne Win directed the coup primarily to cancel numerous concessions for greater autonomy U Nu had made to Burma's rebelling ethnic minorities. He judged that the Prime Minister's policies would lead to the break-up of the Burmese Union. Added incentives were a succession of domestic economic crises, the government's establishment of Buddhism as the state religion, corruption and inefficiency in the bureaucracy, and the virtual disintegration of U Nu's ruling party.[15] Foreign policy issues and contacts with foreigners were not important motivations for the coup or priority items on the reconstruction agenda. Thus, in the early months after the coup, there was considerable continuity in foreign policy; indeed, in some spheres the Revolutionary Council undid some of the Burmanization measures of the previous government. The decision to nationalize foreign trade was postponed for two years, for example. Relations with the major powers remained open and satisfactory. Ne Win negotiated for a new aid agreement with the Soviet Union, and allowed a number of Chinese experts into Burma. New aid commitments also came from the United States and West Germany.[16]

About one year after the coup, however, the Revolutionary Council inaugurated measures to bring the Burmese economy under government control. As a first step, Ne Win announced that 'for political reasons' no more foreign investment would be permitted into the country.[17] In February 1963 the government nationalized the country's banks – including the Chinese bank which was a major conduit for communist funds. From early 1964 until the end of 1965, the government successfully nationalized the import and export trades, most wholesale and retail outlets and, finally, the remaining large foreign corporations. Army institutions took over most of the enterprises and, lacking know-how, trained personnel, capital and experience, quickly ran them to the ground. Indian immigrants who controlled a large portion of the retail and importing firms in Burma received no immediate compensation for their sequestered properties. Many chose to return to India but found it difficult to obtain exit permits. Those who succeeded were allowed to take only immediate personal possessions – excluding jewelry and savings. Bank notes of large sums were demonetized, thus destroying the savings of those who hid their funds rather than place them in the nationalized banks. Most non-Burmans had property ownership and employment rights seriously curtailed. The effect of all these policies was to terminate foreign control of the economy, and to centralize economic decision-making authority in the hands of the government. Between 1963 and 1968, 150,000 Indians of an estimated 700,000 left Burma.[18] Most of the British and Anglo-Burmans went to England.

At the same time that the government launched its drive to gain control of the national economy it also fundamentally altered policies toward all foreigners. Starting in June 1963, many foreign correspondents were asked to leave the country. By 1966 the government had effectively centralized control over incoming foreign information. The Burmese News Agency replaced all foreign news services which had hitherto distributed external news to Burmese newspapers. Ava House Ltd, a subsidiary of the Burma Economic Development Corporation, was appointed sole importer of foreign books and periodicals. The government took over the Burma Translation Society and placed it under the Ministry of Information, with instructions to censor or prohibit translation of all materials that dealt with the cold war, incited criminal instincts, contained pornography or pandered to superstition.[19] The censorship policy thus revealed a concern with both the moral and cultural sensibilities of the Burmese and political and ideological problems. Finally, in 1966 the Revolutionary Council suspended publication of all privately owned foreign-language newspapers – the main target being the Chinese journals.[20] Within four years after the coup, then, Burmese had access to only that foreign information approved by the government, and the outside world knew little about Burma except that which the government news sources provided to the few remaining foreign correspondents. A few journalists visited Rangoon throughout the 1960s, but as they were prohibited from travelling around the country, their reports were based on little more than tourist-type impressions gained during a stay of several days in Rangoon. It is not entirely surprising that the Burmese authorities did not welcome foreign journalists, since virtually every piece of interpretive writing on Burma during the early years of the Revolutionary Council was highly critical of the government's economic performance.[21]

Limitations on information from the outside world did not apply solely to the news media. Within six months after the coup, the government directed the Ford and Asia Foundations to phase out their economic and cultural programs, and eventually to leave the country. Student and scholarly exchanges under the Fulbright program were terminated. The British Council, which maintained an active program in English language instruction and exchange of scholars, had to close down. By the mid-1960s, the faculty of the University of Rangoon was fully Burmanized, the language of instruction was no longer English and most of the curriculum was radically altered to suit 'Burma's needs'. The government even rejected an offer by the Rockefeller Foundation to finance construction of a museum for storing some of Burma's antiquities.[22] Showing virtually no sympathy toward any foreign cultural presence in the country, Ne Win ordered Burmese Lions and Rotary Clubs to disband.[23] Finally, the government placed a number of restrictions on the information activities of foreign diplomatic missions. Embassy libraries were forced to close because they could not obtain a required government license, and embassy staff were prohibited from showing any 'propaganda' films to the Burmese public. A decree required foreign missions to submit all publicity releases to the Burmese Foreign Ministry before distribution to the Burmese press or public.

Foreign missionaries, doctors and teachers left the country, as the government either expelled them directly (the missionaries) or passed legislation prohibiting foreigners from practising medicine. This eliminated not only those physicians who were associated with foreign religious organizations or aid programs, but also many Anglo-Burmese (who held British passports) who had spent their entire life in the country. The government took these measures despite an acute shortage of physicians in the country.[24]

The Revolutionary Council no more welcomed foreign tourists than it did private investment or doctors or university teachers. Burma had never been a great tourist attraction because of its climate and distance from the major metropolitan countries, but prior to the revolution, approximately 10,000 foreigners visited annually (see Table 5.1). Tourist visas were easy to obtain, but by February 1963 Burmese consuls abroad were required to submit all visa applications to Rangoon – which meant, in effect, that even for transit purposes a visitor had to wait a month or more to obtain the necessary documents. In 1964 the government reduced the time of entry

Table 5.1   *Numbers of Tourists, Burma and Malaysia Compared*

	1963	1965	1966	1967	1968	1969
Burma	10,000	2,007	2,682	1,646	2,561	6,853
Malaysia	n.d.	23,225	49,915	42,602	50,588	53,071

Source: The Far East and Australasia: A Survey and Directory of Asia and the Pacific, Annual (London: Europa Publications, annually).

permits to only twenty-four hours, which effectively put an end to tourism. With no passengers destined for Rangoon, foreign airlines terminated their stopovers in Burma. The only remaining access to the country by the mid-1960s was with the tiny and aged Burmese Airways, from Calcutta or Bangkok. Finally, the Revolutionary Council rejected a major proposal to help build a highway from the southern tip of the Malayan peninsula to Calcutta. Part of the highway would have gone directly through Burma. The government made the decision primarily on strategic grounds, but fear of easier access to the country by foreigners was a consideration as well.[25]

On the ingress dimension of foreign policy, then, the Revolutionary Council had transformed Burma from a society accessible to many, to one sealed off from virtually all outside contacts. The thousands of foreign government officials, scholars, missionaries and tourists who roamed the country in U Nu's days had all departed under government order. All that remained were several hundred Chinese, Soviet and European technical experts, a handful of correspondents and a small diplomatic community. The latter group could hardly be said to lead a normal diplomatic life, however, for the government erected an effective bureaucratic screen between itself and personnel of foreign embassies. If a second secretary of an embassy wanted to meet with an official in the Ministry of Transportation, let us say, he had to submit a special request to the Burmese Foreign Ministry; and Burmese officials were instructed not to accept invitations – even to social functions – from foreign diplomats, without special authorization. This was not only a problem for low-level Burmese officials. Ne Win reportedly never met with foreign diplomats – with the occasional exception of the Chinese ambassador.[26] Diplomats soon came to regard an appointment to Rangoon as a period of exile.

The Revolutionary Council's attitude toward foreign aid was no less hospitable. Although in his first year as Chairman, Ne Win had sought assistance from several foreign quarters, one year later his attitude changed considerably. American economic assistance ran its course, and the government halted work on the incomplete Rangoon–Mandalay highway project. Washington received no further request for aid. The major donor of assistance during the 1960s was China, which granted Burma a credit of $80 million, and sent over 300 technical experts to direct development projects. However, the crisis in Chinese-Burmese relations during the period of the Cultural Revolution (see below) ended that program. Soviet offers to step into the breach were spurned.[27] When Sino-Burmese relations were restored in the early 1970s, only 35 percent of the

Chinese credits had been used up[28] – in part because the Chinese during the 1960s had insisted on building strategically important bridges in areas under Burmese communist control, while the Ne Win government had obviously different priorities. The United States did maintain a small program of military equipment transfers (worth approximately $27 million) throughout the decade, but when the commitment ended in 1971, Ne Win did not request a renewal and announced that to remain dependent upon the United States for money and military hardware was 'intolerable'.[29] A trickle of funds came from small loans secured abroad, and a few foreign technicians came to Burma during the period after the coup, but basically the Ne Win government practised a form of extreme self-reliance. The foreign aid component, so prominent in U Nu's days, did not fit into the Revolutionary Council's plans for developing the country.

By 1965 or 1966, Burma had become a hermit nation. All but a handful of foreigners had left, and no new foreigners were admitted to the country. However, a hermit not only makes himself inaccessible to others, but also ceases to participate in the activities of the external community.

Burma's Externally Directed Activities

One would not expect a relatively poor country to establish an extensive diplomatic network, particularly with those countries with which it had few interests or problems in common. But we would expect even the smallest, least developed country to maintain reasonably high levels of diplomatic and commercial interchange with its immediate neighbors, particularly if they share common traditions, religion, language, and the like. There would be nothing particularly unusual if Burma did not take an active role in global affairs, despite U Nu's propensity to do so during the 1950s. But the Revolutionary Council's diplomacy displayed such a pronounced lack of interest in *all* external realms that it must be considered highly unusual.

In the decade under review, Burma refused to join any of the new and growing Southeast Asian regional cooperative endeavors, whether technical, economic, diplomatic, or military. The government never displayed interest in participating in ASEAN, Maphilindo, the Asian Development Bank, SEAFET and ASA. Of the nineteen intergovernmental organizations operating in the region during the decade, Burma belonged to only one – the Colombo Plan which it had joined upon gaining independence in 1947. The Burmese even refused to join such politically innocuous organizations as the Asia-Pacific Postal Union, or the Association of Natural Rubber Producing Countries.[30] Ne Win, who was otherwise a reasonably peripatetic leader, did not make his first trip as head of state to Southeast Asia until 1968, when he visited Singapore and Malaysia. He used that occasion to announce what was already obvious: Burma was not interested in schemes of regional cooperation and was committed to finding its own path to development.[31] On security matters Ne Win's proposed solution to the area's problems was permanent neutralization,[32] but there is no evidence that he promoted his scheme with any active diplomacy.

If Burma's activities in Southeast Asia could be characterized as 'low profile', in the Third World subsystem they were virtually non-existent – again, a radical contrast from the pattern of the 1950s. Ne Win quickly abandoned U Nu's leadership role in the non-aligned movement. At the 1964 Cairo Conference, Burma was one of the few countries represented by its Foreign Minister rather than head of state or government. A Burmese voice was seldom heard at that conference.[33] During the Sino-Indian conflict in 1962 Ne Win made a weak attempt at mediation, but this was the only occasion of such diplomatic activity and, notably, it took place at the beginning of his period of leadership. His government's attitude toward the group of non-aligned states was summed up by one Burmese diplomat: 'We are in principle opposed to all blocs . . . Once you form a non-aligned bloc, your independence is lost.'[34]

At the global level, Burma maintained its membership in all United Nations organizations – but that did not mean that it participated actively. The former Burmese ambassador to the United Nations recounted that he seldom received instructions from Rangoon on how to vote on issues in the General Assembly, and thus had little choice but to abstain. The Burmese delegation listened to debates and sent home reports – but these seldom evoked directions for any further action.[35] At the Geneva Disarmament Committee, the Burmese delegate rarely took part in substantive discussions; in fact, he rarely made an appearance at the meetings.[36] Burma's participation at the global level thus came to reach symbolic proportions only; Burma's delegates did not participate if by that term we mean introducing diplomatic initiatives, engaging in debate, or publicizing a particular point of view.

Little growth occurred during the 1960s at the diplomatic institutional level. Slowing the trend of the previous decade, the Revolutionary Council created only two new embassies during its first twelve years in power. The figure does show an increase, but the reality behind it suggests otherwise. The government used several of the embassies or ambassadorships as sinecures, as places to send potential or actual opponents of the regime, or as honors bestowed upon loyal government officials whom the regime wished to retire or replace. The presence of an embassy in a foreign capital did not mean, therefore, that Burma actually conducted business with the country in question.[37]

The level of diplomatic activity can also be measured in terms of the number of treaties which a government signs or adheres to. For the U Nu period, 1947–61, the Burmese government concluded or adhered to an average of eight bilateral or multilateral treaties per year. In the period of the Revolutionary Council, through 1970, this figure had declined to less than three annually. By contrast, Ghana, Malaysia, Tanzania and even Nepal – all countries with populations significantly smaller than Burma's – had figures of 10·9, 6·5, 5·1 and 3·7 respectively.[38]

Decline of foreign-directed activity is indicated, finally, by the travel, study and employment of Burmese abroad. The government placed strict limits on the number of Burmese who could work for foreign organizations, including United Nations agencies. Those Burmese who had been educated abroad were singled out for severe restrictions.[39] The government also drastically reduced the numbers of students it sent abroad for university and postgraduate training. Only inexact figures are available for the 1950s, but at least several thousand Burmese went abroad – largely to England and the United States – annually for study. The figure had declined to 378 in 1968.[40] Compared to most other developing countries, that figure is extremely low. A comparable Southeast Asian country, Malaysia, sent 7,687 students abroad in 1965, or 37 percent of its total university student population (a percentage quite typical of developing countries); for the period 1962 to 1970, slightly over 1 percent of Burma's university students went abroad – a figure far below all other developing countries for which UNESCO has statistics.

There were only two exceptions to Burma's almost total non-involvement abroad. First, Ne Win was a prolific traveller. He made several visits to Peking before his venture to Southeast Asia in 1968. But he also travelled to Washington, Delhi, Rawalpindi, Moscow and Tokyo. Yet his visits were usually surrounded with so much secrecy that it was difficult to judge what they accomplished. Compared to U Nu, moreover, the numbers and variety of destinations for state visits declined appreciably. Countries such as Yugoslavia, Egypt and Israel, with whom U Nu kept in constant contact, were dropped from Ne Win's itinerary.

Second, the trade patterns of the 1950s which displayed considerable diversity were maintained throughout the period under review. In 1970, for example, Burma's exports went, in rank, to Sri Lanka, Singapore, England, India, Japan, Indonesia and Malaysia (note the high proportion of trade with developing nations, a pattern found among few other countries of the Third World). Its imports for the same year came primarily from Japan, India, England, West Germany, the United States, Hong Kong and China, in that order. No single country accounted for more than 20 percent of Burma's export markets or sources of supply.[41] The most notable change in the trade figures was the precipitous decline in the value of Burma's exports. In the pre-coup days, Burma's exports averaged approximately one billion *kyats* (about $250 million); by 1967–8 the figure had declined to 525 million *kyats*, or approximately $135 million. The explanation for the decline does not lie in a deliberate government policy choice consistent with other forms of isolation, however. Agricultural mismanagement, the nationalization of rice milling, American competition through PL 480 rice exports, poor weather, better rice strains developed in other countries and rapidly increasing domestic demand for rice were all contributing factors.

Despite Ne Win's travels and the diversified foreign trade pattern, there is little doubt that the degree of change in the other indicators of externally directed activities, and the policies toward penetration, constitute an example of foreign policy reorientation and restructuring. Although the Revolutionary Council continued to use the rhetoric of non-alignment, in reality its policies demonstrated almost complete indifference to events and trends in the external environment that did not directly impinge on Burma. It maintained contacts – at least until 1967 – with the Chinese (more out of necessity than desire, apparently) but otherwise our photograph displays a pattern consistent with the concept of isolationism. It does not fit the ideal type as closely as Bhutan did before 1958, but with the exception of Cambodia since 1975 and possibly Albania, no other nation in recent history has so effectively sealed itself off from the outside world and displayed so little concern about issues which confronted other nations in the region and in the global system.

The economic costs of these policies were substantial. Almost all foreign observers of Burma in the 1960s (and even today) have documented the decline of living standards in Rangoon, the innumerable frustrations consumers faced in obtaining even simple necessities of life (with no exports, the government cannot import), bureaucratic incompetence and corruption, black market activities and sagging production figures. To achieve self-sufficiency, how much was the Ne Win government willing to pay? The amazing persistence of the regime in pursuing policies that had demonstrably failed economically will probably remain a mystery for some time. Here, however, we can raise the question why the government reoriented and restructured the country's foreign relations in the first place.

Explanations

Explanations for Burmese foreign policy behavior in the 1960s are difficult to present authoritatively, because interviews with policy-makers are impossible to obtain and because the top leadership – aside from some turgid campaign-style statements and several ideological tracts – seldom commented publicly on foreign policy issues.[42] Thus, we have to make numerous inferences from scattered comments, published anecdotes and the personal histories of the main actors.

Three types of explanations can be related to the Burmese attempts to seal off their country and to reduce drastically the level of regional and global diplomatic activity. The first – which is the most prominent in the literature on Burma – emphasizes immediate external security threats. The second argues that isolationism was a response to the domestic insurrections. A third line of analysis, which generally has been ignored, emphasizes the values and attitudes of the Burmese in general, Burma's historical record under colonialism, and the world views, perceptions and personal experiences of some segments of officialdom, the military members of the Revolutionary Council and the Burmese leader Ne Win.

The three types of analysis are not necessarily exclusive. What we want to do, however, is to demonstrate that simple deterministic explanations focusing on a single variable such as the threat from China do not sufficiently account for the broad range of isolationist behavior. While the Burmese were vitally concerned with their relations with China, the evidence indicates that the regime perceived a much more ephemeral threat facing the country, namely, the vast foreign presence in Burma and the consequences it was having on Burmese independence and society. The variety of isolationist policies appeared to reflect deep-seated historical attitudes toward foreigners, elite perceptions of the 'lessons' of the colonial experience and the impressions gained from the post-colonial period under U Nu. Those analyses which assess Burma's behavior from a cold war perspective have generally failed to take into account the personal, socio-cultural and national historical experiences that conditioned policy choices.

Most discussions of Burmese isolationism argue that it was a carefully conceived strategy to cope with the threat from China. China was and continues to be Burma's main foreign policy problem because alone among the major powers, Peking became directly involved in the Burmese communist insurrection by providing funds, arms, propaganda services and moral support. These activities were undoubtedly of great concern to Burmese officials, and it is possible that Burma closed down some of the foreign presence in the country to prevent the Chinese from claiming that Burma was veering toward the imperialist camp. According to Seymour Topping, for example, 'Ne Win apparently regards [a balance] as essential to his policy of avoiding any irritation of Peking that would invite pressure . . . Confronted by [the Chinese] levers of power . . . Ne Win has responded by adopting a policy of non-involvement in the cold war.'[43] Almost six years later another observer wrote: 'Hoping that China will not increase its activity, [Ne Win] has shaped a foreign policy intended to make Burma as inconspicuous as possible, a policy of giving no offense to its giant northern neighbor.'[44]

This line of reasoning has some plausibility, but it does not muster sufficient evidence to provide an answer to the *totality* of Burmese foreign reorientation and restructuring. Indeed, Ne Win throughout the 1960s adopted a hard line against Chinese subversive activities, while maintaining respectably cordial relations at the state-to-state level – at least until 1967. This suggests that though he was concerned with the China problem, he was not so fearful of the Chinese that he would radically alter Burma's foreign policy orientation for that reason alone. In 1967, Chinese militia troops headed by Burmese insurgents slipped into Burma and cut deeply into the Shan states, Kachin state and across the Salween River. Eventually it controlled the northeast tip of the country.[45] The Burmese response was to order a major and partly successful counteroffensive.

In the non-military realm, the government was no less vigorous in handling the China problem. Chinese attempts to proselytize during the Cultural Revolution led to anti-Chinese riots in Rangoon, where several members of the Chinese embassy were lynched. In the face of Burma's refusal to offer apologies, Peking launched a furious propaganda attack against Ne Win's 'fascist, reactionary' government. For the first time, it also publicly offered support to the White Flag communists, support which had been going on for years, but which was never previously admitted by Peking. Ne Win reacted by demanding the Chinese to withdraw their 300 technical experts, by imprisoning 200 Burmese China sympathizers, by expelling the Chinese News Agency correspondent and by shutting down the pro-communist Chinese newspaper in Rangoon. These were hardly the actions of a regime in awe of Chinese power.

Such actions were of course immediate responses to a crisis. But even in more normal periods throughout the 1960s Burma did not fear to express views that diverged considerably from those promoted by the Chinese. Burma's diplomatic position on a variety of regional issues such as Laos and Vietnam differed from Chinese opinions on these matters – and the Burmese, despite Chinese efforts, refused to line up diplomatically behind Peking.[46] There is not much evidence, then, to support the view that the Burmese were so fearful of Chinese diplomatic pique or subversion that they would adjust their domestic and diplomatic policies solely to meet Chinese desires. Ne Win undoubtedly placed various restrictions on foreign embassy activities and on the local press to reduce the cold war gamesmanship carried on in Rangoon. Other actions might also be linked to a concern with China. But it is hard to understand how the China problem contributed to the dramatic reduction of students sent abroad, the banning of beauty contests, non-participation in the Geneva Disarmament Committee, lack of interest in the non-aligned movement and many other actions described previously.

Was isolationism a response to internal insurgency? In a country racked by insurrection, a government cannot guarantee the safety of tourists, aid advisers, missionaries, and the like. The Burmese therefore asked all foreigners to leave. Some evidence supports this type of reasoning. Rebel incursions and raids often took place along the Rangoon–Mandalay corridor, a major tourist route. Even though most of the fighting took place in relatively remote areas in the northeast of the country, few villages and towns in the more populated areas of the south were completely free of harassment. Indeed, the headquarters of the Red Flag (pro-Soviet) communist rebels was located in the mountains only 100 kilometers from Rangoon. Under such circumstances, exclusion of foreigners made sense.[47] Yet other governments, including U Nu's, faced with the same sorts of insurrectionary problems, did not respond in such an extreme fashion. Moreover, it is impossible to link the actions of guerrillas with Burma's non-involvement in United Nations and other global affairs, its marked indifference to regional cooperative programs, its rejection of aid offers, its restrictions on Burmese travel abroad, to say nothing of turning down the American offer to build a museum to house some of Burma's most precious antiquities.

To understand the main lines of Burma's isolationism, if not *every* exclusionist policy, it is necessary to take an excursion into Burma's past, to try to find the roots of xenophobia and to explore Burmese (and not cold war analysts') perceptions of foreigners and the outside world. We start with Burmese society in general, and work our way through circles of ever-decreasing size until we have covered all the important policy-making segments – the bureaucracy, the military leadership and Ne Win personally.

To begin, we must not assume that the policies of the U Nu government represented, given Burma's past, some natural progression from the colonial to the post-colonial situation. A former high-ranking Burmese diplomat summed up the problem in the following way: 'In many ways the [exclusionist] policies of the Ne Win regime are more consistent with Burmese attitudes and traditions than were those of U Nu. U Nu's internationalism and cosmopolitanism were the real aberrations.'[48]

All peoples have some conception of their national past, often romanticized to include elements of national greatness and purity. Nationalist movements in nineteenth- and twentieth-century Europe, as well as anti-colonial crusades throughout Africa and Asia, fought their struggles not only to achieve an image of a modernized and independent future, but also to resurrect a past golden age. Nationalist movements often envisage the future in terms of the past. For the Burmese nationalist movement in the first four decades of this century, the images of pre-colonial Burmese society (pre-1850s) had a particular attraction. Burma has been effectively sealed off from the rest of the world. Formidable geographical barriers separated it from India and China, and these 'contributed to [a] consciousness of exclusiveness and to an emphasis on the uniqueness of Burma's pristine Buddhist tradition'.[49] Burmese ethnocentrism was based partly on religious criteria. Although the Buddhists were traditionally tolerant of all religions, many Burmese never saw foreigners as models to emulate because, despite their technology, their religions were not equally worthy. But material considerations also played a role in the generally negative evaluations the Burmese made of the British and all foreigners. It is clear from English and French accounts of Burmese life in the mid-nineteenth century that the Burmese then were fundamentally better off than they were to become under British rule. One British envoy in 1828 wrote that Burmese peasants compared favorably to their European counterparts in wealth, and that the laboring classes were well fed, clad and housed. There was little beggary, and land ownership was equally distributed.[50]

But many colonial observers and travelers characterized the Burmese as lazy and shiftless, failing to understand that not all societies are founded on the principle of wealth accumulation, and that Theravada Buddhist ethics do not sanctify the pursuit of material acquisitions. Quite the contrary: those values placed priority on renunciation and doing good deeds to others to gain religious merit; distribution, not increased production, was the aim of social policy. Pre-colonial Burmese economic behavior closely reflected the principles of the all-encompassing church. Hence, the drive for economic development in Burma came from external pressures rather than from indigenous initiative.[51]

Anthropologists such as Nash[52] emphasize that whatever the long-run impact of British rule on Burma, the vast majority of the Burmese were hardly touched intellectually by the experience. There was no revolution of agricultural techniques, no influx of machines, no rapid expansion of industry, no greatly widened mental horizons, and certainly no revolution of rising expectations. Many Burmese, however, had a strong sense of pride and believed that aside from some technology, they had little to learn from foreigners. The foreigners, moreover, invariably tried to change their way of life and hence were not welcome.[53]

If rural Burmese peasants did not understand directly the impact of colonialism on their lives, the educated elites, including the leaders and members of the various nationalist movements, could hardly fail to appreciate what was going on around them. Except for some minimal educational services, the evidence shows clearly that the average Burmese's economic fortunes declined during seventy years of colonial rule. The British had begun the process of destroying the traditional order without replacing it with either economic or social welfare.[54] On a national basis, the British changed the Burmese economy, which had been self-sufficient, to one geared for exports. Subject before only to the vagaries of weather, the Burmese under colonial rule became vulnerable to fluctuation in world rice market prices, currency values and availability of markets. Burmese economic life, once characterized by security and relative plenty, was now insecure and subject to a discernible impoverishment – a condition that the Ne Win regime has not yet been able to reverse.

For the Indians and British, fortunes were relatively easy to make in Burma. Few Burmese profited from these successes. Indian immigrants cornered the retail trade and introduced to the Burmese peasant the institution of the money-lender. When the British had succeeded in gaining control of the rice-milling factories throughout Burma, they reduced prices paid to the cultivators at a time when world prices were increasing. Between 1870 and 1930, agricultural real wages in lower Burma may have fallen 20 percent[55] and Burmese rice consumption fell anywhere from 10 to 25 percent during the last two decades of British rule.[56] In landholding, the record was equally unimpressive. Prior to colonization, Burmese peasants 'owned' their land, but they considered it a part of their patrimony and not an exchange commodity subject to mortgage and foreclosure.[57] The British changed all of this; the Burmese, under British laws, had to pay for their land; and to obtain funds, they had to borrow at usurious rates from Indian money-lenders. The development of lower Burma into a major rice export producing area created a huge class of migrant laborers, thus helping break down traditional Burmese society based on the family and village. Sarkisyanz reports that by the time of the 1921 Census, only one-half of the agriculturalists in lower Burma owned their land. Money-lenders owned most of the remainder. British and Indians came to hold control over all of the non-agricultural sectors of the economy as well. There was little 'trickle down' effect from industrial and commercial enterprises since wages were extremely low and since the colonial authorities, responding to the importunings of those who held economic power, failed to pass any welfare legislation. The consequences of colonialism were grim for those Burmese who entered the cash economy. Sarkisyanz summarizes:

> Under the British rule Burma's village relations were disrupted, the Burmese local officials disassociated from the populace, and the individual released from the restraints of custom and tradition; much of rural Burma became relatively impoverished while a part of the Buddhist monastic order became demoralized. The social balance stabilizing pre-British Burma, with its 'egalitarian character of society' was upset by the colonial system. The colonial administration failed to fill the gap left by its displacing the medieval Burmese regime. Through these social dislocations, to Burma's Buddhist traditionalism, the world order seemed no longer a moral order, and human society no longer an image of it.[58]

Burmese government officials in the 1950s and 1960s often alluded to their memories of the colonial experience and some proposed reverting to a policy of isolationism as a means of protecting traditional values and avoiding tutelary and dependent relationships which they considered to be demeaning or exploitative. Recall that this was the second generation of Burmese government officials. The first had been trained under the Indian civil service, was largely educated in British-type institutions or in England, spoke English and generally fashioned its personal and professional lives on English models. The second generation, which fought against the British system, held different values: its models were Burma's pre-colonial past, Marxism and nationalism.

Lucian Pye's study – the only systematic examination of Burmese administrators' and politicians' attitudes in the post-colonial period – emphasized the conflict between modern and traditional values. He points out that the early leaders of the nationalist movement wished to see changes in Burmese life, but not of the kind that would be inconsistent with important Burmese traditions.[59] He also suggests (p. 157) that, lacking a sense of independence during the U Nu years, the typical Burmese official or politician had a 'pervasive and self-destroying suspicion of others, of all that is foreign'. The acculturation process, according to Pye, tended to reinforce distrust toward those who were anxious to help, that is, toward foreign aid officials, academics, missionaries, and the like. The Burmese held a 'deeply felt sensation of being changed and manipulated by others'.[60] There was a genuine ambivalence toward modernization. It represented as much a threat as a promise because it involved, during the colonial and U Nu periods, foreign controls and paternalism as well as the erosion of traditional forms of personal and economic relationships.

Exact numbers of foreign advisers attached to the government in Rangoon during the 1950s are not available, but the comments of bureaucrats and politicians interviewed by Pye indicate that they could do few things of national importance without the supervision of foreigners. Burma's ambassador to the United States and the United Nations, for example, revealed that most of the aid requests he presented to Washington had been drafted by American aid experts, and not by Burmese officials.[61] Whatever may have been the officials' views on the policies of the Ne Win regime, at least they were freed of foreigners peering over their shoulders and making continuous judgements about their lives, politics and economics.[62]

Some Burmese officials also based anti-foreign attitudes on their perceptions of the modernization process in neighboring countries, particularly in Thailand. They judged that development through foreign tutelage resulted in the destruction of indigenous culture, modesty and piety. As one official put it, 'We would rather do without foreign exchange than have the corruption tourists would bring.' He pointed to Bangkok, a city of massage parlors, brothels and night clubs designed to serve American soldiers and tourists, as the thing, above all, the Burmese wanted to avoid.[63]

In sum, many Burmese officials expressed what some would call 'xenophobic attitudes' because of their images of the pre-colonial past, their personal experiences under foreign tutelage and their pessimistic assessments of the nature of development as it was promoted by foreigners. They tended to idealize traditional Burmese society, particularly the society of the pre-colonial Ava kingdom, with its characteristics of equality, piety and built-in welfare mechanisms. Colonialism had largely destroyed that culture and contributed little except an elite democratic political order that did not function successfully in the hands of the Burmese. Post-independence politics did not fulfill nationalist aspirations either, because most of the institutions were run by, or under the heavy influence of, foreigners, people who for the most part did not understand Burmese society and who, like the British and Americans, placed the accumulation of wealth, profits and savings as the *sine qua non* of development. Looking to the future, they rejected development models which, as in other Southeast Asian countries, resulted in external dependence, unchecked urbanization, official corruption and public immorality.

There is no way of knowing what proportion of government officials shared these attitudes. The respondents of Pye's interviews did not represent a particular percentage of all Burmese bureaucrats. It is likely, however, that those whose formative years were in the 1930s and who received their education in Burma rather than in England probably held views similar to those outlined above. It is significant, too, that when the military took over in 1962, no exodus of bureaucrats, either to the rebel groups or abroad, took place. But what of the top-level military decision-makers? Aside from the recollections of colonialism was there something particular in their collective history that disposed them to adopt policies of exclusion and national self-sufficiency or dislike of foreigners?

The present Burmese army had its origins in the 'Thirty Thakins', a group of socialist-nationalist youths who went to Japan early in World War II for military training. Most had belonged to socialist groups in Rangoon University during the 1930s, and held a strong antipathy against both the British and capitalism as it had developed in Burma. Returning to Burma in 1942, they created the Burmese Independence Army (BIA) which collaborated with the Japanese imperial forces in driving the British from the country. The army had three main organizational characteristics that distinguished it from the Burmese forces under British command: (1) it excluded all members of Burmese minority groups (Chins, Karens, Shans, and the like); (2) it restricted its recruitment to only part of the country; and (3) it was broadly based, class-wise.[64] The Thakins and their army took over the government of towns in the Japanese-controlled areas of Burma and generally provided the leadership which would one day replace the British colonial government. The rural-based Thakins appealed for support on a platform of anti-colonialism, but unlike many such movements which emphasized the economic depredations of colonial administrations, the Burma Independence Army and its spokesmen emphasized the moral decay of the Burmese under British rule. An editorial of the *Delta News* claimed in 1942:

> We Burmese peoples were originally high minded and cultured, while we followed the traditional, cherished Buddhism. However, for one hundred years the white Indian [British] government dirtied our clean minds and made our civilized minds savage. Thus the character of the Burmese people was ruined . . . Destroy the old and dirty mind which was bewitched by the white Indian and adopt a new, clean mind . . .[65]

After 1945, veterans of the BIA took command of the new national army. Many of the officers, including some of the original Thirty Thakins, had been heavily influenced by Japanese militarist ideas, with emphasis on the special virtues of the military in designing a social order based on loyalty, discipline and sacrifice. According to Ba Maw, Burma's wartime president, the Burmese army leaders 'were quick [to] pick up the paranoia bred by pre-war Japanese militarism'.[66]

Thakin Aung San led the fight for Burmese independence and when that was secured in 1947 the unity between the military and the government was symbolized in his person. His assassination along with most of his Cabinet shortly after assuming power was to lead to an alienation between civil and military authorities later, however. The pious U Nu, much admired and respected at home and abroad, could make effective appeals in terms of long-range aspirations and the virtues of Buddhism, but he had little talent for inspiring social and bureaucratic discipline, with the result that the Burmese military became increasingly disillusioned with his leadership. A foreign diplomat described how the military leadership saw their country after several years of independence: 'The British ran the government and big business, the Hill Tribes were in the army, the Indians and Chinese had the commerce, and American Baptists were subverting Buddhism. So what do you expect?'[67] Unfortunately for U Nu, except for the formal vestiges of British rule and the declining position of the Hill Tribes in the Burmese army, he had done little to change the other aspects of foreign penetration of Burmese society.

The 1962 Revolutionary Council was composed of eleven colonels, five brigadiers and one general – Ne Win. Of these, Ne Win was the sole representative of the 'Thirty Thakins', but nine of the other members had served in the BIA. As a collective unit, one observer characterized it in its early years as 'intensely suspicious of foreigners and of Burmese intellectuals who have worked with, or have known, foreigners'.[68] These officials saw themselves as the main agents of Burmese modernization; only they could instill order, efficiency and discipline, and overcome the corruption and political bickering of the U Nu government. Yet, as von der Mehden points out, the military's commitment to modernization did not preclude sensitivity to traditional Burmese values.[69] While the military regime sought to reduce the Buddhist influence in politics, in other ways – particularly in its puritanism – it tried to set an example of how Burmese, in the old tradition, should behave. On assuming power, the Revolutionary Council banned beauty contests, required civil servants to wear the traditional *longyi* and insisted that members of the military forces not display wealth or indulge in conspicuous consumption.[70] The Ministry of Information censored all domestic and foreign literature which it deemed offensive to Burmese moral as well as political sensitivities. The other measures to protect Burmese from contacts with foreigners have already been outlined.

Yet none of the ideological tracts of the Revolutionary Council, or its sole party, the military-led Burmese Socialist Programme Party, made self-sufficiency or isolationism either an official guide to policy or an important policy objective. The themes of those tracts emphasized humanism, socialism and the need for national discipline. Indeed most pronouncements of the party or the Revolutionary Council were bathed in obscurity, so that the roots of the anti-foreign attitudes must be located in the historical experiences of the military's upper echelons, in their perceptions of colonialism – which did not differ markedly from those of many civilian government officials – and not in ideological principles. That Ne Win and his colleagues would place little emphasis on democracy or the British legal tradition is not hard to understand: their early years were spent studying anti-imperialist literature, training under the Japanese on Hainan Island (not exactly a Paris or London) and fighting the British under the auspices of Japanese militarists. Most of the Burmese military elite had enjoyed none of the cosmopolitan experiences of other Burmese officials of the 1920s and 1930s, and had few sympathies for the way that transplanted British institutions functioned in post-colonial Burma; U Nu's regime, for example, was typified by constant factional warfare and bureaucratic inefficiency. As one military official explained, 'We have had enough of western trained intellectuals!'[71] The military also shared many of the attitudes of the bureaucrats of the U Nu period, including a strong aversion to various forms of foreign tutelage, a dislike of private enterprise as they had seen it practised under colonialism, a commitment to some form of socialism, and abhorrence of development as it was being experienced in Thailand. Where they differed from the bureaucrats was their strong commitment to modernization, their puritanism and their anti-intellectual bias. We might predict that people with such backgrounds and values would be highly ethnocentric, but unfortunately we lack a document or speech which clearly demonstrates the sources of the Revolutionary Council's xenophobia.

We can only offer a number of quotes from observers and participants alike, which reveal fairly consistent Burmese anti-foreign attitudes and perceptions of threat coming from foreign penetration into the country.[72]

(1) Ne Win, 1965: '[Bilateral aid] does not help, it cripples. It paralyzes. The recipients never learn to do for themselves . . . In the end they lose control of their country.'

(2) Ne Win, 1962: The government took over the universities because political activity in them 'had led to foreign ideological penetration of the country'.

(3) Ne Win, 1967: 'Unless we Burmese can learn to run our own country, we will lose it.'

(4) Ne Win, 1968: 'We want to be left alone to pursue our own way of life.'

(5) Ba Maw, former President of Burma, 1963: 'In the primary revolution the colonizing foreigners hand over to nationalists who speak their own tongue . . . Now come the men who never had the benefits of a foreign education, who are really of the people. This applies to almost every member of the Revolutionary Council.'

(6) Official of the Burma Socialist Programme Party, 1964: 'In our party, we don't want any of your western educated sophisticates.'

(7) Government official, 1968: 'We are not yet able to welcome [tourists] hospitably.'

(8) Government official, 1969: 'The thing you must never forget about us is that we are obsessed with our national identity.'

(9) Government official, 1969: 'If they [foreigners] think that our [economic policies are disastrous, that is alright]; we know then they won't want to interfere in our affairs.'

(10) Government official, 1976: 'Bangkok is very conspicuous when we look abroad. We will do anything to avoid becoming another Bangkok.'

(11) Information Minister, 1971, speaking to publishers, booksellers and theatre managers: '[You must] help eliminate culture that is repugnant to Burmese society.'

(12) Seymour Topping, 1963: '[These is a] deeply rooted distrust of foreigners in Burma, xenophobia among members of the Revolutionary Council. [They have] an intense desire to eliminate the vestiges of the old dominant foreign cultural and economic influences.'

(13) Dennis Bloodworth, 1964: '[Ne Win's] ideal is a Burma in almost monastic isolation, a neutral socialist state that works out her own formula for salvation and stands aloof from all foreign involvement.'

(14) Joseph Lelyveld, 1969: 'If progress meant turning Mandalay into Indianapolis . . . if it meant having foreigners everywhere insistently showing them foreign ways of doing things, haughtily or even humbly pointing out their errors and shaping their future, then they simply were not having any.'

We cannot automatically assume that a small sample of statements such as these represents or indicates an entire world view, or that actions clearly express motives and attitudes. However, in the case of Burma there is such consistency both in quoted statements and in the observations of correspondents and academics with long experience in Burma, that establishing causal links between life experiences, the attitudes outlined and the actual policies of exclusion and non-involvement does not seem to be taking methodological license. The theme of xenophobia, fear of foreign penetration, the desire to re-establish a Burmese society based on romanticized notions of the past, the recollections of the bitter colonial experience and the period of Japanese military tutelage are too pervasive to be dismissed as mere anecdotal evidence. The question may be raised, nevertheless, to what extent did isolationism reflect the views of the military and the bureaucracy (or at least their upper echelons) as groups, or the preferred course of action of the decision-makers, particularly General Ne Win?

Attitudes and Perceptions of Ne Win

In the first year after the coup, the Revolutionary Council took few new directions in economic policy; indeed, it postponed the previous government's nationalization orders of the import and export sectors for a two-year period, and for a while it continued to invite foreign investment. These policies can be attributed largely to the moderate Aung Gyi, who virtually ran the government for a four-month period in late 1962 when

General Ne Win went abroad for a rest cure. Upon his return to Rangoon, Ne Win dismissed Aung Gyi from his position and banished him to a remote village in the north. The influence of two orthodox Marxists – Brigadier Tin Pe and U Ba Nyein – began to grow at this point. Most of the economic nationalization policies, as well as some of the exclusionist directives, derived from their advice and plans. This conclusion is supported by later events: in 1972 and 1973, when the Burmese government began slowly to move away from its strict isolation by accepting new foreign loans and inviting foreign companies to drill for oil in the offshore waters, Ne Win fired U Ba Nyein; Tin Pe had left the government some time before. Despite the influence of these two advisers, particularly in economic policy, Ne Win was a strong man who made all the fundamental decisions himself. Those who incurred his displeasure were summarily dismissed.[73] It is therefore inconceivable that Ne Win would have accepted the advice of Tin Pe and U Ba Nyein for almost a decade if he did not fundamentally agree with the lines and policies they were proposing. The analysis must thus turn to the ultimate fount of authority in Burma, to Ne Win.

Ne Win's few policy statements and speeches do not reveal in *principle* any particular orientation toward foreigners. There are some clues, however, that suggest a strong fear that foreigners, and the foreign policies of other countries, constituted direct threats to Burmese independence and culture. For example, he made an explicit linkage between Burma's domestic factionalism and insurgency, and the cold war in the global system. In his view, Burmese politics did not revolve around local – that is, the appropriate – issues: Burmese politicans viewed their country's problems through the spectacles of foreigners:

> [The two blocs] created an impact on small nations and on newly independent countries, including Burma. Hence, among our people there are those who prefer the Eastern bloc and those who prefer the Western bloc. Even if the number of such persons who are thus committed is small we suffer a loss. When the Eastern and Western blocs quarrel their partisans among our people also quarrel. This drives a wedge in our national solidarity.[74]

Further statements in this speech rationalized some of the exclusionist measures as necessary to regain Burmese control over the economy. A later section on 'Prevention of Foreign Influence' attributed a number of policies to the need to root out the social and cultural, as well as economic, consequences of imperialist control. Included among the culprits were 'degenerate songs and music' (p. 102). The General Secretary of the BSPP, in his report, claimed that most of the exclusionist measures were taken to 'prevent domination [by] foreign influences' in Burma and to uproot influences which were 'not in accord with the social revolution of the Revolutionary Council' (p. 104).

While these comments focused on the evil consequences of imperialism, they did not reveal all the attitudes underlying Burma's isolationism because the exclusionist measures were applied equally to the 'imperialist' and socialist countries. Although 300 Chinese technicians had remained in Burma until the crisis during the Cultural Revolution, most other aid projects from East Europe and the Soviet Union were phased out along with those from the West, and Burma rejected further offers of assistance. Thus while Ne Win and his party officials may have railed against imperialism, the fact remains that their policies were directed against all foreign influences. Moreover, his pronounced lack of interest in all global and regional issues reveals no selectivity. If his prime concern had been imperialism, he might at least maintain active contacts with the leaders of the non-aligned movement who also shared his concerns. Whatever his public statements, then, the evidence suggests that Ne Win displayed a pronounced aversion to and fear of *all* forms of foreign penetration into Burma, and particularly with those forms of external influence which did not coincide with his conceptions of Burmese piety, culture and economic socialism.

His interest in these areas was highly personal. A few anecdotes reveal his attitudes. Despite his own interest in horse-racing, he banned the sport because he believed gambling on this foreign imported sport was not consistent with the frugality required under socialism. He personally issued the directives banning beauty contests and requiring civil servants to wear traditional clothes. To emphasize his attachment to Burmese ways and his commitment to wipe out corruption, he dealt ruthlessly with transgressors and those who in his opinion did not vigorously suppress foreign influences. For example, he divorced his fourth wife ostensibly because her sister was caught dealing in the black market. In 1976 he dismissed his Trade Minister for failing to 'execute the duties as regards Western dances' and for inadequately squelching 'the snowballing stereo menace'.[75] This act came after Ne Win had marched into a New Year's party held at a hotel near his residence, ordered the rock musicians to stop playing and personally smashed their instruments.[76]

Ne Win was born in a lower middle class family of a Burmese father and Chinese mother. During his early youth he found employment as a postal clerk, but his political ideas were formed primarily through his associations with Rangoon University students. The predominant current of thought among them in the 1930s was a blend of humanist socialism, Marxism and, of course, strong nationalism. After returning from Japanese military training on Hainan Island, he launched a successful military career, partly in collaboration with the Japanese, whose notions of a Greater East Asia Co-Prosperity Sphere he did not reject until the end of the war.[77] As a military commander he emphasized discipline and loyalty; although he did not intervene in politics, he made it clear on numerous occasions that he was profoundly affected by the century of colonial rule and by the powerful grip the English, Chinese and Indians had on the Burmese economy.[78] Lacking experience in foreign travel, higher education, diplomacy, or familiarity with British principles of constitutionality and legality, it is not surprising that his model of government did not derive from Western sources. His conception of capitalism, moreover, was based on his perceptions of the Burmese experience under colonialism. The *Burmese Way to Socialism*, the Revolutionary Council's first lengthy ideological pronouncement, characterized capitalism as 'the inclination to lie, to exploit others, not to have the hands dirtied, to be a parasite on others, to shirk, to be selfish . . .'[79] Finally, it has been reported at least once that Ne Win personally disliked foreigners.[80] This view is supported partially by the fact that on his numerous and lengthy trips abroad for medical purposes (usually to Austria or England), he was known to lead a reclusive life, interested neither in touring nor in making contacts with foreigners.

There is a striking parallel between Ne Win's political style in Burma and his aversion to foreigners and to diplomatic involvements. He was and continues to be a secretive political leader. From the beginning, he rarely made public appearances – on the average, only three per year.[81] Between the 1962 coup and 1968 he gave only one press conference. Much of the time he was absent from the country, but even when present, few people knew how he spent his time aside from playing golf. As the country's economic fortunes declined, his appearances became even rarer, and he seldom spoke about the country's difficulties.[82] Nor did he seek to create a personality cult. He received no accolades from the press – indeed he was seldom even mentioned in the newspapers. His photographs did not adorn the walls of government offices, nor did they appear in newspapers. When he met foreign guests (not a frequent occurrence) they were not usually accorded public welcomes in Rangoon, but were whisked off by helicopter to some remote resort area, the main amenity of which was a golf course. Given these facts, is it possible to hypothesize that a country's orientation toward the outside world may be partly a reflection of the strong leader's personality characteristics that seem to shun human contact? Such a line of reasoning would not explain sufficiently Burma's foreign policy reorientation, but some of the more extreme aspects of policy restructuring seem to emerge from considerations other than pragmatic calculation, ideological commitments or historical recollections of the colonial and post-colonial periods. This hypothesis cannot be taken too far, however, because since the late 1960s there has been a slight opening up of Burma, but no discernible change in Ne Win's political style. Yet after Ne Win's demise we could expect to see some of the more idiosyncratic aspects of Burmese policies toward foreigners changed.

Before we conclude with a brief outline of recent developments, we must now try to rank the relative importance of the various explanatory factors discussed above.

Unlike the case of Bhutan where a concrete set of external events prompted foreign policy reorientation, Burma's dramatic change must be seen as the response to a more ephemeral perception of threat. This evidence suggests that Ne Win, many of the military leaders and perhaps important segments of the civil service regarded Burma as a highly penetrated state. The colonial and post-colonial periods had made deep impressions on these people; not only was the economy under the control of persons considered as foreigners, but many were riled at the paternalism and dependence implicit in the activities of the missionaries, foreign aid and governmental advisers, visiting academics, and all the others. To many of the policy-makers, the image of the 'good future' was modeled more on an idealized version of the isolated Ava kingdom of the early nineteenth century than it was on Western industrial society – and particularly of its offshoots, such as Bangkok.

Many observers have noted the high degree of xenophobia among the Burmese and their officialdom. But perhaps this term is too vague. While some have claimed that Ne Win personally did not like foreigners, it is also true that he did not care to mix with his own people. So, xenophobia must be disaggregated into more discrete sets of attitudes. These would include: fear of being manipulated by foreigners; fear that foreign aid programs would be used to re-establish or maintain the post-colonial private enterprise system which meant, in effect, continued domination of the economy by foreigners and minorities; fear that certain types of cultural influences would corrupt Burmese manners and morals; fear that the spill-over of the cold war would further disunite an already fragile political order; and a feeling that Buddhist social ethics are more humane than the ethics displayed in private enterprise. The Burmese, in short, wanted some aspects of Western technology but not the social and cultural baggage or the political and economic dependence that came with it.[83] Aside from Ne Win's personal feelings, there is little or no evidence that Burmese xenophobia – if we can use that as a shorthand term – included an actual dislike of foreigners as *individuals*. Descriptions of anthropologists and travellers indicate quite the opposite.

The policies of the Ne Win regime, then, can be seen primarily as a reaction to the westernization and exploitation of Burma from the 1850s until the military coup, reflecting a complex amalgam of nativist, socialist, nationalist and xenophobic attitudes. The problem of China and internal rebellion no doubt account for some of the exclusionist policies, but the overall withdrawal of Burma from the international system reflects deeper concerns about Burma's past and future. Ne Win equated Burmese nationalism with self-sufficiency. The Burmese, in his view, must learn to run their own country, otherwise their political, economic and cultural institutions will be buried under the onslaught of Western (including socialist) communications, fads and dissolute life – to say nothing of their diplomatic competition. A weak central government would also result in the breakup of the Burmese union, with the minority states becoming puppets of China or of the other great powers. While Ne Win may not hold the intention of keeping Burma isolated for ever – the costs of doing so have been very great – he took the view that it could not re-enter the international system until it had ended the ethnic and communist insurgencies, and until the Burmese had restored enough faith in their own culture and values so that they could pick selectively from foreign ideas and practices without being overwhelmed by them.[84]

We must rank first, then, Ne Win's military experiences, his associations with the wartime Japanese, his purported dislike of foreigners and the more dissolute aspects of their social and cultural lives, and his perceptions, memories and attitudes toward the colonial and post-colonial periods as basically conditioning his exclusionist, puritan and non-involvement policies. Except for those problems that touched immediately upon Burma, Ne Win was not interested in international affairs; without leadership from the top, with no sense of direction or guidance, Burma's diplomacy abroad just wilted. The broad range of exclusionist policies also reflected Ne Win's consistent fears of excessive foreign penetration and prolonged foreign tutelage, conditions which he thought exacerbated Burma's domestic quarrels and its inability to organize the socialism that was necessary for economic modernization and national unity.

Several key advisers such as Te Pin and U Ba Hyein come next in importance. Their role in nationalizing the economy and various measures to expel some foreign elements appears particularly notable. The government rigidly adhered to a policy of total economic socialization, despite the economic ruin it brought to Burma. A slight opening to the outside world occurred when these men were ousted from the government.

The general support of the upper echelons of the civil service must rank next. This is not to suggest that the bureaucrats unanimously approved of all of the new government's stern measures. But it is clear that the U Nu order had come to such straits by 1962, including the virtual dissolution of the country, that important segments of the bureaucracy could appreciate the need for more discipline. We can speculate, nevertheless, that as many of them had been educated abroad and were familiar with Western-style living, they must have privately opposed the austerity imposed on their lives through declining incomes and lack of access to foreign imports.

Some aspects of the exclusionist policies can be seen, fourth, as a response to the domestic rebellions. With attacks on the Rangoon–Mandalay rail line and sabotage throughout the country, any government might have placed restrictions on the travel of foreigners. And certainly the government was suspicious of the missionaries, for they were most active in the areas populated by the Chins, Kachins and Shans and were thus suspected of aiding their insurgencies. As the dangers of the rebellions receded in the early 1970s, tourists were again permitted to visit, but still received only seven day visas.

The Chinese factor, while important in some areas of policy, should not be overrated. Closing down embassy libraries and the directive to have all embassy-produced films and news releases screened through the Foreign Ministry were probably instituted to put an end to the little 'cold war' that Chinese, Russian and American diplomats were conducting in Rangoon. Chinese proselytizing activities might have been the target as well. But most of the other restructuring activities do not seem relevant to the delicate character of Burmese-Chinese relations.

The most important external factor appeared to be not so much the Chinese, but the war in Southeast Asia and Ne Win's concern that it might spread to involve Burma. There is little direct evidence of this proposition, but the Burmese government did release numerous statements calling for an end to the hostilities and occasionally referred to Ne Win's proposal for the naturalization of the entire Indochinese peninsula. Burma's lack of interest in any form of Southeast Asian cooperation may have arisen from a fear that any linkages with militarily involved countries such as Thailand or possible ultimate targets such as Malaysia would drag it into unwanted complications. This line of reasoning is at least plausible, but at best it accounts for only a portion of the change in Burma's externally directed activities.

In sum, we are arguing that Ne Win's personal history, attitudes and perceptions – broadly conceived – serve as a sufficient explanation for many but not all of the aspects of reorientation and restructuring. In other words, in his absence many of the policies would have taken different guises, or would not have been instituted at all. Yet, given the known attitudes of important segments of two key elite elements – the upper bureaucracy and military – it is likely that Burma would have turned inward in 1963 under any new regime. It is the seeming excesses of policy rather than the general policy directions themselves which can be linked to Ne Win and a few key advisers. To repeat: the U Nu years represented a significant departure from Burmese traditions and were not an inevitable progression from the colonial era.

Retreat from Isolationism?

Despite some significant advances in health and literacy, as well as a few military victories against the insurgents,[85] the economic costs of the isolationist policies have been very high. The fetish with complete nationalization, even down to the street hawkers of Rangoon, created a flourishing black market, widespread corruption and lowered productivity. With steadily declining rice export earnings, imports of consumer goods ceased. Periodic riots by university students and several planned coups by the military indicate that the costs of isolation were more than many were willing to bear. Nevertheless, most of the exclusionist policies and international non-involvement have continued into the late 1970s. No government official has claimed that Burma would open up again. Yet Burma has cautiously amended its hermit-like existence of the 1960s, but not to the extent of restructuring policy. Its practices still come close to the isolationist-type discussed in Chapter 1, but there have been a few changes.

Ne Win's trip to Singapore and Malaysia in 1968 – five years after the coup – indicated that he was interested in establishing some minimal contacts on a bilateral basis with regional states. Exchanges of students and technicians have taken place, and there is now a direct air route between Malaysia and Burma, but that is the only extent of the opening to the southeast. For tourists, visas can now be obtained for seven days, so that the number of visitors has now increased to about 18,000 annually.[86] In 1969 Rangoon served as the venue of the Southeast Asian Peninsular Games. More important, perhaps, was the increasing number of trips abroad by Burmese Ministers to investigate new economic cooperation possibilities. These resulted in loans from the World Bank and the Asian Development Bank. Burma subsequently joined the latter organization – its first membership in a regional group since 1947. Also on the economic front, the government allowed foreign companies to drill for oil and to help reconstruct Burma's inland oil fields. Few new discoveries were made, but the mere act of allowing foreigners to undertake any venture was a significant change from the policies of the 1960s. Finally, Ne Win became somewhat more interested in establishing personal contacts with foreign leaders. In 1974, for example, he visited India, Bangladesh, Pakistan, Malaysia, Australia, Singapore, Indonesia and Yugoslavia. His trips to Australia and Yugoslavia were the first to those countries.

These actions indicate a gradual turning away from some of the more extreme forms of isolation in the 1960s. But in so far as they have been done slowly, and only in a very few policy sectors, there seems to be no overall strategy to overturn the policy directions of the last twenty years. A pragmatic moving away from some of the policies which for over a decade had demonstrably led to economic catastrophe is all that is involved. The end of the Vietnam war may also have prompted Ne Win to increase his contacts in Southeast Asia, no longer fearing that to do so would compromise Burma's neutrality or drag it into cold war politics. Yet Burma remains essentially an inward-looking state, closed to most outsiders, not yet strong enough to meet the outside world without fear of being engulfed by it.

Notes: Chapter 5

1 *New York Times*, 16 July 1968.
2 For a general review of Burmese foreign policy during the U Nu period, see William C. Johnstone, *Burma's Foreign Policy: A Study in Neutralism* (Cambridge, Mass.: Harvard University Press, 1963).
3 ibid., p. 90.
4 ibid., p. 95.
5 ibid., p. 206.
6 S. Bhattacharya, 'Burma: neutralism introverted', *Australian Quarterly*, 37 (March 1965), p. 51.
7 *New York Times*, 3 December 1963.
8 Ruth Pfanner, 'Burma', in F. H. Golay *et al.* (eds), *Underdevelopment and Economic Nationalism in Southeast Asia* (Ithaca, NY: Cornell University Press, 1969), p. 236.
9 An interesting description of great power intrigues in Burma is by Alexander Kaznacheev, a Russian diplomat stationed in Rangoon who defected to the West. See his *Inside a Soviet Embassy* (Philadelphia, Pa: Lippincott, 1962).
10 However, in 1958–9 Ne Win reviewed all foreign aid programs and ended the stay of two American advisory groups. He also refused to renew contracts with twelve Soviet agricultural experts. Johnstone (pp. 142–4) claims these were economy moves and adds that during the same period the Burmese government entered into a number of new aid agreements.
11 Pfanner, in *Underdevelopment and Economic Nationalism*, p. 239.
12 ibid., pp. 213–15.
13 Far Eastern Economic Review, *Yearbook 1963*, p. 60.
14 Sir Richard Allen, 'Recent developments in Burma', *Journal of the Royal Central Asian Society*, 52 (January 1965), p. 11.
15 Moshe Lissak, 'The military in Burma: innovation and frustrations', *Asian and African Studies*, 5 (1969), pp. 148–9.
16 Far Eastern Economic Review, *Yearbook 1963*, pp. 60–3.
17 ibid., p. 63.
18 Richard Hughes, 'In the land of the nationalized noodle-hawker', *Sunday Times* (London), 22 December 1968.
19 Donald Eugene Smith, *Religion and Politics in Burma* (Princeton, NJ: Princeton University Press, 1965), p. 295; Far Eastern Economic Review, *Yearbook 1977*, p. 33.
20 Robert A. Holmes, 'Burma's foreign policy toward China since 1962', *Foreign Affairs*, 45 (Summer 1972), p. 248.
21 Of the several dozen interpretive articles on Burma appearing in the major English, French and American newspapers during the 1960s, only one could be said to present the

military regime's policies in a reasonably sympathetic light. See Joseph Lelyveld, 'Mandalay must not become Indianapolis', *New York Times Magazine*, 5 January 1969, pp. 30–9. All other articles concentrated on the economic decline of Burma and ignored achievements in literacy, health care, education and other social sectors. The Burmese government is partly to blame for the one-sided view because it discouraged interviews with government officials.

22 C. D. Cook, 'Burma: the era of Ne Win', *World Today*, 26 (June 1970), p. 262.

23 *Frankfurter Allgemeine Zeitung*, 19 March 1976.

24 Pfanner, in *Underdevelopment and Economic Nationalism*, p. 261.

25 Interview with Burmese diplomat and former high-level financial official with the Ne Win government, Ottawa, 5 December 1975.

26 *New York Times*, 22 April 1962; Dennis Bloodworth, 'Burma's way to socialism', *Observer Foreign News Service*, 18 June 1963; Dennis Bloodworth, 'Burmese revolution at critical stage', *The Observer*, 1 March 1964.

27 Joseph Lelyveld, 'Mandalay must not become Indianapolis', *New York Times Magazine*, 5 January 1969, p. 30.

28 *Financial Times*, 2 May 1973.

29 *New York Times*, 24 January 1972.

30 Data from Michael Haas (ed.), *Basic Documents on Asian Regional Organizations* (Dobbs Ferry, NY: Oceana Publications, 1974), 4 vols.

31 Résumés of comments by Ne Win during his visit are in the *Straits Times*, 25 April 1968.

32 Jon A. Wiant, 'Burma 1973: new turns in the Burmese way to socialism', *Asian Survey*, 14 (February 1974), pp. 175–6; Raymond Solhac, 'La Neutralité Birmane', *Politique Etrangère*, 32ᵉ année, no. 2 (1967), p. 150.

33 Bhattacharya, 'Burma: neutralism introverted', p. 56.

34 Quoted in *Japan Times*, 21 September 1969.

35 Interview with former Burmese ambassador to the United Nations and to Washington, 16 November 1976, Edmonton, Canada.

36 Michael J. Sullivan, 'Conference at the crossroads: prospects of the Committee on Disarmament', *International Organization*, 29 (Spring 1975), p. 399, fn.

37 Figures on the numbers of embassies are derived from the lists in the *Statesman's Yearbook*, annual. Confidential interview with Burmese diplomat, 5 December 1975.

38 Figures from Peter Rohn (ed.), *World Treaty Index* (Santa Barbara, Calif.: Clio Press, 1974).

39 *Asian Recorder*, vol. 9, no. 35 (1963), p. 5375. The rationale was that the Burmese government had paid for the higher education of most professionals and these in turn owed a debt to Burmese society. Those who had been educated abroad were assumed to be the one least likely to return to Burma when their foreign employment ended.

40 UNESCO, *Statistics of Students Abroad, 1962–1968* (Paris: UNESCO, 1972). Figures from other sources differ. The Far Eastern Economic Review *Yearbook 1969* (p. 113) says that between 1962 and 1967 only 357 students went abroad–46 paid for by the Burmese government and 311 by host states. It also points out that most of the students were in fact government employees.

41 United Nations, *Yearbook of International Trade* (New York: UN, 1973). Somewhat different figures, though not a different pattern, are in Far Eastern Economic Review, *Yearbook 1970*.

42 Smith's *Religion and Politics in Burma* contains a full discussion of the various pronouncements of the Ne Win government. These sources focus on economic issues, attacks on religion, the need for discipline, the humanitarian aspects of socialism, and the like. One looks in vain, however, for government explanations for the total change in foreign policy. See esp. ch. 8.

43 'Burma's aims: socialist state poised between East and West', *New York Times*, 30 December 1963. The title of the article demonstrates Topping's cold war analytical point of view.

44 *Japan Times*, 1 September 1969; see also Bhattacharya, 'Burma: neutralism introverted', pp. 64–5.

45 Many accounts were reported in the press. See, for example, Sterling Seagrave, 'Report on Burma', *The Atlantic*, 225 (April 1970), p. 35; *Sunday Times* (London), 19 November 1967.

46 Holmes, 'Burma's foreign policy toward China since 1962'.

47 A high-level Burmese official told the author that during the 1960s the Ne Win government was much more concerned with the ethnic minority rebellions and internal collapse of the nation than it was with China. Interview, 20 June 1976, Vancouver.
48 Interview with former Burmese ambassador to the United Nations and to Washington.
49 Emanual Sarkisyanz, *Buddhist Backgrounds of the Burmese Revolution* (The Hague: Nijhoff, 1965), p. 5.
50 Recounted in ibid., p. 137.
51 There is considerable debate whether devotion to Buddhism is a barrier to development. Mya Maung, 'Cultural values and economic change in Burma', *Asian Survey*, 4 (March 1964), pp. 757–64, emphasizes the inconsistencies between Theravada Buddhist principles and the requirements of development. Hla Myint, the eminent scholar at Oxford, argues an opposite point of view. Emanuel Sarkisyanz, 'The social ethics of Buddhism and socio-economic development in Southeast Asia', *Asian and African Studies*, 6 (1970), pp. 7–22, summarizes some of the debate as it applies to Burma.
52 Manning Nash, *The Golden Road to Modernity: Village Life in Contemporary Burma* (New York: Wiley, 1965).
53 F. S. V. Donnison, *Burma* (London: Benn, 1970), p. 23.
54 Sarkisyanz, *Buddhist Backgrounds of the Burmese Revolution*, p. 9.
55 John Furnivall, *An Introduction to the Political Economy of Burma* (Rangoon: Peoples' Literature Committee and House, 1957), p. 77.
56 Sarkisyanz, *Buddhist Backgrounds of the Burmese Revolution*, p. 141.
57 J. R. Andres, *Burmese Economic Life* (Stanford, Calif.: Stanford University Press, 1957), pp. 15, 65.
58 Sarkisyanz, *Buddhist Backgrounds to the Burmese Revolution*, p. 148.
59 Lucian W. Pye, *Politics, Personality, and Nation-Building: Burma's Search for Identity* (New Haven, Conn.: Yale University Press, 1962), p. 112.
60 ibid., p. 139.
61 Interview, Edmonton, Canada, 16 November 1976.
62 John Badgley, 'The union of Burma: age twenty two', *Asian Survey*, 11 (February 1971), p. 157.
63 Harold Sieve, 'Burma's nationalized nightmare', *Daily Telegraph*, 5 November 1968. A high-level Burmese official echoed this view to the author, suggesting that Burmese restrictions on tourism and some forms of censorship were in part motivated by fear that foreign tourists would come to Burma only if the Burmese supplied the 'amenities' available in Bangkok—which they were not willing to do. Interview, 20 June 1976. He emphasized that, in his opinion, Bangkok was no longer a Thai city.
64 Dorothy Guyot, 'The Burma Independence Army: a political movement in military garb', in Joseph Silverstein (ed.), *Southeast Asia in World War II: Four Essays* (New Haven, Conn.: Yale Southeast Asian Studies Monograph No. 7, 1966), p. 53.
65 Quoted in ibid., p. 58.
66 Quoted in Martin Woollacott, 'Burma road to iron-bound xenophobia', *The Guardian*, 25 April 1974.
67 Quote from a foreign diplomat in ibid.
68 *Daily Telegraph*, 17 July 1963.
69 Fred R. von der Mehden, 'Politics and the military in Burma', in John P. Lovell (ed.), *The Military and Politics in Five Developing Nations* (Kensington, Md: Center for Research in Social Systems, 1970), pp. 219–20.
70 James F. Guyot, 'Political involution in Burma', *Journal of Comparative Administration*, 2 (November 1970), p. 314.
71 Quoted in 'A country goes underground', *The Times* (London), 12 February 1964.
72 Quotations from the following sources: *The Hindu* (New Delhi), 6 February 1965; *The Times* (London), 2 May 1962; *The Hindu* (New Delhi), 27 July 1967; *Straits Times*, 25 April 1968; *Daily Telegraph*, 17 July 1963; *The Times* (London), 12 February 1964; *Sunday Times* (London), 22 December 1968; quoted in Joseph Lelyveld, 'Mandalay must not become Indianapolis', *New York Times Magazine*, 5 January 1969; ibid.; interview, Vancouver, 20 June 1976; Far Eastern Economic Review, *Yearbook 1972*, p. 133; *New York Times*, 30 December 1963; 'Burmese revolution at a critical state', *The Observer*, 1 March 1964; *New York Times Magazine*, 5 January 1969.
73 Private interview, Ottawa, 5 December 1975.
74 Burma Socialist Programme Party, Central Organizing Committee, *Party Seminar 1965:*

Speeches of Chairman General Ne Win and Political Report of the General Secretary (Rangoon: Sarpay Beikmah Press, 1966), p. 14.
75 Reported in *Straits Times*, 8 January 1976.
76 The press mentioned this episode to illustrate Ne Win's aversion to foreign cultural penetration. According to a Burmese official, however, Ne Win was furious because youths were dancing while units of the Burmese army had just suffered heavy casualties during an engagement against insurgents. Interview, Vancouver, 20 June 1976.
77 George McArthur, 'Burma's road to socialism', *Japan Times*, 14 April 1976.
78 *International Herald Tribune*, 21 September 1973.
79 Quoted in *Party Seminar 1975*, p. 102.
80 Anthony Paul, 'Burma's road to ruin', *Asia Magazine*, 25 December 1974, p. 6.
81 *International Herald Tribune*, 21 September 1973.
82 *The Guardian*, 16 August 1972.
83 Interview with Burmese official, Vancouver, 20 June 1976.
84 ibid.
85 The communist insurgents were weakened as much by their internecine warfare, including assassinations and executions, as by Ne Win's military pressure.
86 Far Eastern Economic Review, *Yearbook 1977*, p. 131.

6

Restructuring Chinese Foreign Policy, 1959–76: Three Episodes

Thomas W. Robinson

Introduction

From the inception of the Chinese communist regime in Peking in 1949 down to the most recent period, the foreign policy of that country has been in a state of almost constant flux. A general policy orientation, once adopted or forced upon the regime by circumstances, never continued for more than four or five years at most. Changes were not only relatively frequent but radical, moving within a relatively short time between pugnatious intervention, one-sided alliance commitment, total isolation, extreme involvement and reversal of alignment. Frequently, such radical changes were closely associated with equally severe swings in the political pendulum of domestic politics. Just as often, however, changes came in response to pressures from the international environment. There is no clear causal relationship between domestic and international factors as determinants of Chinese foreign policy. Indeed, there is probably a complex, reciprocal interaction between international and domestic factors as agents influencing Chinese foreign policy formulation and execution. Whatever the exact nature of that relationship, apparently either the chemistry of the process or the objective requirement to take extreme measures to confront critical challenges produced wide gyrations in foreign policy that were unprecedented in Chinese policy and perhaps in the foreign relations of any modern state.

In terms of the typology of foreign policy restructuring advanced in Chapter 1, the Chinese case is unique. Chinese policy has gone through four transitions since the early 1950s, three of which find no parallel among the cases in this book and may be the only instances of their kind in the post-World War II era. The first transition occurred during the late 1950s, when Peking shifted from *modified dependence* on the Soviet Union to *extreme self-reliance* and rejection of any foreign model or security relationship. The second, during the middle and late 1960s, moved the country from self-reliance to the even greater extreme of total, self-imposed *diplomatic isolation* characteristic of the Cultural Revolution. The pendulum was bound to swing back, once the Cultural Revolution excesses had peaked, and a third restructuring set in during the early 1970s. Emerging from isolation, China now decided to adopt a posture of *diversification* in foreign relations. She sent her ambassadors back into the field, joined the United Nations and established contact for the first time with a wide range of states, including her former worst enemy, America. But having thus retreated from the Cultural Revolution extreme, China now found it necessary to adopt yet another stance to the outer world, *relative dependence* on the West for protection against its new worst enemy, the Soviet Union. Precisely the opposite policy from that of Peking's first foreign policy orientation, this new phase and the restructuring that accompanied it occupied Chinese policy attention during the middle and late 1970s.

Over the entire first quarter-century of Chinese communist foreign policy, Peking occupied, by force or design, all four of the possible foreign policy ideal types outlined in the first chapter and restructured its diplomatic stance four times. Indeed, indications are that Chinese foreign policy will once again undergo massive change in the early 1980s, from modified Western dependence to a combination of modified self-reliance and diversification, that is, an out-and-out balance of power policy.

What is one to think of a state that made extreme changes in its foreign policy so often and within such a comparatively short time? Perhaps the changes were not so extreme; perhaps they were mere tactical shifts and thus do not approximate the ideal types. As will be made clear below, all four instances do fit the typology; significant changes were made in level of external involvement, policies toward external penetration, direction of involvement and degree of commitment.

While the Chinese instance thus falls within the bounds of the overall analytic framework of this book, explanations for such extreme behavior need to be made. Three sets of factors – domestic, great power and systemic – intersected in a differential manner to produce these changes. Their comparative strength varied over the quarter-century of our concern and they are sufficient to explain, in a general manner, why Chinese foreign policy changed so often and why it swung from one extreme to another. It was, moreover, the change in the specific weight of each with time and the differential manner in which they impacted as a group on China that caused Chinese policy to fluctuate in the manner that it did.

Most of the variation in Chinese policy can be traced directly to domestic determinants, including demands of the physical environment, influence of the Chinese (particularly the party's) past, the influence of personality (especially that of Mao Tse-Tung) and the demands of economic modernization through socialism. At times, Chinese foreign policy change can be traced almost entirely and without delay in time to major changes in the internal order. Such was the case, for instance, during the Cultural Revolution. At other times, reversal of the political pendulum at home initiated a chain of events abroad and changes in Chinese attitudes toward them that constrained Peking within a few years to make foreign policy choices it would not necessarily have taken earlier. Such was the case of the influence of the Great Leap Forward in 1958 or the split with the Soviet Union in 1960.

The second factor of influence was the looming presence, and therefore the exceeding importance, of the United States and the Soviet Union. Chinese foreign policy had to take into account the policies and actions of the nuclear super-powers before any overt action in the international arena could be taken. Indeed, Chinese policy since 1949 can be divided into four rather neat phases, each occupying roughly a decade. From 1950 to 1960, China leaned far to the Soviet side to compensate for what Mao and his associates thought was an overriding security threat from the United States. During the 1960s, Peking attempted to wish away its problems with Russia and America. It did so first by thumbing its nose at Moscow while continuing to have nothing to do with Washington and second, during the Cultural Revolution, by withdrawing into itself and presuming the super-powers would let it conduct its internal revolution without interference.

Mao got away with the resulting game of bluff until the worst disorders of the Cultural Revolution were past, but then found to his dismay that the Soviet threat had grown so imminent that he was forced to adopt a policy precisely the reverse of that of the 1950s. Thus, in the 1970s China leaned heavily in the direction of the United States as a counterweight to the Soviet military build-up on China's northern border and deliberately fostered the construction of a grand alliance of all relevant non-Soviet powers. Finally at the end of the 1970s, China seemed to have begun a new phase in its foreign policy, this time choosing the only remaining untried option: balance between Washington and Moscow. This would gain for China the policy independence that she had been unable to obtain in any of the three previous policy choices, enable her to interrupt the inexorable drift toward war with Russia and maximize the prospects for successful economic modernization during the last two decades of the twentieth century.

The final factor of influence is the changing character of the international system. In flux since the breakdown of 1914, the systemic base of international relations continued to change rapidly after 1945. China, just as much as the United States and the Soviet Union, was pushed along by the rush of changes that stemmed from the globalization of international politics, the end of colonialism, the demands of modernization and development, the invention of weapons of mass destruction and instantaneous means of delivery, the internationalization of mass movements and ideologies, and the emergence of a host of 'global issues'. Just as the others, Peking found its range of policy choices constricted and its long-term policy goals constantly frustrated. And like the others, China often did not know what was happening to the system as a whole or to its own policy initiatives until very late. Or, if Peking did at last understand the situation, it was unable to fit such changes into its world view and adjust near-term policies to cope with these secular changes. Indeed, because of its special ideological preconceptions, both national, cultural and Marxist, and because of its relative unfamiliarity with the outer world, the Chinese communist leadership was singularly ill-equipped during most of the period under analysis to deal successfully with international systemic changes.

This chapter does not, of course, intend to recount the history of latter-day Chinese foreign policy nor to analyze in detail its development since 1949. What we are after is to demonstrate that the four changes in Chinese policy noted above are indeed examples of foreign policy restructuring, that is, that they represent a series of foreign policy actions deliberately taken to alter the previous policy in a fundamental manner, are measurable (or at least evident) along a significant number of geographic and functional dimensions, and were completed within a reasonably short period of time.

To accomplish that, we proceed as follows. First, we write three case studies of Chinese foreign policy, tracing the four transitions noted above. (For purposes of clarification, the last two, diversification and relative dependence, will be treated together.) This discussion includes reference to the data base essential to convince the reader that the four cases of policy change were indeed fundamental. On that basis we outline, second, a model of the Chinese foreign policy restructuring process, noting in particular the range of causal variables. Third, we indicate what actions were 'fundamental', that is, what decisions by the Chinese constituted, and what activities at the great power and systematic levels acted as catalysts for, restructuring Chinese policy.

Transition I, 1957–61: from Modified Communist Dependence to Extreme Self-Reliance

Having achieved a broad measure of success at home during the eight years since 1949, and having provided for the state's security by fighting the Americans in Korea and allying with the Soviet Union, in 1958 the Chinese Communist Party suddenly veered course in both domestic politics and foreign policy. In the course of two years, the domestic political and economic scene was transformed from orderly progress and confidence in the future to a desperate attempt to assault all problems at once. The result was severe setbacks on the economic front and fratricidal strife in politics, breaking apart the hitherto solidly united leadership. In foreign policy, the party first deliberately re-radicalized its relationship with the United States by assaulting the Nationalist-held Offshore Islands, then engaged India in a border war and finally challenged the bloc leadership of China's security guarantor, the Soviet Union. The result was defeat by the Americans in the Quemoy Crisis of 1958, alienation from and the rearmament of India, and long-term decline in relations with Moscow eventuating in military confrontation a decade later. Thus, in both domestic and foreign spheres, China by 1960 came under severe strain and was forced, at home and abroad, to adopt a policy of self-reliance, made the more extreme by Mao Tse-Tung's decision to make a virtue out of this necessity.

It is tempting to argue that the decisions stemming from the failure of the Hundred Flowers Campaign in mid-1957 can be traced directly to the operation of Mao's own personality. The best way to explain the entire chain of events down to the recovery from the Great Leap and its associated policies abroad would then be to understand how Mao personally initiated the process.[1] Indeed, most explanations of the entire Great Leap era, even at this late date, center around Mao Tse-Tung.[2] Thus, it was Mao himself who saw the necessity to break through to a much higher level of agricultural production; it was Mao who conceived of the people's communes as the specific organizational means to that end; it was Mao who by force of his own personality motivated the Chinese people as a whole enthusiastically to engage in otherwise intolerable kinds of labor and to work at a hectic pace for so long without demand for material compensation; it was Mao who deceived himself into thinking that the Great Leap was an enormous success just when it was teetering on the edge of disaster; and it was Mao who personally overcame the Great Leap-engendered opposition at the 1959 Lushan Plenum and who thereafter directed the three-year recovery process, even if from the 'second line' of the Chinese leadership.

But in retrospect it has become more clear that factors not particularly associated with Mao's psyche must also be drawn in to explain the new departure. One major element was the necessity to suppress the bold student/intellectual opposition manifested during the Hundred Flowers Campaign and to engage in a new energetic campaign to educate the population in the verities of Marxism-Leninism and the righteousness and rightfulness of Chinese Communist Party rule.[3] Most communist parties would have reacted in a fashion similar to the Chinese when they instituted the late 1957 Anti-Rightist campaign, out of which emerged the Great Leap. Moreover, purely economic analysis quickly concludes that strong new measures in both agriculture and industry were necessary to avoid first stagnation and then being overwhelmed by the resurgence of China's traditional economic problems: feeding and employing a very large population, the impossibility of increasing arable land area and the lack of surplus capital for industry.[4] Finally, in retrospect it is apparent that popular criticism of the party for its undemocratic character was reflected within the party itself as criticism of the autocratic nature of Mao's own rule. The personal and political differences that surfaced first in 1959 and more broadly at the outset of the Cultural Revolution in 1966 were already present in outline form in 1957 and perhaps even at the Eighth Party Congress in 1956.[5]

Whatever the range of causes of the Great Leap Forward, it radicalized the party's policy domestically and caused enormous changes throughout the country. Domestic radicalization also carried over into foreign policy. It is true that the mechanism transferring radicalization from one sphere to the other is not entirely clear. Also, as we note below, part of the reason for making major changes in Chinese foreign policy stemmed directly from the international sphere. Nonetheless, one can perceive causal linkages. For instance, the enthusiasm of the Great Leap made the Chinese leadership think that any obstacle could be overcome if only enough energy and force was applied against it. This mood undoubtedly affected Peking's foreign policy decision-making just as much as it did attitudes toward internal matters. Moreover, the economics of the Great Leap spilled over into foreign policy. By 1957, it was clear that neither the Soviet Union nor any other country would supply funds for China's capital construction at the very high level required. In fact, the net flow of funds was already turning back in favor of the Soviet Union. It follows that China was forced by her international economic environment to risk the Great Leap just as much as she was so forced by her domestic economic environment.

The enormous creation of new human capital through the added work effort of the populus produced two further effects. One was to convince the leadership that almost any task could be overcome merely by party-led popular energies. The other was the promulgation of a new instrument of foreign policy. Mao and his associates thought that the Great Leap-produced surplus of human energy could be used at will for foreign policy purposes as well as at home. And since China had plenty of as yet unattained objectives on its foreign agenda, there were many places where such energies could be applied. Of course, the domestic politics–foreign policy linkage worked both ways. The leadership saw the need continually to infuse the population with motivations to work even harder. Since during the Great Leap the domestic supply of such motivations was constantly being used up, the leadership was constrained to turn to the foreign sphere, engendering crises or taking advantage of situations, to use them for mass mobilization purposes at home.

On these bases, it seems possible to explain the timing of the radicalization in Chinese foreign policy as well as part of the sequence of events. Thus, the attack on Quemoy and Matsu in the summer of 1958 seems to stem directly from Great Leap radicalization earlier that year.[6] The Chinese decision to bring to a head the border differences with India in 1959 seems clearly associated with the need to infuse the people with additional ardor, just as it appears to follow from Peking's perception that it would easily best New Delhi militarily.[7] Further, the decision to break with the Soviet Union, although surely not coming all at once in 1960, nonetheless was at least partially precipitated by Soviet unwillingness to finance successive Chinese five-year plans and from Soviet criticism of the Great Leap as the wrong way for China to extricate itself from its economic problems.[8] Finally, China's abject refusal of Kennedy's grain offer in 1961, at the nadir of the Great Leap-induced depression, stemmed not merely from Chinese pride but also from the feeling that the Great Leap in the end would provide the country with the wherewithal to overcome its difficulties, which Mao always regarded as temporary.[9]

But domestic explanations are insufficient of themselves to explain the enormous changes that came about in Chinese foreign policy after 1957. Several influences stemmed from the changing configuration of Chinese national power and interests relative to those of the Soviet Union and of the United States. Others arose out of the changing nature of international relations as a whole. Let us inspect each in turn. One need only consider the basis of Sino-Soviet relations up to 1957 to realize that sooner or later the Chinese would want to wean themselves from Soviet primacy within the context of joint opposition to the United States. Movement away from totalistic Soviet direction of the alliance had already taken place as early as 1954[10] and by 1956 it was apparent that China no longer felt so completely constrained by the perceived threat from the United States as to follow every Soviet initiative without question. Moreover, with the passing of Stalin and Khrushchev's subsequent handling of the 'Stalin question' at the Twentieth Party Congress in 1956, the Chinese concluded that Moscow need not be followed in the ideological sphere either.[11] Thus, the internal ties binding Moscow and Peking together began to slacken. In addition, external pressure from the United States was not felt quite so severely in Moscow, for in 1955 the United States began gingerly to move toward a policy of accommodation.

The resultant of the Sino-Soviet changes was that Peking concluded it had obtained sufficient strength within the alliance to push Moscow into more direct, stringent action against the United States. It was this set of forces, and perceptions, as well as Great Leap Forward radicalization, that induced Peking in the summer of 1958 to reopen the Taiwan question through attack upon Quemoy and Matsu. This was a deliberate exacerbation of the issue, which had lain fallow since Peking's previous attempt at forceful solution in 1954. The initial stage quickly brought America and China to a crisis. But Peking found to its surprise that the United States first chose to support the Nationalist garrisons on the Offshore Islands and then was willing to threaten nuclear war. Peking thereupon backed off, ending the crisis.

In Sino-Soviet relations, movement was slower but the trend inexorable. Moscow refused to allow Peking to lead it into possible nuclear war with the United States over Taiwan and therefore publicly divorced itself from this aspect of Chinese policy. Already strained Sino-Soviet relations were further exacerbated. Thus, from the summer of 1958 differences in state relations were added to what was hitherto primarily an ideological dispute. Khrushchev tried to mollify Mao through diplomatic persuasion and by extending Peking a new program of economic and military assistance, including proffering the famous sample atom bomb agreement. But the Chinese did not like the attached policy strings, to say nothing of feeling betrayed by Moscow in the hour of their need (although they eagerly accepted the atom bomb offer). Additionally, the Chinese considered that their new-found internal strength would permit them to achieve their foreign policy ends without firm Soviet backing.

As if to demonstrate the point, in late 1959 the Chinese brought to a head the developing border dispute with India and the associated Tibetan issue. As in the Sino-Soviet case, it is relatively easy to analyze the situation in retrospect. A combination of China's more strongly felt national interest and comparative Sino-Indian power explains much of the timing and the reasoning behind Peking's decision to use force against New Delhi. China strongly felt the need for a secure land link between Sinkiang and Tibet, especially in the face of popular rebellion in the latter province and still incomplete rule over the former. Nonetheless, it is doubtful that Peking would have made the move had it not felt emboldened first by the Great Leap Forward, and second by the desire to teach the Russians a lesson in leadership. Having learned at Quemoy the consequences of incomplete preparations, the Chinese now made sure that the operation against the Indian army would stand a very high probability of success.

And successful it was, at least in obtaining the short-term territorial objectives just noted. On the other hand, that episode plus its follow-on in 1962 precipitated the inevitable reaction in New Delhi: the Indians embarked on a major military modernization program, eventuating a decade later in the Indian nuclear explosion, trained a large army that by the early 1970s made Indians masters of the subcontinent, and opened a security relationship with Moscow. The long-term results were thus highly detrimental to China.

The immediate consequence was further aggravation of the dispute with Moscow. The Soviet Union publicly divorced itself from China's India adventure, unilaterally tore up the atom bomb agreement and decided to take the first steps in the long process of fashioning a new détente relationship with the United States. To his credit, Khrushchev did attempt to stop the descent in Sino-Soviet relations by flying to Peking and taking his case directly to Mao, but the latter was now even less receptive to Russian supplications than during the Taiwan Straits crisis. Khrushchev therefore went home empty-handed but with his mind made up that Mao would have to be put in his place and China stopped from further unilateral actions that could threaten Soviet-American peace.[12]

Under these circumstances the Soviet Union decided to cut its losses with China and to punish Peking for its transgressions. The means chosen was to threaten and then to carry out withdrawal from China of all Soviet economic and technical assistance. This was done rather suddenly, it is true, in the summer of 1960. The Chinese claim it came as a big shock and for no good reason; actually, they knew the Soviets would act in this way and really had no one to blame but themselves. The Soviet Union, of course, became a convenient whipping-boy for Chinese propaganda.[13] Their actions were 'convenient' in the sense that Mao could pin the blame on them for all the Great Leap failures, which by then had become painfully obvious. Not that the effects of the Soviet withdrawal did not hurt; they did and they intensified the resulting economic depression that followed for the next three years.

Most of the burst of foreign policy activism during the Great Leap and the subsequent withdrawal into 'self-reliance' stems from the domestic and foreign developments sketched above. A third set of variables does, nonetheless, enter in, and no explanation of major changes in Chinese foreign policy is complete without them. These reflect the influence on China of the evolution of international relations in the early 1960s. Two changes stand out. First, by the late 1950s East–West relations had progressed to where both Washington and Moscow were willing to retreat from the most threatening aspects of the cold war. True, it took a great deal of patience on Washington's part and facing down Khrushchev in Berlin, the Congo and Cuba to convince the Kremlin that ways other than confrontation existed to carry out foreign policy goals. More positively, America and Russia initiated arms control negotiations in 1958, Khrushchev visited the United States in 1959 and Russia agreed to participate in the Paris Summit Conference in 1960 (a major achievement, even though the Conference itself was aborted by the U-2 incident). These developments all pointed toward transforming international relations from bi-polarity and threat of imminent East–West conflict to a looser relationship between and, concomitantly, diversity within the two camps.[14]

The second unmistakable trend was the vast increase in the number of new states produced by decolonization. None of the several dozen newly emergent governments wanted to mortgage its foreign policy future by attaching itself to either bloc. All therefore proclaimed a kind of neutrality between East and West and sought to build a third force impervious to American and Soviet control. In the short run, of course, some of these countries became arenas for Soviet-American competition, as East and West regarded the 'newly emergent forces' as a marketplace for hawking their respective ideological wares. Still, even at the outset, it was clear that sooner or later most Third World countries would pull themselves together into some sort of overall organization, however loose, and set forth a common attitude toward the competing camps.[15]

If the outlines of these trends were evident in Washington and Moscow, they were not in Peking. There seems no doubt that China was 'behind the times' in its evaluation of the forces of international change. Not only did it resist the notion of mutually useful East–West compromise but it also saw the growth of Soviet military strength and decolonization as unambiguous evidence of a major opportunity to overcome once and for all the imbalance of power hitherto thought to be so heavily tilted toward the capitalist countries. China therefore pressed the Soviet Union to take advantage of the new situation.[16] And when told by Khrushchev that Moscow saw things differently, Mao openly proclaimed that China would now succeed to the mantle of leadership that the Soviets were vacating.[17] Thus, differing Soviet-China perspectives of the nature of international order exacerbated tensions between the two communist powers already high as a consequence of the trends and actions noted previously. Only when the Soviet Union abjectly refused to move in the directions demanded by Peking and sought to punish Mao for his ideological and political transgressions did China begin to realize that these systemic changes in international relations (however nascent they were at the time) significantly contributed to widening the gulf between them.

With regard to decolonization, again Peking was out of phase with developments in Third World states, with the thinking of their leaders and with how decolonization affected the nature of the structure and the international system. Mao and his associates asserted that decolonization made even more graphically evident the tilt in East–West relations against the United States.[18] The Peking leadership thought, moreover, that Third World states would naturally ally themselves to the socialist camp and that China herself would be the broker in the coming marriage between socialism and developmentalism. Was not China, after all, a developing Third World country herself, and were not the benefits of socialism to China obvious to all who cared to look? And if Third World countries were, upon decolonization, led by imperialist-appointed lackeys, would it not be merely a question of time and a little bit of external assistance from China, the Soviet Union and other socialist countries before genuine socialist revolution would occur throughout Asia, Africa and Latin America, just as it had occurred in China? Why should not China, therefore, encourage anti-Westernism on the part of newly independent countries, on the one hand, and do its part in subverting the bourgeois leadership in those same countries in preparation for the inevitable socialist revolution, on the other? And if the Soviet Union was so foolish as not to see the opportunities in these countries or was so stupid as not to lead the socialist camp in carrying out such a dualistic policy, was it not China's duty first to criticize Moscow for its errors, next to insist that the job be done correctly, and finally to replace Soviet leadership with its own?

It should be stressed that self-reliance was also a necessary and inevitable outcome of the collision between the overly forward policies of the late 1950s and the natural reaction to China's environment to those same policies. Self-reliance was another, more positive, name for enforced isolation precipitated by the break with Moscow, the continued estrangement from the United States and the as yet unfulfilled relations with the newly decolonized states of the Third World. It was possible for the next few years to 'get away with' self-reliance in foreign policy, although it cost China dearly at home, merely because the United States and the Soviet Union were busy competing with each other for primacy in international politics, because neither regarded China as a necessary (or, in the case of Moscow, a desirable) contributor to its struggle with the other, and because in its state of relative weakness China was a threat to neither. The period of self-reliance in Chinese foreign policy thus began with and was symbolized by the withdrawal of the Soviet advisers in the summer of 1960. It lasted straight down to the Cultural Revolution, when China for essentially internal reasons decided to adopt a policy of near-total isolation from the outer world.

It remains to document these changes through reference to various indicators noted in Chapter 1, and other measures specific to the case. These can best be presented by contrasting those indicators that reflect foreign policy activism of the 1957–9 period and those that evidence retrenchment of the 1960–2 period. It must be borne in mind that throughout this time China was still almost totally isolated from the West, including Japan, and that therefore most of its transactions were with the other socialist countries, non-ruling parties and (to some extent) with developing states of the Third World. It should also be remembered that China under communist leadership did not engage in certain activities that normally serve as important indicators of policy direction and change. Treaties are a good example. Other standard indicators were not germane to China in this period, for example, voting patterns in international organizations, since China was not a member of the United Nations or any of the multitude of international technical organizations.

Nonetheless, there are ample data to make the case. For instance, in the period of policy activism and dependence China greatly increased the number of students sent to socialist countries;[19] stepped up its trade with the Soviet Union and the communist states of Eastern Europe;[20] increased the frequency of visits abroad by state leaders – again mostly to other socialist countries;[21] signed new trade and cultural agreements with those same countries calling for measurable increases in such ties;[22] and continued to receive and exchange large numbers of books, periodicals and media material, especially with Moscow.[23] There are, of course, no comparable data with Western countries since China had no ties with them. The only relations with the West possible in that era were those of mutual emnity and isolation. Quantitative studies that have been done clearly show this vehement anti-Westernism in China's policy.[24] Thus, without exception practically every speech, press conference, party statement, *People's Daily* editorial and radio broadcast that dealt with China's foreign relations was of this singular character. (Hong Kong, to be sure, continued to be an exception. Its role as China's 'window on the West' remained unchanged during these years, as it did before and after.) One other indicator of more than symbolic note is China's first change in Foreign Ministers. Chou en-Lai, the epitome of rationality and moderation in foreign policy as at home, was replaced at the outset of the Great Leap by Ch'en Yi, who proceeded to make a name for himself as China's leading hawk.

The period of enforced self-reliance was accompanied by a near reversal in almost every one of these indicators as well as the appearance of others that graphically illustrate the change in policy. Thus, the number of treaties signed with the Soviet Union and other East European states, save Albania, declined precipitously.[25] The best symbol of the change was a series of 'letters' the Chinese sent to the Soviet Communist Party criticizing in detail its policies at home and abroad, thus bringing into the open the seriousness and advanced state of the Sino-Soviet dispute.[26] One need also look no further than the vehemence of Chinese speeches at the series of international communist conferences in Moscow, Bucharest and elsewhere during those years. The epitome of discord was the abrupt departure from Moscow of the Chinese delegation to the Twenty-second Soviet Communist Party Congress in protest against Khrushchev's open criticism of them and his removal of Stalin from the Red Square Mausoleum.

Needless to say, once the Soviets withdrew their experts and advisers from China, the number of Chinese delegations going to the Soviet Union also declined greatly, to say nothing of the number of Chinese students resident in that country and East Europe.[27] Trade with the Soviet Union, which always has been the best quantitative indicators of the nature and direction of Chinese foreign policy, declined precipitously. Soviet diplomats were also restricted in their movements inside China, tourists and other delegations now were unwelcome. Soviet books, periodicals and media material stopped flowing into the country in such massive amounts, and the Sino-Soviet Friendship Society, hitherto a mass organization assertively of 100 million people, was shut down entirely.[28]

Finally, China made a fetish of its self-reliance. It pointed with pride at supposedly superior native designs.[29] It refused to redirect its trade from the socialist countries to the West. It did not take up the slack in cultural exchanges and tourism left from the break with Moscow by sending or receiving similar numbers with other countries. It prohibited from export the majority of Chinese domestically produced written material. It began crash projects for making at home products that could easily have been imported or whose technologies could have been obtained abroad to ease the transition to native production (shipping and jet aircraft are good examples of this propensity). Finally, in education things foreign came under increased suspicion, even though renewed emphasis was of necessity placed on expertise and technical knowledge as opposed to 'redness' and ideological training.[30]

Transition II, 1965–9: from Extreme Self-Reliance to Isolation

By 1965, China had worked its way free from Soviet-imposed economic problems and had emerged from the depression induced by the Great Leap Forward. The years from 1962 through 1965 were ones of genuine progress and steady recovery. By the end of the period the country was back, economically if not politically, to where it had been in the late 1950s. In foreign policy, China had made the break with the Soviet Union more or less permanent and had reaped a number of benefits at Soviet expense within the international communist movement. Moreover, it had made some progress in the Third World and had avoided further tangles with the United States in the Taiwan Straits. Thus, in domestic and foreign developments the country was poised for a lengthy period of progress and influence.

A few setbacks had occurred along the way and a few problems remained on the horizon. Chou en-Lai's African tour in 1963 had gone poorly,[31] as China discovered that newly independent African states did not take kindly to the suggestion that their current leadership were mere way-stations to socialism and that the former colonies had really not been freed from domination by their former colonial masters. In Southeast Asia the Vietnam war brought an increasing degree of American involvement and held out the possibility that, were the Americans to invade the North, China would have to intervene militarily.[32] With regard to the Soviet Union, some in Peking wondered aloud whether things had not been carried too far. Not only ought it be necessary to stand with the Russians against the United States in Vietnam, they said, but it was also possible that ideological opposition to Soviet leadership might soon take on state-centered, then territorial and finally military form with which China was ill-equipped to deal. Finally, by vehemently practising the virtues of self-reliance which it so loudly proclaimed, Peking needlessly kept itself away from many states in the Third World and the West. This was no better symbolized than by the continuing yearly refusal of the General Assembly to admit China to the United Nations.

None of these trends, whether positive or negative, can account for the change in Chinese foreign policy that occurred in 1966. For this, one must look almost entirely to internal causes and more particularly to intra-party developments. The outbreak of the Cultural Revolution in mid-1966 is almost a pure case of a domestic change causing a variation in foreign policy. It is true that Mao came to his judgement concerning the ideological corruption of the party at least partly as a result of his analysis of what had gone wrong in the Soviet Union.[33] Still, the foreign policy of isolation, 1966–9, was merely the external manifestation of the Cultural Revolution.

Indeed, that policy was an attempt to insulate China from the rest of the world while the country was deliberately encouraged to tear itself apart and when it was extremely vulnerable to the unfriendly acts of its self-perceived enemies.

The foreign policy of the Cultural Revolution was thus extremely simple. China would pretend that the outer world did not exist and that, therefore, it could do China no harm and need not be dealt with. To this end, China cut all important diplomatic and economic ties with every country with which it had established relations, postponed the quest to establish relations with other states and avoided involvement directly in any of the issues of contemporary international relations. In particular, Peking recalled all its ambassadors save one,[34] dropped all foreign economic assistance programs, called home students and others temporarily abroad, closed its borders to all but a handful of foreigners, and thumbed its nose at the United Nations.[35]

Of course, China needed to have reasonable assurances that neither the United States nor the Soviet Union would take advantage of its internal travail to threaten its national security. The more important question in this regard was whether American intervention in Vietnam would lead to ground invasion of the North and hence to the necessity of a Chinese military response. This was an acute possibility, for the Tonkin Gulf Incident of August 1964 and American aerial action against the North in February 1966 came during the very period when Mao sought to initiate battle against his intra-party opponents. This threw off Mao's Cultural Revolution timetable and engendered a debate within the leadership as to what course of action to take at home as well as abroad.[36] But by June of 1966 the question had been resolved.[37] Moreover, China established a tacit agreement with the United States, accepting the American promise of no ground attack against the North and offering in return the promise of no major Chinese support for Hanoi's operations in the South.[38] The net result was delay of eight months in the onset of the Cultural Revolution, a cost that Mao apparently thought well worth paying since the American military threat was thereby removed. Having thus secured this objective, and having assured itself also of Soviet non-interference, China was free to deal with its internal problems and to ignore external matters completely.

Indicators of China's self-imposed isolation are abundant. Not only did it take the actions noted above to minimize contacts with other states, but it also introduced major changes in other spheres. Trade dropped precipitously and trade agreements were allowed to lapse or continue only at their previous levels.[39] Foreign ideas and cultural modes of expression were rigorously suppressed within the country and kept from entering from the outside. Tourism and exchanges of persons were completely halted.[40] No new material assistance was sent forth to support revolutionary movements abroad, and Chinese |broadcasts| and publications contented themselves with incantation of Mao Tse-Tung thought.[41] China also seemed to become less interested in competing with the Soviet Union for the allegiance of non-ruling communist parties throughout the globe; while it did not entirely leave the field of battle, mere Maoist sloganeering would not convince many local communists of the innate veracity of the Chinese revolutionary line.

China did try to 'export' the Cultural Revolution in the sense of pointing to itself as the only true example of communist societal change and in that regard Red Guard-like organizations sprang up in several foreign countries.[42] But China did not support such groups materially, telling them explicitly to fight their own battles and to emulate China only to the extent of applying the universal principles of Marxism-Leninism to their own particular cases. The presumption was that the Cultural Revolution would neither spill over Chinese boundaries physically nor negatively affect for long Chinese foreign policy.

For most of the period down to 1969 – the 'active phase of the Cultural Revolution' – this proved to be viable. It is true that in Moscow, Hong Kong and Rangoon returning Chinese students, local Red Guard-like organizations and home-grown Maoists sometimes took matters into their own hands and made trouble for the local authorities. At one point in Hong Kong such activity took a vicious and threatening turn and it seemed that the British authority might be toppled.[43] Red Guard groups also taunted Russian border guards and it was not clear whether the Chinese authorities had lost control of the student revolutionaries or, worse, whether they were actually encouraging them to engage in inflammatory activity. By and large, however, these were minimal problems and China did its best to keep the Cultural Revolution within its boundaries.

This did not mean, of course, that the Cultural Revolution produced no effects abroad. General world appraisal of the rationality of the Chinese leadership and of the stability of its institutions declined precipitously. General esteem of the People's Republic of China was probably lower during these three years than at any time since 1949, despite popular fascination with the ever-changing kaleidoscope of events in the country. The general trend toward diplomatic recognition of Peking was stopped and even reversed, and the Nationalist Chinese lease on the United Nations seat was prolonged.[44]

More importantly, however, the Cultural Revolution caused concrete policy changes in Moscow which, in the end, so severely reacted back upon China as to put an end to the foreign policy of isolation and eventually to the Cultural Revolution itself. The uncivilized and threatening behavior of Chinese mobs in front of the Soviet embassy in Peking and at the Peking airport against departing Soviet embassy dependants, the scuffles induced by Chinese students in Moscow, the constant needling of Soviet borderguards and China's refusal to continue with the border negotiations all induced Moscow to believe that Mao was planning more direct action against the Soviet Union.

The Russians felt it necessary to take two decisions in response. One was to give up any possibility of compromise on substantive issues with China so long as Mao Tse-Tung and his supporters remained in power. Hence, Moscow renewed with vengeance its propaganda attacks against Peking and took every opportunity to recoup pre-Cultural Revolution losses in the international communist movement. More importantly, the Kremlin decided to increase its defense posture along the Sino-Soviet border by building up, slowly but deliberately, the numbers and strengths of ground, air force and riverine units east of Lake Baikal. As corollary, Soviet border forces were ordered to take a much firmer, although still peaceful, stance toward objectionable Chinese behavior at border sites. These latter decisions, although understandable, were nonetheless fateful since they in turn appeared to the Chinese as threatening and pre-emptory. The Chinese were in no mood to allow social revisionist thugs, as they put it, to push around right-speaking and peaceful Chinese citizens. Mao was also anxious to avoid an impression in Moscow of Chinese weakness merely because of preoccupation with internal Cultural Revolutionary matters. Thus, the Chinese responded to Soviet firmness at the border with a toughened patrol policy of their own. It was then only a matter of time before a clash of arms would take place at a point of dispute between the two sides. This occurred in early March 1969 at Damansky (Ch'en-Pao) Island in the Ussuri River.

Transition III, 1970–80: from Isolation to Diversity and Relative Dependence

The two March 1969 Ussuri River border incidents[45] put an end to the era of isolation in Chinese foreign policy and forced Peking once again thoroughly to restructure its external relations. From this point, it became painfully obvious to the Chinese leadership that one of the critical conditions for a policy of isolation – non-interference by either of the super-powers – was no longer viable. China had only itself to blame, since it was the excesses of the Cultural Revolution that precipitated the first incident at Damansky and caused the Russians to act with such lack of restraint on 15 March 1969. The end of the Cultural Revolution-induced isolation would have come in any case, but probably later and surely by Chinese initiation. But as it was, after the early spring of 1969, the security threat posed by the Soviet Union grew so strong and so rapidly that Peking felt it has no choice but to revamp its foreign policy completely. Thus, China sought to restore good relations with the many Third World countries it had hitherto ignored, attempted to establish ties with the industrial powers of Western Europe and Japan, and even opened the door to détente with the United States.[46] China's reaction to the border incidents was characteristically extreme, once the evaluation was made that the Soviet Union acutely threatened its security.

Having ignored the world for the previous three years, Peking now discovered that China's external environment had changed immensely for the worse in that period. The United States was so preoccupied in Vietnam that it ignored the rapidly increasing military power of the Soviet Union. The overall balance between Washington and Moscow had therefore shifted toward the latter. Peking itself had found safety in the drawing off of American attention to Southeast Asia, but it too had more or less ignored the Soviet build-up. But the Soviets, freed by the American preoccupation with Vietnam, could threaten great harm to China without fear of retribution from the United States. Moreover, China found that the Northeast Asian international environment had also changed immensely: Japan had become the area's principal economic power by virtue of its enormous industrial and technological growth. And in Western Europe and the Third World, China discovered that it had, in fact, almost no reliable friends.

These foreign policy shocks merely accentuated what by then had become a very bad situation at home, what with civil strife, provincial rebellion and near-total social disunity produced by the Cultural Revolution. China was therefore forced by unenviable domestic and international circumstances to make major changes in its foreign relations.[47]

By themselves the river border incidents were not overly serious. Casualties were comparatively light, little equipment was lost and the territory in question was not important. It was the severity of the Soviet counterattack on 15 March that surprised the Chinese. Not only did the Russians administer a decisive defeat, but they followed up that action with two highly threatening policy changes. First, the Soviets conducted a well-orchestrated diplomatic-military campaign to force the Chinese to reopen negotiations on the border question, terminated by China in 1964. Thus, throughout the spring and summer of 1969 the Soviets perpetrated a number of increasingly severe border military actions against the Chinese and coupled them with open threats to use nuclear weapons unless China agreed to resume negotiations. This campaign culminated in the forced meeting between Chou en-Lai and Alexei Kosygin at the Peking airport in early September. There the Chinese were made to agree to the Soviet proposal to reopen talks and to cease military activities directed against Russian territory.[48]

Second, the Soviets accelerated the build-up of their military forces east of Lake Baikal, raising the number of divisions from fifteen to around forty-five. They also militarily occupied Mongolia, laid the infrastructure for the presence of a Siberian force three or four times the level reached in 1972, and raised the total number of military effectives facing China from 300,000 to over 750,000.[49] This build-up and the accompanying campaign of threat and force so upset the balance of power between the two countries that, from late 1969 forward, China was no longer able to defend itself against any reasonably large Soviet military incursion anywhere along its border with the Soviet Union and Mongolia. The situation was made the worse by the unpreparedness of the Chinese military. Their major task during the past several years had been to support the Red Guards against the party leadership. The upshot was that China was neither militarily defensible nor economically stable. Having deliberately isolated itself from contact with potential allies, Peking was now face to face with a severe threat that it could not counter with any of its traditional methods. The crisis was therefore as serious as any that the Maoist leadership had faced in its entire half-century of experience.

Of primary importance, therefore, was for Peking to do whatever possible to restore defensibility to China's borders. Since the country was in no shape to mobilize against the Russians, the leadership felt it had no choice but to make peace with its traditional enemies, the United States and Japan. This was probably a harder task for the Chinese to accomplish than is realized, since China would have liked to open the door to Tokyo and Washington on its own terms and at a time of its own choosing. No such luxury was now permitted, although the Chinese did their best to convince the leaders of these countries that each would have to make serious compromises in order to be allowed to station their diplomatic representatives in Peking.

The story of the careful and secret American diplomatic approach to China has been told many times, and the details need not concern us.[50] More important is that the Chinese began to explore the possibilities of ties with Washington, and hence with Tokyo, almost immediately after the Ussuri incidents, although it took the two Western capitals a longer time to pick up the Chinese signals. Vietnam-based differences and domestic political requirements on both sides meant that two full years were needed before the initial breakthrough could occur. During this period, China was so nearly defenseless against Soviet attack that Washington policymakers concluded that American interests dictated support of a strong and unified China, even if communist, and not neutrality in future conflict between the two communist giants.[51]

China did what it could to convince the Russians that force would be met by equal force. At home the regime put as rapid an end as possible to the Cultural Revolution.[52] In essence, this meant imposition of military government and at least the beginning of party reconstruction. In the propaganda sphere, the leadership carried out major campaigns to convince the citizenry of the imminence of war and to encourage them to make whatever preparations they could. Peking also praised the latter-day version of People's War: a militia, tens of millions strong; an enormous air-raid shelter program; stress on self-reliance, especially in food; and verbal taunts at the Russians, daring them to come ahead and be swallowed by the sea of popular resistance. These were weak reeds and the leadership knew it.

More seriously, the party was severely divided between Maoist ideological purists, military opportunists under Lin Piao and organizational-economic modernists led by Chou en-Lai. The resulting disunity was so disruptive that in late 1971 an attempted coup d'état was staged by Lin and his associates.[53] Even though it never came close to success, the very attempt was graphic evidence of weakness in the face of the Soviet threat. Of equal importance, the leadership was so divided that it could not, even during this period of greatest external threat, agree to increase the military budget and redeploy military forces in large numbers against the Russians.[54] Nor could they agree to make the necessary changes in Chinese industry and culture that would have put China back on the road of rapid economic development. Finally, the leadership could not even curtail the pernicious influence of the Maoist radicals (later termed the 'Gang of Four'). Indeed, their influence increased during the six years after the Damansky Island incidents.

Faced with disarray at home, Mao and his associates had to substitute maneuver and bluff in foreign policy. The opening to the United States and subsequently to Japan clearly was part of a strategy undertaken from weakness and designed to convince the Soviets that Chinese policy had more substance than actually existed. The principal element was political reconciliation with the Americans and the Japanese, both of whom were eager to push open the door which the Chinese now left unlocked and slightly ajar. Still, the process took a good three years and by itself was therefore insufficient.

Other instruments of policy had to be brought into play. One was diplomatic. After the spring of 1969, China sent forth an increasing number of ambassadors and other diplomatic personnel to posts vacated at the beginning of the Cultural Revolution.[55] Once reopened, the various near-dormant embassies poured out a torrent of anti-Sovietism. In fact, every aspect of Chinese diplomacy on whatever issue or in whatever region was rigidly subordinated to opposition to Moscow. If the Russians moved in one policy direction, the Chinese would automatically take the opposite tack. Ideological differences with local regimes now meant nothing. Peking offered diplomatic recognition and exchange of ambassadors with every country, even those to whom it had been strongly opposed. This process took much time, however, as China, constrained by its own interests, continued to insist that newly recognized states cut all ties with Taiwan. Although Peking was usually successful in this quest, the concurrent negotiations were so protracted that here too three years went by before a substantial number of additional countries established diplomatic relations with China.[56]

The final aspect of the diplomatic offensive involved entrance into the United Nations. UN membership should have been accomplished long before, but China's own intransigence and its poor reputation during the Cultural Revolution postponed for a full decade the successful General Assembly vote in 1972. Once in the United Nations, Peking used every forum to denounce the Russians. This heavy-handed approach did not gain for Peking the degree of support for which it had hoped and in some instances rebounded to the Soviets' advantage.[57]

In the 1970s, then, Chinese foreign policy purposes were three: first, to attain a degree of security from Soviet attack; second, to support domestic goals, principally political stability during the Maoist succession and economic development thereafter; and third, to restore Chinese influence internationally. Overall, Peking hoped to achieve independence in world politics – and hence the ability to maneuver between various groups of states – and freedom from the threat of war and military defeat. The hoped-for means to these ends was diversification of China's diplomatic ties. In essence this meant attempting to refurbish contacts with Third World countries and revolutionary movements, on the one hand, and establishing diplomatic relations with the major Western nations, on the other.

Because the confused and domestic situation before Mao's passing differed substantially from the relative stability of the more recent period, the emphasis among the three foreign policy goals varied. Before 1976, the succession issue limited Chinese foreign policy to deterring, as best it could, the Soviet security threat. This meant compromising with historic enemies and subordinating all other foreign policy goals to that of anti-Sovietism. After the Gang of Four had been removed in October of 1976, the domestic basis of China's foreign policy added a new and significant element: supporting the Four Modernizations. This meant opening up economic, technological and cultural ties with those states – America,

Japan and Europe – best able to supply the capital, equipment and knowledge critical to the success of modernization.

The overriding importance of these two foreign policy goals – security and development – called into question the degree to which China could pursue the third – establishing a position of independence between the super-powers and her assertion of leadership of the Third World against the United States and the Soviet Union. Increasingly, China found that diversification did not enhance independence, as it had hoped, but that the imperatives of defense and modernization drove it increasingly into relative dependence on the West and to forsaking its claimed natural leadership of the Third World. So long as Peking depended on the West for security and development, China could not appeal to the Third World as its natural electorate. Hence, this element of Chinese foreign policy, initially so stridently expressed upon China's entrance to the United Nations, was for all intents and purposes dropped.

A further problem which the Chinese leadership faced, before and after 1976, was that the Soviet Union would not sit still while China went about appealing to all other states to join a China-led anti-Moscow front. The Soviets countered the Chinese strategy by conducting their own diplomatic offensive in Asia and elsewhere, thus offsetting Chinese activism by strategic and regional initiatives of their own. Although the Soviet offensive was partially directed against the United States in southern Africa, the Horn and the Middle East, the Asian component of Moscow's drive was successful enough in South and Southeast Asia that China suffered a relative setback in its perceived degree of security. By signing 'friendship treaties' with India in late 1971 and Vietnam in late 1978, and by continuing a steady military build-up in Siberia, Moscow was able to prevent the Chinese from improving upon the weak position that it occupied in 1969. By the close of the decade, in fact, China was driven even more into a united front strategy with Japan, the United States and Western Europe. And although each of these states and regions had good reason for agreeing with Peking that Moscow was the common threat, not much came by way of substantive – that is, military – support for China before 1980.

Added to this was the progressive Chinese discovery of their own economic backwardness. This was, of course, obvious to the objective observer long before Mao's death. But the combination of the removal of the Gang of Four and enhanced contacts with the West after 1971 drove home just how far economically China had slipped in the decade since the beginning of the Cultural Revolution in 1965. The new leadership realized with increasing clarity that a long time would pass, and a great deal of catch-up effort would have to be made, before China would enter the ranks of modern nations and first-rate world powers. Moreover, China became even more aware of its military problems vis à vis the Soviet Union and realized it would have to become militarily dependent upon Western arms, technology and diplomatic support for a substantial period. Because this dovetailed with the requirement for outside support for the Four Modernizations, China adopted a policy of economic interdependence and military entente with the West.

The end of the decade, therefore, saw China in a quite different, but not necessarily better, situation than it had been in 1970. In that year it had been diplomatically isolated, internally disunited and incapable of defending itself against the Russians. In 1980 Peking was no longer isolated, had recaptured internal unity and at least had a measure of support against the Soviet Union. But the price was high: cessation of ideological struggle against its former enemies; dependence on the West for defense and the means to modernize; a near-total inability to pursue revolutionary goals in Asia and beyond; and only a marginal gain in overall security against the Russian threat. If China could hold to a policy course of subordinating its long-term ideological and great-power goals to the short-term interest in economic development, it probably would be much better off. The question remained, however, whether the Peking leadership would have the good sense to be patient and let favorable trends stemming from economic development take hold. A rational, pragmatic leadership would surely make the necessary compromises, but given the vast swings in Chinese policy over the previous thirty years it was not at all certain that the Chinese would or could be so patient.

All the qualitative and quantitative indicators quoted in connection with the first two transitions substantiate these major changes in Chinese foreign policy in the 1970s. Reference has already been made to the establishment of diplomatic relations with a wide variety of states. In many instances – the American and Japanese are the most important – the communiqué surrounding the event amounted to treaty-like statements of the degree of closeness between China and the other state.[58] Thus, for example, normalization statements with almost every Western state included the so-called anti-hegemony clause directed against the Soviet Union. This fitted in with China's perception of its leadership – it was not that – of a united front against the Soviet Union. Moreover, in at least the 1978 Sino-Japanese Treaty of Friendship, China induced Japan to make such overtly anti-Soviet statements (which Tokyo had previously avoided) that the resultant amounted to a change in China's favor of Tokyo's policy of balancing between Moscow and Peking.[59] And in the case of the United States, the several communiqués issued upon the visits to China of high American officials during the four years leading up to normalization also amounted to treaty-like statements.[60]

A second telling indicator of China's policy in this period was the frequency and importance of state visits by Chinese and foreign leaders. In the period of the policy of diversification before Mao's death in 1976, Chinese leaders did not travel abroad. Rather, they received an increasing flow of high foreign officials, including the presidents and premiers of all the major Western states.[61] After 1976, when China's dependence on the West became manifest, the flow reversed. Now an increasing flood of high Chinese officials went abroad, many for the first time. They were led by the party and state head, Hua Kuo-Feng, who made a highly publicized visit to Iran and Europe in 1979, and Teng Hsiao-p'ing, who visited the United States in early 1979, shortly after normalization. The number of official delegations between China and Western countries rose so precipitously that, in the case of the United States, by the end of the decade so many Chinese delegations were in that country at any given time that State Department officials gave up even trying to count them.[62]

Students also were sent forth in large numbers, soon rising to between several hundred and over a thousand in each Western country. Such countries as the United States and Canada sent the first contingents of exchange students and technicians to China, and joint agreements of research in science, technology and culture were signed on all sides.[63] Tourism rose dramatically and pressed increasingly on the growing, but still inadequate, Chinese facilities.[64] When China established new air routes with other countries, it did so almost exclusively with Japan, Europe and North America.[65]

Trade also rose by leaps and bounds after 1976.[66] Because it was directed toward industrial countries, China soon found itself with a mounting balance-of-payments problem. A measure of the magnitude of the change in Chinese policy is to be found in its willingness to accept foreign loans, pay interest on those loans and agree to such other un-socialist devices as the establishment of foreign export process zones along the China coast. China went to great lengths in its quest for importation of Western technology, and soon found itself in close working relationship with a wide variety of Western capitalist concerns.[67]

Only the Soviet Union, its East European allies, Vietnam and Cuba were left out. China's policy was to isolate them and to use the improvement of relations with the West as a shield against Soviet military threats. Thus, there was no tourism or other personnel exchanges with these countries, little change in the already low level of trade, no state/party visits of any sort, no new treaties signed other than renewal of the most prosaic, and no attempt to gain the benefits of Soviet and East European technology.[68] Chinese broadcasts and domestic descriptions of the West rapidly took on an objective and positive character, whereas it remained negative and dark when describing the Soviet Union and its followers.[69] It is true that Peking began to lay the groundwork, ever so gently and carefully, for improvement of relations with Moscow and China's eventual extrication from the exclusive embrace of the West. Negotiations were opened in early 1979 on the entire range of Sino-Soviet differences and on some statement or other instrument to replace the denounced Sino-Soviet Treaty of 1950. These negotiations were interrupted by the Soviet invasion of Afghanistan but it seemed probable that they would resume eventually. In late 1979, China dropped the revisionist accusatory label of the Soviet Union, thus indicating its willingness to talk with Moscow about 'questions of principle' as well as of state-centered differences.[70] If the two communist states were to reach agreement on the plentitude of their differences, it would, of course, initiate a new era in Chinese foreign policy, a new restructuring. Indeed, the policy of deliberate dependence on the West was designed to provide the basis in state power for an eventual approach to Moscow to negotiate differences from a position of strength and to achieve thereby foreign policy freedom. But such was China's weakness in the first years of the 1980s and such was the anti-Chinese policy activism in Asia of the Soviet Union that the prospect of major Chinese foreign policy restructuring was still a way off.

A Model of Chinese Foreign Policy

These three instances of restructuring enable us to generalize about Chinese foreign policy. On the basis of the facts presented above, Chinese policy orientations appear to be the weighted average of three mutually interactive elements: a complex of domestic determinants, including national interests as modified by Chinese power relative to that of other states; the foreign policies of other states and parties, particularly the United States and the Soviet Union; and the changing character of the international politic-economic system. Since each of these is the sum of a number of sub-elements and since the whole is interconnected in a complex manner, it is impossible to determine with accuracy what course China will take at any given time. Nonetheless, we know enough about each of the elements, about their linkages and about Chinese foreign policy intentions and behavior to reason with some confidence about how the Chinese conduct their foreign relations, particularly in periods of restructuring.

Domestic Determinants
The most important element informing Chinese foreign policy is the set of domestic determinants. These include: the 'lessons' that Chinese history – particularly the history of the Chinese Communist Party – are thought to hold for the conduct of foreign relations; the constraints and opportunities stemming from China's unique population and geography; its level of economic development and the sociological character of the people; and the operational characteristics of Chinese communist decision-making, including the influence of Chinese 'political culture', the nature of Chinese politics and the political 'style' of its chief decision-makers. But while these components comprise the domestic element, there is no agreement as to how they combine to affect Chinese foreign policy.

At the least, any sophisticated approach must not only take account of domestic priorities but also demonstrate that Chinese foreign policy is the complex product of the interplay among processes occurring at three levels: domestic, great power and systemic. That task is difficult, given limitations of data and the absence of agreed-upon integrative schemes and because the three levels influence each other directly as well as through the medium of foreign policy. A realistic approach must therefore include 'feedback' elements and embed domestic determinants in a large schema.

It is useful to approach the problem through successive approximation. A first stage lists relevant domestic factors:

- Political culture
- Ideological attitudes (including historical memory and philosophical code)

- Institutional and procedural requisites
- Struggle for power (including issues, means and arenas)
- Personality variables.

This small list contains, through sub-categories, most of the domestic ingredients of Chinese foreign policy.

The second stage fits these factors into a workable scheme, as shown in Figure 6.1. Chinese foreign policy is thus the joint product of the five factors, now joined in a definite manner. The struggle for power is the central variable of the domestic Chinese political process. Psycho-cultural variables operate directly on foreign policy formulation and indirectly as they influence the struggle for power. Institutional and procedural requisites influence foreign policy formulation at several different levels, as shown. There are various and changing arenas, issues and means of conducting the struggle for power, while ideological attitudes are subdivided into historical and philosophical components, each with further divisions. China's historical legacy can be included in this scheme at several points: historical memory, domestic and foreign policy issues, and administrative levels on which the struggle for power is conducted. Provision is made for 'feedback' of other states' foreign policies by including foreign policy issues among those over which the domestic struggle for power is fought (such issues may, of course, enter the policy-making process at other spots as well (as noted below)). The third stage introduces propositions, hypothesizes dependence relationships among the variables, or imports whole explanatory concepts. In every case, a literature exists specific to contemporary China or more general work can be found suitable for application to each domestic determinant of Chinese foreign policy.

As in other states, Chinese foreign policy is influenced by foreign events and the actions of other states. Their influence is exerted at more than one point, usually at different times, and with varying degrees of strength. This is evident by considering the three stages of Chinese foreign policy decision-making, as shown in Figure 6.2. These three stages organically connect the domestic political process to the level of foreign policy formulation. The Chinese decision-making group, once formed out of the domestic power struggle, must grapple with a range of foreign policy issues caused by the actions of foreign states or the general character of the international environment. The range of issues is also the product of the group's perception of them and of how it chooses to face them. That in turn is largely determined by the composition of the group – hence, such factors as ideology and personality are already included. The same group may perceive the same issue differently at different times, since domestic pressures and past experience with the issue in question may cause them to change their perception and appraisal of the issue.

Once the issue is defined, the group must consider what decision options exist. Aside from the 'definition of the situation', which is the chief product of the formulation stage, two other important variables influence this second, decisional, stage. These are disposable Chinese power and the structure of Chinese national (including ideological) interests. Both are modified by the group's perception of them, so that there

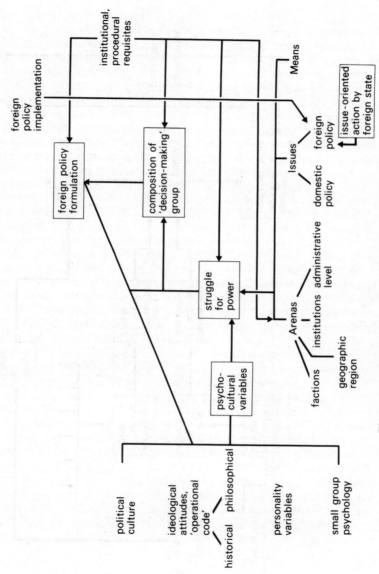

Figure 6.1 *Domestic determinants of Chinese foreign policy.*

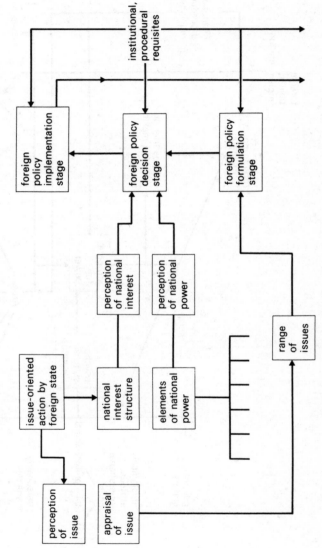

Figure 6.2 *Three stages of Chinese foreign policy formulation.*

exist both objective and subjective definitions of power and interest. However, only subjective appraisal counts for policy purposes. Before power and interest can be used to understand how Chinese foreign policy works, they must be operationalized through relation to specific issues and situations. (Power and interest are time, issue and space relative. It is thus not possible to speak in policy-relevant terms of aggregate Chinese 'power' or of objectively existing, eternal Chinese 'national interests'. Nonetheless, no analysis of Chinese foreign policy is complete without inclusion of the specific operational content of these two factors.)

Implementation, the third stage of Chinese foreign policy-making, follows directly from foreign policy decision. Its effect is dual. On the one hand, it fulfills, in some differentially successful manner, its intended function of responding to the challenges posed by the issue-related actions of a foreign state or the international environment. On the other hand, it possesses the (usually) unintended function of becoming a domestic (for example, intra-party, party versus army, center versus region, and so on) issue itself.

Two policy decision cycles operate, each with a foreign policy/international environment component. In the domestic cycle, inputs from the environment affect Chinese foreign policy *and* Chinese domestic politics. The decision process takes place, either simultaneously or successively, at the domestic and foreign policy levels, and a part of the resultant output is fed back internally to the next domestic political cycle. In the foreign policy cycle, Chinese policy output influences the other state (or states or international environment in general) in three manners: by affecting that state's domestic politics; by being detected as an action that may need response according to that state's self-perceived ideological and psychocultural proclivities; and by causing the state's decision-makers to consider what issue-related components of the national interest are to be invoked, and what elements of power, in consequence, are to be employed. Together with the influences brought to bear from domestic politics, these three trigger the foreign state's foreign policy decision process, with a consequent change in policy output. In turn, these outputs, produced in response to Chinese policy initiatives, become inputs to the Chinese political system, and the process is repeated. This cycle is illustrated in Figure 6.3.

Time is a parametric variable in the Chinese foreign policy cycle, since each stage – perception, decision and implementation – requires time to complete and since delays occur between the actions taken by foreign entities and their perception by the Chinese. Moreover, time differentials are not equal, so that as the domestic and foreign policy cycles are repeated, actions, perceptions and decisions may occur at different (or even simultaneous) times. Thus, a given Chinese foreign policy action may affect the policies of other states, which after a time take action according to their perception of their own interest and power. At some further time, the policies thus adopted may enter Chinese domestic political processes as one of the issues behind the struggle for power. There may also be a delay between the time when China's foreign policy actions are taken and the point when as an issue they enter directly the domestic political arena.

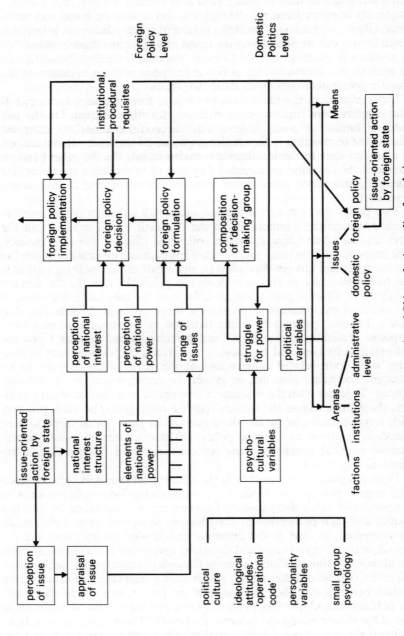

Figure 6.3 *A representation of Chinese foreign policy formulation.*

Finally, the actions of both China and the foreign states may influence Chinese domestic politics simultaneously, for instance by triggering a debate on the merits of actions taken some time previously.

The Chinese foreign policy-making process comprises the time-differentiated effects of all of these causal factors. While the relation of causes, processes and effects appears rather simple, obviously the reality it represents is quite complex. Moreover, Chinese foreign policy is not merely the sum of its actions and policies taken in relation to single foreign states or to single issues. Policies toward many states and with regard to multiple issues must simultaneously be adopted, carried into effect and monitored, as shown in Figure 6.4 and 6.5 for the two- and three-state cases. This further complicates the picture, even more confuses cause and effect in the minds of Chinese decision-makers, requires trade-offs between sometimes incompatible national and ideological interests, and makes necessary differential evaluation of the utility of the several elements of national power. Thus Chinese foreign policy, no different in this respect from that of other major states, becomes an art to manage and a nightmare to analyze.

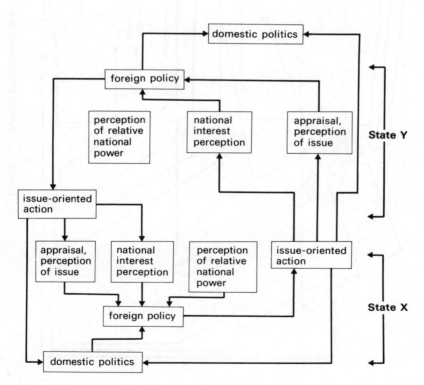

Figure 6.4 *A two-state international system showing domestic and foreign policy components, and kind and direction of decision.*

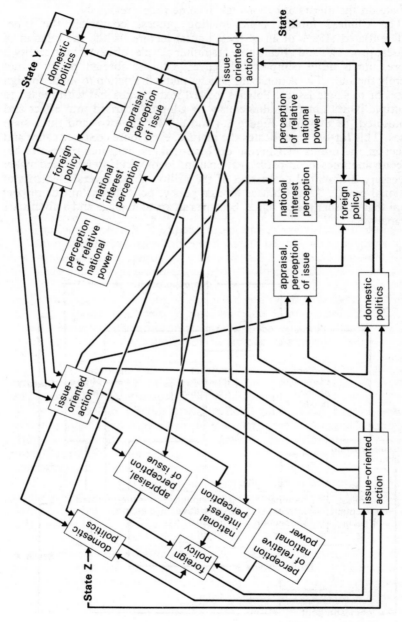

Figure 6.5 *Foreign policy sources in a multi-state system.*

The Sino-Soviet-American Triangle

Chinese policy is directed primarily to its relations with the five or six states that require constant attention and are capable of influencing domestic Chinese developments. They are: the United States, the Soviet Union, Japan, North Korea, Vietnam and (possibly) India. However, the two super-powers, America and Russia, have so vastly affected China that its foreign policy can be analyzed largely in terms of Peking's relations with them alone. Indeed, post-World War II diplomatic history centers on triangular relations among the three, which form a subsystem dominating international politics in form and content. Relations between China and all other states depend directly on the state of play between Peking, Moscow and Washington and indirectly on the ties of Moscow and Washington with other relevant states.

North Korea, Vietnam and India are of importance to China because Peking has been militarily involved on each of their territories and because India now possesses a nuclear capability. Japan is also central to China, but because of lack of offensive military potential, its alliance with the United States and China's inability to influence Japanese domestic developments decisively, Peking has tended to treat Tokyo as a Far Eastern appendage of the United States. Even with regard to India and the two Asian communist states, Chinese policy is largely determined by the character of its relations with the two super-powers – to the early 1960s with the United States, since then with the Soviet Union. So Chinese interests in regard to these states too can be reduced for expository purposes to dependence on its relations with America and Russia.

From China's point of view, the following propositions relate Chinese policy to the policies and actions of the United States and the Soviet Union:

(1) When China perceived the United States to be more powerful than itself or the Soviet Union, it allied with Russia against America. This was the major reason for the Sino-Soviet alliance in 1950.

(2) When China considered the Sino-Soviet alliance to be more powerful than the America-centered alliance system, it acquiesced in attempts by other communist states at military expansion in peripheral areas. This was a major cause of the Korean war and Chinese encouragement of the Vietminh revolutionaries.

(3) When all three parties considered Soviet and Chinese power to balance that of the United States, the resulting equilibrium led to relatively peaceful relations within the triangle. This was the situation from 1953 to 1958.

(4) When mutual fear of nuclear war drove Moscow and Washington to seek détente, the Sino-Soviet alliance began to dissolve. China was forced to adopt a policy of opposition to both super-powers. This was the case from 1961 to 1965.

(5) On one occasion, domestic and international factors combined to make it profitable for China to pursue *no* foreign policy. This occurred during the Cultural Revolution, 1966–9, when Soviet and American power was, in Chinese eyes, mutually balanced and non-threatening to China.

(6) When the Soviet Union threatened China militarily, Peking resolved some of its differences with Washington to construct a proto-coalition against Moscow. This decribes the situation after 1969.

(7) Peking's propensity to involve itself actively with the United States and the Soviet Union is directly related to the intensity of campaign-style economic development programs and inversely related to the level of political disagreement in the party leadership. The former tendency is illustrated by the Great Leap Forward in 1957–9, and the latter by the P'eng Teh-Huai affair in 1959–61 and emerging Cultural Revolutionary differences in 1964–6. The differential character of economic development and political disagreement imparts a cyclical character to Chinese domestic politics, and hence to Chinese policy toward the United States and the Soviet Union, albeit attenuated and with a varying time-lag.

(8) Given the party's greater concern with domestic matters and its tendency to pursue a foreign policy course, once established, until it is in obvious need of revision, Chinese relations with the United States and the Soviet Union often are not amenable to rapid short-term alternation. This helps to explain the overly slow improvement in Sino-American relations after 1969 in the face of Soviet military threats, and the continued decline in Sino-Soviet relations after 1963 below the point where China retained control of the situation.

Thus, the history of the triangle since 1949 indicates that the basic direction of Chinese foreign policy has been determined by the character of Chinese relations with the Soviet Union and the United States.

Chinese military, economic and third state policies followed closely the outlines of these fundamentals. Militarily, close cooperation with Moscow during the 1950s was succeeded in the 1960s by emphasis upon independence from both super-powers. China soon produced its own nuclear weaponry, renewed emphasis on its own strategic and tactical military philosophy, began producing many components of a modern military machine and became a factor in the world nuclear deterrent equation. But instead of being able to use its new military power to drive the Americans from the Taiwan Straits and Southeast Asia, in the 1970s China found itself threatened by the Russians from the north and, in league with the Indians, from the southwest. Meanwhile, the Americans were still firmly in place in the northeast (that is, Japan and Korea) and the east (Taiwan and the Philippines). Exiting from the Southeast Asian disaster, the United States left behind a divided, if still communist, Indo-China, a North Vietnam leaning visibly toward Moscow, and a surprisingly strong group of non-communist states in the rest of the region. China had to protect itself against the serious Soviet threat and thus felt constrained to agree with Washington to neutralize the Taiwan Straits region, cease opposition to the American–Japanese security tie and acquiesce in a slight lessening of tensions in Korea.

Economically, the same pattern has prevailed. Reliance upon Soviet assistance during the 1950s and adoption of the Soviet model of development at home was succeeded, perforce, by stress during the 1960s on autarchy and diversification of trade away from the Soviet Union abroad. Melioration of Chinese relations with the United States following the Sino-Soviet border classes accentuated this trend by developing trade with Washington and its Western allies. China also attempted to forestall close Soviet–Japanese economic relations by offering to sell to Tokyo virtually all of China's surplus oil. The Soviet threat was felt deeply enough that the principle of self-reliance was dropped and replaced by a policy of accepting interest-bearing long-term loans from foreign states. In general, leaning economically to one side or another meant quicker development of the Chinese economy, whereas isolation from both sides implied difficult economic times at home and a general decline in economic contacts abroad.

Chinese policy towards states other than America and Russia has also depended on its relations with Washington and Moscow. During the period of near-total enmity with the United States, friends and allies of America were ipso facto enemies of China. Japan and India are good examples: when Tokyo signed an alliance with Washington, China declared every Japanese government to be unfriendly; until the mid-1960s the warmth of Peking's relations with New Delhi was inversely related to the ups and downs of India's friendliness with Washington. Peking invented 'people's diplomacy' as a means to establish unofficial relations with unrecognized states, and thus to put pressure from below on regimes friendly to the United States to change their policy. 'National liberation movements' were supported in states whose governments were considered to be pro-American but not in neutralist or pro-Chinese states.

Once Peking and Washington began to seek détente, however, Chinese policy changed. Japan is again a good example: Peking came to terms with Tokyo as concerns recognition, greatly increased the level of Sino-Japanese trade, encouraged the Japanese to continue the Japanese-American Security Treaty, and signed an anti-Soviet Peace Treaty with Tokyo. Once the Sino-Soviet break came in 1960, moreover, Chinese energies went to countering Soviet influence in those areas and institutions to which it had access. Given the lack of Chinese influence in Eastern Europe and in the America-centered alliance system, Peking concentrated on battling the Russians ideologically within the non-ruling communist parties throughout the world and on competing for the favor of newly independent states in Asia and Africa.

Chinese foreign policy is thus the product not only of domestic conditions and of the party's perceptions of China's relative power, national interests and ideological goals, but also of the necessity to deal with the nuclear super-powers. Most other states did not count as factors of major importance in formulating Peking's general foreign policy.

The International System
An analysis of Chinese foreign policy restructuring must be expanded to include the influences of the structure of and trends within the international political-economic system as a whole. A series of system-wide factors operates parametrically on all members and constitutes a fourth level of analysis. Many of these factors change slowly and affect states

unequally. Hence, they are often ignored in short- to medium-term analysis. Yet they are responsible for much of the general direction of world political activity and are the prime agents accountable for longer-term change in the entire international system. There are four groupings of such factors: the global distribution of power; the number and kind of economic actors; technology; and the relation of man to his natural environment. Each influences Chinese foreign policy.

Power is distributed laterally across the northern hemisphere, and concentrates in five areas: North America, Europe, the Soviet Union, East Asia and the Middle East. In Europe and Asia, geography and politics bifurcate power into eastern and western sectors. The situation was not always thus: in 1880, global political and economic power was concentrated in Western Europe. Within a century, power has dramatically dispersed throughout the globe. But the process must now dramatically decelerate: only India and Brazil remain candidates for great power status. Therefore the twentieth-century revolution in world politics is largely over. One conclusion follows immediately for China. Peking cannot depend upon defining the 'Third World' into existence as a naturally united entity able to counter the industrialized North and holding interests naturally in harmony with those of China.

World politics is a whole, for the first time in history, also because of advances in transportation and communication. Certain kinds of power can now be applied nearly instantly at vast distances, while information is no longer slow to spread or facts easy to conceal. Moreover, decolonization has brought the number of states member of the international system to near its potential maximum. But although global politics is unified in these senses, it has fragmented along several new lines. China, like others, has little control over the direction of these changes. Divisions are no longer simply ideological, as during the cold war (although the residual division of the developed world into America-centered and Soviet-centered alliances continues). Rather, they are economic and geographic. Aside from the Sino-Soviet-American triangle, which dominates political-military aspects of world politics, there is also the economic split into industrialized/developed and the agricultural/developing countries. A further division is between the Western industrial triangle of nations (the United States, Western Europe and Japan), the Soviet-led socialist group, the oil-rich developing countries and the residue of poor Afro-Asian states.

China does not fit easily into any of these groups: it is neither fully industrialized, basically agricultural, essentially resource-exporting, nor really poor. But Peking must pay attention to these divisions and cannot merely act as if it were the natural leader of the 'world countryside' against the 'world city'. China's in-between developmental status makes it doubtful that it can for long continue to participate in world economic activity merely as a self-proclaimed 'Third World' developing country.

Technology is one of the driving forces changing the contemporary world. It passes national boundaries with relative ease and in certain spheres, for example, military hardware, technological change forces states to keep abreast of their opponents. If anything, the rate of technological innovation is increasing. China must thus move even faster in order to domesticize foreign technology and accelerate the rate of its own innovation. Indeed, its entire program of development and modernization depends on catching up technologically; China cannot perpetually remain one or two technological generations behind, for each new wave of technological progress quickly obsolesces preceding modes of production. Equally important, each higher level of technology is more costly than the previous level, so that the price of remaining in the competition rises at increasing rates. China thus has no choice but to 'stay in the game', since it must compete with the Russians and the Americans and must overcome its legacy of backwardness. The technological race therefore imposes increasingly severe constraints on the foreign political options open to Peking. Because technological innovation emanates for the most part from the developed (and capitalist) Western states, China must keep open channels of communication, information exchange and trade with them. This further constrains Chinese policy to a more narrow set of policy options than the party would prefer ideologically.

The final group of exogenous factors is perhaps of the greatest relative importance to Chinese policy. China is constrained by very high population, relatively low economic development and a disadvantageous geographic setting. But these factors limit the effectiveness of many other countries as well, thereby impinging on Chinese foreign policy from two directions. For instance, the growing global shortage of food makes it more difficult and expensive for China to purchase grain when it is short of food. Since China's own production occasionally falters, and since China's population is still increasing, it must constantly be ready to enter world markets to cover shortfalls. In extreme circumstances, China cannot aid other food-short countries but must compete with them for available stocks.

It follows that China must modify its opposition to Washington longer, and with regard to more issues, than it would otherwise prefer, since the Western countries, principally the United States, will continue to be the main food suppliers. The same case can be made concerning oil policy. China has supported the OPEC policy of large increases in prices because it wishes to gain influence in the Middle East and the Third World and because it views these measures as generally anti-Western. But to the extent that such support solidifies OPEC price levels, China contributes to the higher costs of the very Western industrial goods that it desires, thereby weakening the West in general, which it now wishes to strengthen for anti-Soviet reasons. This contradiction could force Peking to choose between supporting OPEC, selling oil to Japan at less-than-OPEC prices, or waffling between support or changing its oil policy entirely.

Conclusion

Any realistic examination of Chinese foreign policy change must take into account the complex connections between four levels of analysis: domestic, foreign policy, international political (in our case, Sino-Soviet-American relations) and international systemic. Each informs a part of

Chinese foreign policy and each is partially the product of the factors comprising the other three domains.

On balance, Chinese foreign policy turns out to be not startlingly different from those of other major states in terms of causal factors and, generally, results. Despite ideological pretensions and laudatory goals, processes and trends over which Chinese policy-makers have had little control, much less knowledge, have determined much of Peking's relations with the external world. Like the rest, China is being pushed along by the press of events and unforeseen contingencies. Despite a very strong domestic government ruling over a state united (Taiwan excepted) for the first time in over a century, China in reality has had surprisingly little control over its foreign relations. At the outset of the new regime, China became a major participant in world politics, playing a major part in precipitating, solidifying and continuing the East–West split. But as time progressed and as Peking moved more surely on to the international scene, it found to its dismay that its freedom of initiative declined instead of expanded. Although China's advancing power allowed it the comparative luxury of ceasing to fear invasion, foreign control of its economy, or unequal legal status, the more active it became, the higher were the barriers that its designated enemies, not unnaturally, threw up before her.

At the end of a quarter-century, then, Peking's foreign policy appeared increasingly to be the product of a rational response to internal, external and systemic demands, subject to the same forces and obeying the same 'rules' of politics as did the other states. Chinese foreign policy would not be the same were a non-communist government suddenly to appear in Peking; but China's ideologically induced departures from established patterns of international behavior appeared to be declining in number and importance. The 'style' and many of the goals of Chinese foreign policy remained undeniably communist, as did some of the means. But an increasing proportion of both goals and means were relatively indistinguishable from those that China qua China would have adopted anyway, while many of the twists and turns of policy, as well as the general drift of events, seemed understandable on the same grounds that explain the behavior of most other states.

Notes: Chapter 6

1 Dick Solomon, *Mao's Revolution and the Chinese Political Culture* (Berkeley, Calif.: University of California Press, 1971).
2 Parris Chang, *Power and Policy in China* (University Park, Pa: Pennsylvania State University Press, 1975).
3 Mu Fu-sheng, *The Wilting of the Hundred Flowers: The Chinese Intelligentsia Under Mao* (New York: Praeger, 1962).
4 Jan S. Prybyla, *The Political Economy of Communist China* (Scranton, Pa: International Textbook Co., 1970), ch. 8.
5 Roderick MacFarquhar, *Origins of the Cultural Revolution* (New York: Praeger, 1972).
6 Jan H. Kalicki, *The Pattern of Sino-American Crises* (New York: Cambridge University Press, 1975), p. 168.
7 Alan S. Whiting, *The Chinese Calculus of Deterrence* (Ann Arbor, Mich.: University of Michigan Press, 1975).

8 Donald Zagoria, *The Sino-Soviet Conflict, 1956–1961* (Princeton, NJ: Princeton University Press, 1962), pp. 334–5.

9 Roderick MacFarquhar (ed.), *Sino-American Relations, 1949–1971* (New York: Praeger, 1972).

10 Philip Mosely, 'The Moscow–Peking axis in world politics', in Howard Boorman *et al.*, *Moscow–Peking Axis* (New York: Harper, 1957).

11 Robert Bowie and John Fairbank (eds), *Communist China 1955–1959: Policy Documents with Analysis* (Cambridge, Mass.: Harvard University Center for International Studies and East Asian Research Center, 1962), documents 7 and 13.

12 David Floyd, *Mao Against Khrushchev: History of the Sino-Soviet Conflict* (New York: Praeger, 1964).

13 Alexander Dallin *et al.*, *Diversity in International Communism* (New York: Columbia University Press, 1963), pp. 670ff.

14 Paul Y. Hammond, *The Cold War Years: American Foreign Policy 1945* (New York: Harcourt, Brace & World, 1969).

15 Cecil Crabb, *The Elephants and the Grass: A Study of Nonalignment* (New York: Praeger, 1965).

16 Edward Crankshaw, *The New Cold War: Moscow versus Peking* (Harmondsworth, England: Penguin, 1963).

17 Jen-min Jih-pao, 'The leaders of the CPSU are the greatest splitters of our time', *Peking Review*, 4 February 1964, 7 February 1964.

18 Michael B. Yahuda, *China's Role in World Affairs* (New York: St Martin's Press, 1978), pp. 145–69.

19 Herbert J. Passin, *China's Cultural Diplomacy* (New York: Praeger, 1963), p. 6.

20 Gene T. Hsiao, *The Foreign Trade of China: Policy, Law and Practice* (Berkeley, Calif.: University of California Press, 1977), p. 11.

21 *Activities of Chinese Communist Personalities* (Washington, DC: Joint Publications Research Service), Yearly Culmination, 1957, 1958, 1959.

22 Douglas M. Johnston and Hungdah Chiu, *Agreements of the People's Republic of China, 1949–1967* (Cambridge, Harvard University Press, 1968), pp. 229–74.

23 Author's conversations with Soviet scholars and librarians at the Institute of Oriental Studies, Moscow, 1–20 July 1972.

24 'Sino-Soviet interaction: a quantitative assessment', Project Triad, BSR 2953A (Ann Arbor, Mich.: The Office of National Security Studies, June 1967); Franz J. Mogdis, 'The verbal dimension in Sino-Soviet relations: a time series analysis' (Ann Arbor, Mich.: ONS Studies, Bendix Aerospace Systems Division, September 1970); Franz J. Mogdis and Karen S. Tidwell, 'A quantitative assessment of Sino-Soviet relations, 1950–1967' (Ann Arbor, Mich.: ONS Studies, Bendix Aerospace Systems Division, 1970).

25 Johnston and Chiu, *Agreements of the People's Republic of China*, pp. 229–74.

26 Floyd, *Mao Against Khrushchev: History of the Sino-Soviet Conflict*, p. 147.

27 Passin, *China's Cultural Diplomacy*, p. 6.

28 Joint Economic Committee, Congress of the United States, *An Economic Profile of Mainland China*, Vol. 1: 'General Economic Setting', Part 1: 'Main lines of Chinese communist economic policy' by Arthur G. Ashbrook, Jr, pp. 15–44, and 'The tempo of economic development of the Chinese mainland 1949–1965' by Ta-Chung Liu, pp. 45–76 (Washington, DC: Government Printing Office, 1967).

29 Hans Heymann, Jr, 'Acquisition and diffusion of technology in China', in *China: A Reassessment of the Economy* (Washington, DC: Government Printing Office, for the US Congress, Joint Economic Committee of Congress, 1975), pp. 678–729.

30 Allency H. Y. Yang, 'Red and expert: Communist China's educational strategies of manpower development', unpublished dissertation (Berkeley, Calif.: University of California, 1965).

31 Bruce D. Larkin, *China and Africa, 1949–1970* (Berkeley, Calif.: University of California Press, 1977), pp. 65ff.

32 Donald S. Zagoria, *Vietnam Triangle* (New York: Pegasus, 1967), pp. 63–98.

33 John Bryan Starr, *Continuing the Revolution* (Princeton, NJ: Princeton University Press, 1979).

34 *China Quarterly*, 'Chronicle and documentation', nos 30–2, April–June 1967, October–December 1967.

35 *China Mainland Review*, 1, 1 (June 1965), *et seq.*
36 Uri Ra'anan, 'Peking's foreign policy "debate", 1965–1966', in Tang Tsou (ed.), *China in Crisis*, Vol. 2, (Chicago: University of Chicago Press, 1968), pp. 23–72.
37 Alan S. Whiting, 'What Nixon must do to make friends in Peking', *New York Review of Books*, 7 October 1971, pp. 10ff.
38 Harry Harding and Melvin Gurtov, *The Purge of Lo Jui-ch'ing: The Politics of Chinese Strategic Planning* (Santa Monica, Calif.: Rand Corporation, R-548-PR, February 1971).
39 Jacques Guillermaz, *The Chinese Communist Party in Power, 1949–1976* (Boulder, Co.: Westview Press, 1976), pp. 486–7.
40 Annual article on China in *Asian Survey*, VII, 1 (January 1968).
41 See the relevant analysis in *Trends in Communist Media* (Washington, DC: Foreign Broadcast Information Service, 1965–1968). Almost without exception these analyses refer to translations of Chinese broadcasts and other material in *Daily Report on Communist China* (Washington, DC: FBIS, 1965–8) for the same period.
42 Thomas W. Robinson, 'China's revolutionary strategy in the developing world: the failure of success', RAND P-4169, published in *The Annals*, 386 (November 1969), pp. 64–77.
43 Hong Kong, *Report for the Year 1967* (Hong Kong: Hong Kong Government, 1968), ch. 1.
44 Robert Sutter, *Chinese Foreign Policy After the Cultural Revolution, 1966—1977* (Boulder, Co.: Westview Press, 1978), pp. 3–10.
45 Thomas W. Robinson, 'The Sino-Soviet border dispute: background, development, and the March 1969 clashes', RAND P-6171-PR published in the *American Political Science Review*, 66, 4 (December 1972), pp. 1175–1202.
46 Sutter, *Chinese Foreign Policy*, pp. 11–24, 113–48.
47 Robert G. Sutter, *China Watch* (Baltimore, Md: Johns Hopkins University Press, 1978).
48 Gene T. Hsiao (ed.), *Toward Sino-Soviet Reconciliation* (New York: Praeger, 1974).
49 Thomas W. Robinson, 'Soviet military involvement in recent Sino-Soviet border clashes', in Steven Kaplan (ed.), *Mailed Fist, Velvet Glove: Soviet Use of Force* (Washington, DC: Brookings Institution, 1980).
50 Henry A. Kissinger, *White House Years* (Boston, Mass.: Little, Brown, 1979), pp. 684–708.
51 Thomas W. Robinson, 'The Sino-Soviet border conflict and the future of Sino-Soviet-American relations', RAND P-4461, June 1971.
52 Jurgen Dommes, *China After the Cultural Revolution* (Berkeley, Calif.: University of California Press, 1975), pp. 9–28.
53 Michael Y. M. Kau (ed.), *The Lin Piao Affair* (New York: Institute of Arts and Sciences Press, 1975).
54 Sydney Jammes, 'The Chinese defense burden', in *China: A Reassessment of the Economy* (Washington, DC: Government Printing Office, 1975 for the Joint Economic Committee, US Congress), pp. 459–66.
55 *China Quarterly*, 'Chronicle and documentation', 1970, 1971.
56 *China Quarterly*, 'Chronicle and documentation', 1973, 1974, 1975.
57 Samuel Kim, *China, the United Nations, and World Order* (Princeton, NJ.: Princeton University Press, 1979).
58 The two relevant documents in the American case are the Shanghai Communiqué, *Peking Review*, 1972, no. 9, pp. 4–5, and the two statements on normalization, *Peking Review*, 1971, no. 51, pp. 8–15.
59 See, for example, the normalization statements between China and Australia and New Zealand, *Peking Review*, 1972, no. 52, p. 3; the Philippines, *Peking Review*, 1975, n. 24, pp. 7–10; the Federal Republic of Germany, *Peking Review*, 1972, no. 42, pp. 4–8; Greece, *Peking Review*, 1972, no. 23, p. 20; and Belgium, *Peking Review*, 1973, no. 18, p. 73. The two relevant Japanese-Chinese documents are the joint statement upon normalization, *Peking Review*, 1972, no. 42, pp. 12–18; and the Friendship Treaty, *Peking Review*, 1978, no. 33, pp. 7–9.
60 The Kissinger visits are covered in *People's Daily*, 16 July 1972; *Peking Review*, 1973, no. 8, p. 4; 1973, no. 46, p. 10; 1974, no. 49, p. 4; the Ford visit is in 1975, no. 49, pp. 4ff.; the Vance visit in 1977, no. 36, p. 7; and the Brzezinski visit in 1978, no. 21, p. 4.
61 Central Intelligence Agency, *Activities of Important People's Republic of China Officials*, yearly summary for 1972–80 (Washington, DC: Government Printing Office, 1972–80).

62 Author's conversations with chiefs of the relevant Department of State offices, 1979 and 1980, and Scholarly Committee Communications with the People's Republic of China, *China Exchange Newsletter* (Washington, DC: National Academy of Sciences Issues for 1978–80).

63 These agreements, of which over twenty had been signed between the United States and China alone by mid-1980, can be followed through the *China Quarterly*, 'Quarterly chronicle and documentation', 1977–80; and Alfred C. Julien and Robert E. Slattery (eds), *Report on International Educational Exchange* (New York: Institute of International Education, 1978).

64 US Department of Commerce, US Travel Service, *Foreign Visitor Arrivals, 1967–1977*, and yearly thereafter.

65 The Sino-Japanese air agreement was signed in 1972, the European and links during 1973–7 and the American in 1980.

66 Central Intelligence Agency, 'China: international trade 1977–78' (Washington, DC: Library of Congress, 1978), and yearly thereafter.

67 National Committee for US–China Trade, *China Trade Review* (Washington, DC: bimonthly, 1972–) has many articles detailing these changes as they apply to all nations.

68 *China Quarterly*, 'Quarterly chronicle and documentation', 1976–80.

69 *Trends in Communist Media* (Washington, DC: Foreign Broadcast Information Service, weekly, 1972–80).

70 *New York Times*, 10 November 1979, p. 3; *Washington Post*, 26 April 1980, p. A21.

7

An Abortive Attempt to Change Foreign Policy: Chile, 1970–3

Jacques Zylberberg and Miguel Monterichard

Chile's foreign policy during the Popular Unity (*UP*) coalition government headed by Dr Salvador Allende Gossens constitutes a good example
of a radical attempt to restructure foreign policy by a small peripheral
country. For three years the left-wing populist government did its best to
implement a programme with the double goal of autonomous development
of Chile, and breaking off dependent relations with the United States.
Chile serves as a case not only of foreign policy restructuring, but also of
disintegration. We shall begin by examining the evolution of Chile and the
development of its relations with the international environment, an evolution which led to the establishment of a relatively autonomous nation-state
within the overall framework of structural dependence. Then we shall
analyze the Allende government's attempts to cut dependence bonds both
inside and outside the country and to restructure its qualitative and quantitative position vis-à-vis the rest of the world.[1]

From independence to 1970, the history of Chile can be divided into
four phases: a period of expansionist autonomy, a moderate dependence
on European imperialism, a period of withdrawal and crisis, and finally,
structural subordination to the United States. These progressive changes
in Chile's international roles did not, however, occur at the same pace in
the areas of culture, economy and geo-politics.[2]

The legal independence of Chile was formally proclaimed in 1818. In
1830, after twelve years of disturbances. Diego Portales established an
authoritarian, oligarchic regime that extended Chilean hegemony over the
Southern Pacific region and the tacit subordination of Peru and Bolivia.
To the military vocation of the region was added a commercial one: the
grain merchants in Valparaiso turned, in addition to Peru, to California to
sell wheat during the gold rush in the American West. Chile's expansionist
policy had its greatest success during the Pacific war (1879–84) when it
divested Peru and Bolivia of their mining regions in the south. Chile's
local supremacy allowed it to play a subtle balancing game in South
America with Brazil and Argentina.[3]

The success of the expansionist policy changed Chile's role in interna-
tional affairs; the 'robber baron', which had become 'the policeman' of the
Southern Pacific region, nevertheless became tied to the economy of
Europe through Chile's mining and grain exports. From 1880 to 1929,

saltpeter and grain poured into Europe so that Chile could obtain currency in order to pay its debts, to finance an European-style consumerism among the elite and the middle classes, and even to permit some shy industrialization at the local level. The role played by European powers in the Chilean economy was limited by Chile's geo-political autonomy, which was sustained by distances, by the European powers' activities in Africa and Asia, by the conflicts which set these powers against one another, and by the growing influence of the United States.[4]

Changes in both the domestic and the external environments further undermined the influence of Britain and Europe in Chile's economy. Local population growth made continued grain exports impossible; the invention of a substitute for saltpeter cut down exports of that product, and the 1929 crash hastened Chile's economic decline. Between 1929 and 1940 Chile was plunged into an economic, political and social crisis. The drastic decrease in saltpeter and grain exports to Europe meant that the American-controlled copper industry would now take a dominant economic role in Chile despite an effort at progressive industrialization directed toward substitution of light finished products. Chile's internal weakness during its period of involuntary isolationism made the task of any potential guardian nation easier: the United States would be only too happy to take the vacant protectorate. Only in the local culture did European influence continue, primarily through modest immigration to Chile.

After World War II, American interests covered Chile with a network of bonds which progressively satellized the country. The arrival of the United States in the 'Cono Sur' was not accomplished suddenly. Already at the beginning of the century, the Braden Company entered the copper sector. Both a large growth in the copper sector of the national economy and the support by the Chilean political elites of the anti-communist thrust in the United States helped mold Chilean-American bilateral relations into a system of structural dependence.[5]

Dimensions of Dependence

After 1940 Chile, which had always tried to contain any attempts at American, Brazilian, or Argentinian hegemony within the hemisphere, ceased to be a medium-sized, independent power in the Southern Pacific region. Due to American pressures during World War II, Chile eventually declared war on Germany in spite of rather strong internal resistance by various pressure groups.[6] During the cold war Chile adhered to the Inter-American Defense Treaty of Rio and banned the communist party from 1946 to 1958. In exchange, it received from the United States an average annual income from foreign aid of $12·5 million. In 1952 Chile signed the Mutual Security Act with the United States, a treaty which opened the way for American military officials' increasing penetration of the Chilean army through officer training programmes, joint naval man-euvers and consultations on defense policies. After this agreement was signed, annual American aid until 1961 averaged more than $45 million, of which about 4 million dollars went to the army. During the Cuban crisis the United States pressured Chile to participate in the Cuban blockade, in spite of the Alessandri government's reservations. In return, Chile received increased military and civil aid. Thus, after 1960 Chile was one of the principal beneficiaries of the Alliance for Progress, created to counterbalance Cuban influence and to develop Latin-America. From 1962 to 1970 the United States and international organizations granted an average of $160 million per year in aid to Chile, of which about $10 million went to the army. These figures obviously do not include all the American money going to Chile, such as the secret contributions made to assure the election of President Frei over the leftist candidate, Allende, in 1964.

It is likely that geo-political factors played a dominant role in the United States policy of massive aid to Chile: the central empire faced competition from the Soviet Union and Cuba, and the Chilean elites were themselves threatened by the most powerful communist party in Latin America. American gifts and credits granted for security reasons also encouraged a permissive policy on the part of the Chilean government toward increasing American economic influence.[7]

A number of figures reveal the extent of Chile's increasing dependence on the United States, and its virtual satellization. From 1960 to 1970 Chile's foreign debt increased from $598 million to $2·9 billion, an increase of over 397 percent. One-half of this debt was owed to American sources. A large part of foreign trade – 37 percent of Chilean imports came from the United States whereas only 18 percent of Chilean exports went to the United States – depended on short-line terms of credit of $220 million granted by American banks. The equilibrium between the balance of payments and the national budget had been helped by aid from the United States, the IDB and IBRD, which had totaled more than 1·1 billion dollars between 1964 and 1969. Moreover, foreign interests – of which 70 percent were subsidiaries of American companies – directly controlled almost all of the most dynamic and critical areas of the economy by the end of 1970: machinery and equipment (50 percent); iron, steel and metal products (60 percent); petroleum products and distribution (over 50 percent); industrial and other chemicals (60 percent); rubber products (45 percent); automobile assembly (100 percent); radio and television (nearly 100 percent); pharmaceuticals (nearly 100 percent); office equipment (nearly 100 percent); tobacco (100 percent); and advertising (90 percent).[8]

In the critical copper industry, American firms controlled more than 80 percent of the production. Copper represented in the Chilean economy about 10 percent of the gross national product, and 70 percent of the export revenues; it supplied nearly 100 percent of the foreign currency reserves and 12 percent of the total fiscal revenues. The enormous size of the foreign companies controlling Chilean copper – in this case Anaconda and Kennecott – had produced a situation of a state within the state. As Moran points out: 'no domestic decision about the rate of economic development, the strength of the balance of payments, the level of aggregate employment, the breadth of social welfare programmes could be made without a careful calculation, from outside, of how the foreign copper companies might be going to exercise their discretionary power'.[9]

Contemporary history generally shows that this discretionary power was not always exercised in a way favorable to the national interests of Chile. The multinational companies tended to develop an economic rationality which rarely took into account the needs of the host country. To take an example, Chile was not rewarded after the Korean war for its 'new treatment' policy, which gave tax advantages to mining companies in order to encourage them to increase investments and production – this, in spite of the fact that Anaconda was earning income at least two times greater from its Chilean mines than from its non-Chilean production units. These corporations reacted rather timidly to these fiscal enticements and to the 'favorable economic climate'. Chile was responsible for 22 percent of world copper production in 1945 and 14 percent in 1960. As regards the local refining of copper, the case of Kennecott, traditionally more conservative than Anaconda, was particularly interesting and ironical to the Chileans. Kennecott announced in New York – not long after the last speech promoting a good 'climate for foreign investment' had ended in the Chilean Congress – that the Europeans were demanding more electrolytic copper for their electrical needs, and that therefore Kennecott would spend more than 100 million dollars to build a new refinery to treat Chilean copper – in Maryland! This episode in the policy of 'nuevo trato' is a good illustration of the dependence paradox: throughout the twentieth century, Chile, for reasons of local development and industrialization, wanted copper production to be increased to provide more Chilean side-benefits, such as the extension of the smelting industry, local refining and an increase in revenue. While some benefits did accrue, the copper companies generally ignored Chilean national interests while reinforcing Chile's dependence on the foreign copper markets.[10]

Cultural Penetration
After the Cuban panic, American cultural penetration in Chile grew rapidly. Although hard data on American cultural and ideological action are difficult to obtain, it is possible to outline several important domains of cultural activity. For example, the USIA's budget for Chile doubled after 1958. This body played an important role in the direct and indirect transmission by the Chilean mass media of material – often propaganda – developed in cooperation with the American authorities. Cultural exchanges between the United States and Chile also grew considerably during the 1960s. Thus, in addition to student scholarships, the Ford and Rockefeller Foundations, among others, financed programs in which Chilean universities established formal connections with the University of Minnesota, the University of California and Notre Dame University. The 'Peace Corps' sent several dozen volunteers to work in Chile. The discovery of the Camelot Plan (a research program organized by an American university to study means of combating revolutionary activities in Chile) convinced the Chilean left, rightly or wrongly, that the cultural dissemination activities of official or private representatives of the United States were part of an overall plan of cultural infiltration.[11]

Cultural exchanges by government and universities came on top of a plethora of religious activities of American origin, as well as extensive penetration of the Chilean media. The following figures for the 1960s are indicative of a typical dependence or neo-colonial situation:

- 96 per cent of films and television series shown on Chilean television came from the United States;
- 46 percent of all the programmes of the two main television channels of Santiago originated in North America;
- subsidiaries of three North American firms dominated the Chilean advertising market: J. Walter Thompson, McCann-Erikson and Grant Advertising;
- RCA and Odeon dominated the recording industry;
- 150,000 copies of the Spanish edition of *Reader's Digest Selections* were sold locally;
- a large majority of the print media carried comics drawn in the United States.[12]

The Chilean state was not, however, a simple colonial enclave of the West in general, or of the United States in particular. Chilean society was diversified enough in its internal structures to be able to claim a certain autonomy, even if, since 1945, the structural presence of the empire had not stopped increasing. Chilean governments often tried to get concrete advantages, especially in the economic sector, in which Chile had made quite a strong effort since 1945 to develop heavy industry. This industrialization, however, was slow since it had always depended on the external aid of foreign technology and on export income. Nevertheless, the Chilean industrial sector produced 20 percent of the national product in 1970, compared to the 10 percent produced by mining. These figures suggest a structural difference between Chile and most neo-colonial economies of the Third World.[13]

Initial Attempts at Diversification: Enter Frei

Between 1964 and 1970, Eduardo Frei's Christian Democratic government launched some domestic and external diversification programmes to reduce dependence. In the copper and petrochemical industries, for example, the government obtained majority control by buying back 51 percent of the shares. Taking advantage of the increasing flood of copper sales in Western Europe (70 percent of production was sold to West Germany, England and Italy compared to 15 percent to the United States) and of Christian ideological and social ties, Frei increased cultural and economic exchanges with Western Europe. Technical, financial and cultural cooperation, as well as private exchanges with German and Belgian Catholic Groups, especially with the 'Misereor Foundation', grew dramatically. The Chilean government re-established diplomatic relations with the Soviet Union and Hungary, organized official contacts with Cuba and even went so far as to engage in some timid trading with Havana in spite of the economic blockade declared by the OAS. The Frei administration also helped form a group of copper producers, CIPEC, and joined the non-aligned nations' conferences as an observer. Chile underlined its growing autonomy vis-à-vis the United States by playing an organizing role in the establishment of a Latin American group, the Special Committee on Latin American Coordination (CECLA) within the OAS. Finally, Frei's government was also a founding member of the Andean Pact which proposed sectoral integration in the field of industry and led to the establishment of protective barriers for regional production and mechanisms for controlling foreign investment.[14]

The Frei administration's copper policy represented a considerable innovation in the history of Chilean mining. The important points of Frei's 'Chileanization policy' were:

- Chilean control of the price of copper. Henceforth, the Chilean authorities chose between the best of two world reference prices (United States and London);
- a massive increase in production, smelting and refining investments, and in production and income;
- Chileanization of the ownership of 51 percent of Kennecott's mineral deposits;
- nationalization of Anaconda, which had chosen to be expropriated and compensated rather than share its property with the Chilean state.[15]

Despite these programmes, Chile's economy remained highly vulnerable to decisions made in Washington and in the boardrooms of American companies. Relatively uncontrolled private investment flows continued apace, with the most modern sectors of the economy becoming increasingly controlled by outside forces.

The Christian Democratic administration supported in the realm of foreign policy the sub-regional status quo that emerged from the war of the Pacific, trying to preserve Bolivia's status as a weak country dependent on Chilean goodwill for access to the Pacific and to maintain stable relations with Peru by pursuing a policy of balance, of which the military ratio was an important component. At the same time, it courted the friendship of Ecuador. The traditional pattern of policy toward Argentina was thoroughly defensive: first, Chile tried to prevent the deterioration of the bilateral balance; second, Chilean diplomacy watched carefully, and was ready to counteract, any close rapprochement amongst Chile's three neighbors; third, while the development of economic ties was a desirable objective, the Chilean economy was not to become too dependent on Argentine products or markets; and finally, Brazil was to be treated as Chile's 'natural friend' under the assumption that it was in the Brazilian interest not to allow Argentina to achieve a position of economic or political domination over Chile.[16]

Enter Allende

The emergence of the Popular Unity represented above all the focusing of a general reaction against Frei's government. The Christian Democrats had stirred many aspirations, but the state of the Chilean economy made it impossible to satisfy all of them. The partial failure of the Frei administration and the slowing down of its reform programmes provided electoral opportunities for a broad coalition of center-left and left parties. The heterogeneous coalition agreed in promoting the themes of national independence, recovery of national resources, the struggle against oligarchy and state appropriation of monopolies. These themes generated electoral support from segments of the middle class as well as the urban and rural proletariat and sub-proletariat. Allende's programme mixed then a Leninist approach with a certain amount of demagoguery, which we can call 'rhetorical populism'.[17]

Internal Restructuring
For the Allende government, the opening phase in the struggle against dependence was to launch internal structural reform, principally of the economic structures. This priority is indicated by the preamble to the programme of the *Unidad Popular (UP)* coalition:

> What has failed in Chile is the system which does not correspond to present day requirements. Chile is a capitalist country, dependent on the imperialist nations and dominated by bourgeois groups who are structurally related to foreign capital and who cannot resolve the country's fundamental problem . . . The only alternative, which is a truly popular one, and one which therefore constitutes the Popular Government's main task is to bring to an end the rule of the imperialists, the monopolists, and the landed oligarchy, and to initiate the construction of socialism.[18]

The platform of the *Unidad Popular* emphasized that the first stage on the road to independence involved state control of the economy. 'Infrastructural reform' was to take precedence over 'superstructural reform'. State ownership, centralized planning and centrifugal economic development were the goals that would guide the steps taken by a government that was at once nationalist, populist and Leninist. It was scarcely concerned with the double structural contradiction between, on the one hand, a desire for autonomous industrialization and a need for financial and technical contributions from the world market, and on the other hand, the conflicting requirements for investment capital and popular consumption. During the populist euphoria, everything seemed possible, and the expansion of working-class consumption and state control of the economy proceeded rapidly. The state launched its undertaking to organize the economy into three sectors – public, mixed and private. The bureaucratic takeover was effected by three procedures designed to permit legal 'socialization' of the economy: parliamentary sanction of nationalization, purchase of stock by the government development agency (CORFO) and establishment of government management, under various pretexts, over private companies.

By the time of the 1973 coup, the *Unidad Popular* had succeeded in acquiring state control over the mining sector, the primary industrial sector and almost all the principal means of production, including the banking and foreign trade sectors in their entirety, a minor part of the means of commercial distribution and an important number of the huge private agrarian landholdings (haciendas). The government also placed high priority on the expropriation of foreign interests. Eighteen months after the 1970 elections, the *UP* had successfully taken control of the majority of foreign companies operating in Chile. The expropriation of American interests was pressed with particular dispatch. In July 1971 the Chilean Congress authorized the nationalization of the copper mines of the Anaconda, Kennecott and Cerro de Pasco companies, to be followed in July 1972 by the nationalization of ITT interests which had been under government management since September 1971. During 1971 the government 'bought back' the chief iron and nitrate mines and the foreign banks, including the Bank of America and the First National City Bank. Finally, in 1970 the government appointed 'interventores' (public directors or interveners), to run the subsidiaries of the Northern Indiana Brass Company and the Ralston Purina Company, and in May 1971 the subsidiary of the Ford Motor Company. This list, although incomplete, shows that in eighteen months the *UP* had assumed control of the principal American interests in the primary, secondary and tertiary sectors.[19]

Various American retaliatory measures sharply reduced the trade between the two countries. The American share of Chilean imports dropped from 37 percent in 1970 to 16·6 percent in 1973; the American share of Chilean exports declined from 14·3 percent in 1970 to 8·5 percent in 1973. The United States reduced foreign aid disbursements to Chile from 90·9 million dollars in 1970 to 26·6 million dollars in 1973. There was also a drastic reduction in short-term lines of bank credits, from 220 million dollars in 1970 to 20 million dollars in 1973. However, this rupture of the complicated economic web that bound the two countries, brutal though it was, did not prove fatal to all parts of the private enterprise sector in Chile, and still less did it succeed in eliminating that country's financial and technological dependence on foreign sources.[20]

The Chilean Left, in 1970 still fired with the spirit of elementary Leninist dogma, gave absolute priority to the 'economic infrastructure' upon which national culture was perforce contingent and hence not an immediate problem. The Allende government lacked the time to tackle the problem of foreign cultural penetration. Moreover, the *UP* programme concerning the question of culture tended to be somewhat vague. That document maintained that 'the social process, which will begin when the working class wins power, will develop a new culture which considers human labour with the highest regard, which emphasizes the desire for national assertion and independence, and which develops a critical understanding of present reality'. In two areas, however, there are indications which point to the existence of an indirect policy of promoting media autonomy and cultural diversification. Policies adopted by the Central Bank (Banco Central de Chile) resulted in a diminished influx of foreign magazines, films and cultural products in general, and a reduction in the foreign travel of Chilean citizens. The J. W. Thompson advertising firm terminated its operations in Chile, and RCA and Odeon lost their dominant position in the Chilean record and film industries. Cultural and social exchanges with Western Europe, Latin America and Eastern Europe showed a significant increase, thus reducing the impact of American cultural penetration. The government made an effort to encourage the spread of a populist and socialist counter-culture by establishing an integrated Chilean school system and through state support of leftist material in state and private media. The state television channel became in effect a propaganda tool of the *UP*, which reduced its North American program content in favor of leftist propaganda. Chile Films, a government creation, drastically reduced (by at least 50 percent) the import of films from the United States. A private publishing house which had been a large distributor of imported cultural materials, including comics, became the pro-government publishing firm Quimantu, dedicated to the communication of socialist reality. Aided by state subsidies, both direct and indirect, leftist groups purchased several radio stations and a daily newspaper, the *Clarin*, which they used to set up another daily, the *Puro Chile*, as well as several weekly and monthly publications. However, the government did not succeed in reducing significantly the output of foreign news releases and North American comics, but *UP* policies did contribute to a greater diversification in the cultural market and to the diffusion of an anti-imperialist mystique. Finally, as regards higher education and scientific research, the Allende government showed respect for university autonomy. Pre-existing university exchanges with the United States were not significantly affected, but academic bodies which so desired were evidently successful in setting up new exchanges, particularly with Cuba and Eastern Europe.[21]

Concerning military dependence, the *UP* programme was as imprecise as its stand on cultural dependence. The two countries were under equal compulsion to avoid direct confrontation. After a series of skirmishes – United States evacuation of the small American airforce bases on Easter Island, Punta Arenas and Quintero, and the cancellation of the February 1971 visit to Chile of the aircraft carrier Enterprise – there was an apparent return to the status quo. Allende could not afford to make a direct attack on the Chilean military, and Washington certainly had no wish to break off its privileged relationship with an army that was, on the whole, pro-Western. As early as 23 March 1971, in the interview which he granted to C. L. Sulzberger, Allende declared his intention of maintaining complete dissociation between geo-political and economic problems in his conflict with the United States: 'We will never do anything against the United States or contribute to injuring its sovereignty . . . We will never provide a military base that might be used against the United States, Chile will never permit its territory to be used for a military base against any foreign power – by anybody.[22]

Allende felt constrained to accept the continuation of privileged military relations with the United States. These were particularly visible in joint naval maneuvers – the Unitas operations – reciprocal officer exchanges, maintenance of a permanent American Military Mission, and increasing American military credits: $11·7 million in 1969, $0·8 million in 1970, $13·3 million in 1972 and $15 million in 1973. Prevented from putting an end to institutional relations between the military of the two countries,

Allende would bend his efforts toward co-opting part of the High Command into the Cabinet, while certain leaders of the Left endeavored to establish communications with non-commissioned officers and with simple conscripts. Subsequent events have shown that the great majority of officers remained basically hostile to the regime. The permanent American Military Mission in Chile remained active and had frequent contacts with local officers, contacts which were partially responsible for the growing rift between the army and Allende. The only attempt at diversifying military contacts was the Commander-in-Chief of the army's trip to the Soviet Union in April 1973, which did not produce any concrete results.

External Restructuring

The Chilean government sought to protect its internal restructuring policies by a systematic recourse to classic diplomatic measures for diversifying Chile's international relations and escaping from overwhelming American influence. Allende during the three years in office sought to implement his initial electoral promises:

> The main lines of emphasis of the Popular Government's Foreign Policy are: the assertion of full political and economic autonomy for Chile, the establishment of diplomatic relations with all countries, irrespective of their ideological and political position, on the basis of respect for self-determination and in the interests of the Chilean people. Ties of friendship and solidarity will unite Chile with dependent or colonized countries, especially those who are fighting for their liberation and independence; the promotion of strong inter-American and anti-imperialist sentiments based on foreign policies which are the expression of entire nations rather than on policies formulated solely by foreign ministries. Efforts by nations to achieve or maintain self-determination will be given decided support by the new government as a basic condition for the existence of international peace and understanding. As a consequence, our policy will be one of alertness and action in defence of the principle of non-intervention and we shall resist any attempt by the imperialist nations to discriminate, pressure, invade, or blockade. We shall reinforce our relationships, trade and cultural exchanges, and friendship with socialist countries.[23]

This election rhetoric, like many of Allende's statements and policies, was based on two ideological paradigms – populism (Third World solidarity) and socialism (revolutionary solidarity) – both used to justify the principal goals of Chilean foreign policy: dissociation from the United States and national independence. Allende himself, with his Foreign Minister Almeyda, assumed direct control of a policy that gave Chile a high visibility on the international scene from 1970 to 1973.

Under the Allende government, Chile increased the number of its diplomatic missions from forth-eight to fifty-seven. It established new connections – ranging from recognition to the sending of a diplomatic representative – with Barbados, Trinidad, Cuba, Guyana, Bangladesh, the government in exile of Norodom Sihanouk, China, North Korea, North Vietnam, Libya, Nigeria, Congo, Albania, East Germany, Guinea, Madagascar, Tanzania and Czechoslovakia. This completed the normal-ization of international relations program instituted by President Frei, who had already established missions in Eastern Europe and Algeria. As Soto has remarked, Chile, whose 'network of external relations has been spread equally over the United States and Cuba; the U.S.S.R., and the People's Republic of China; the two Germanys; has encompassed Latin America, Western Europe, Eastern Europe, and part of Asia and Africa . . . has become the only Latin American nation able to display such a wealth of foreign relations . . . '[24] In practive, all these new embassies were to play but a limited role, given the personal leader-ship of Chilean foreign policy.

Personal contacts between Chilean and foreign leaders provide a better indicator of Chilean disengagement from the United States. In July 1971 Allende traveled to Argentina to meet its President – who returned his visit in October 1971 – and from 24 August to 4 September 1971 he visited Peru, Colombia and Ecuador. This first series of visits to immediate neigh-bors was aimed at the consolidation of a nationalist bloc facing the United States and Brazil. During this period of populist good fellowship Almeyda, following on the visit of the Minister of Economic Affairs to Peking in April 1971, traveled to the Soviet Union, Poland, East Germany, Czechoslovakia, Bulgaria, Romania and Yugoslavia. Later that year, Allende risked playing host to Fidel Castro. Populism then yielded for a time to revolutionary rhetoric, but only to make a strong comeback in April and May 1972 when delegations from all the world crowded into Santiago to attend the meetings of UNCTAD III. In November and December 1972, with the country in the throes of domestic crisis, Allende put on an impressive display of diversification diplomacy: brief meetings with the Peruvian and Venezuelan presidents, official visits to Cuba, Mexico and Moscow, and condemnation of multinational corporations at the General Assembly of the United Nations. During the following spring the Chilean President, in the company of Carlos Rafael Rodriguez, the Cuban Vice-Prime Minister, carried out his last foreign mission, to put the seal of approval on the installation of the Peronist leader Campora as President of Argentina. In September 1973 the domestic crisis and the coup prevented Allende from making yet another projected Third World voyage, this time to Algeria for the Conference of Non-Aligned Nations. A comparison of the diplomatic traveling abroad done by Frei and Allende indicates that the *UP* leader's essential innovation was in replacing Western Europe as a new ally by the Socialist camp.[25]

International economic relations indicate better than diplomacy how fundamental was the shift – not always premeditated – in Chile's external orientation. The Chilean priority was to reduce its dependence on United States economy, but following its own calendar. One has to wonder at the lack of judgement on the part of Allende, who having devoted half a lifetime to denouncing the evils of imperialism, somehow assumed that the United States was going to finance his domestic experiment in socialism.

Caught unawares by the progressive cut in the flow of money from Washington, the *UP* was forced to go to its neighbors and the socialist camp for alternative sources of funds and credits to finance its economic restructuring. Too engrossed in its populist and socialist projects and its Third World activism, Chile had neglected the markets of Western Europe which could have partially compensated for the degeneration of economic relations with the United States. The aid from the socialist camp was erratic. China increased its purchases of copper, concluded a maritime agreement, and granted tied loans to the approximate value of $72 million. This credit was not in fact turned to account, since China's imports from Chile remained non-existent while Chinese sales to Chile grew only from nil to $300,000 in 1971, $23·1 million in 1972, and back to an insignificant sum ($400,000) in 1973. Numerous economic agreements were signed with the Soviet Union and Eastern Europe, including Yugoslavia and Romania; loans from these countries were devoted chiefly to the mining and industrial sectors. According to the United Nations statistics, promised Soviet bloc aid (though not always forthcoming) which had amounted to some $47 million in the sixteen preceding years, climbed to $155 million in 1971, $405 million in 1972, and then fell to $21 million in 1973. This erratic socialist aid contributed neither to the development of heavy industry, nor to a resolution of the consumer tie-ups and shortages created by the slump in the domestic economy and the curtailment of American imports.

Imports for general consumption came now mainly from Latin America. Cuba, in its role of symbolic partner-in-chief, set up air links with Chile, made that country a gift of 40,000 tons of sugar, and proceeded to increase its sales to Chile (which in 1970 had stood at $3,000!) to $13·1 million in 1971, $9·9 million in 1972, and after Allende's visit to Havana and the signing of a trade agreement, to $34·9 million in 1973. Mexico, in 1972, made credits available to the sum of $72 million, but no trade exchanges took place either in 1972 or in 1973. Argentina, on the other hand, advanced a series of credits for consumer goods in 1971 and 1973 which pushed its share of the Chilean import market from 10 percent to 15 percent, while Chilean exports to this neighbor remained at a standstill. Although most of these changes appeared to implement Allende's economic diversification policies, the gains were inadequate to meet Chilean needs. After three years of improvising policies for foreign trade and economic agreements in order to replace the American presence, Chile developed only two insufficient poles of diversification – Latin America and the socialist bloc.[26]

Extending the ambassadorial network and undertaking the set of economic agreements signed with Latin America and the socialist camp represent the only concrete, if limited, achievements of the Allende government's diversification policies. The United Nations Treaty Series record only three agreements between Chile and the Western countries – Denmark and the United States – since 1970. A comparison of the list of treaties and agreements made by the Allende government with the equivalent record of the preceding Frei government shows a drop in the number of formal agreements signed by Chile from 1970 (see Table 7.1).

Table 7.1 *Treaties and Agreements Signed by Chile*

Signatory with Chile	1964–70 (Frei's administration)					1970–3 (Allende's administration)				
	Economic	Cultural	Misc.	Military	Total	Economic	Cultural	Misc.	Military	Total
Multilateral	1	2	1	1	5	3	—	—	—	3
World Bank	5	—	—	—	5	—	—	—	—	—
Inter-American Development Bank	3	—	1	—	4	—	—	—	—	—
Israel	—	1	—	—	1	—	—	—	—	—
Italy	2	—	—	—	2	—	—	—	—	—
Japan	1	—	1	—	2	—	—	—	—	—
Great Britain	1	2	—	—	3	—	—	—	—	—
USA	3	—	1	—	4	1	—	—	1	2
Argentina	2	—	—	—	2	—	—	—	—	—
Brazil	—	1	—	—	1	—	—	—	—	—
Denmark	1	1	—	—	2	1	—	—	—	1
Germany	2	2	—	—	4	—	—	—	—	—
					35					6

Sources: Peter Rohn, *World Treaty Index*; United Nations *Treaty Series*.

The populist nature of the Allende government led to a preference for symbolic acts over practical results.

Chilean activity in international organizations tended to follow the policy lines developed by the preceding Christian Democratic government, but with a tougher style, and with no reluctance to oppose American positions. In the OAS, Chile was a member of the informal nationalist coalition of Peru, Venezuela, Colombia, Mexico and Argentina. These nations supported Panama unreservedly on the Canal question, demanded the lifting of the economic boycott of Cuba and called for radical reform of the statutes of the OAS, as well as in the structure of the Inter-American Development Bank.[27] In most international bodies, Chile under Allende maintained a position closer to Mexico than to that of Castro, a claim which is borne out by Allende's speech to the UNCTAD III in Santiago, April 1971:

> We cannot, with a wave of the hand, change the way the world is, with all its injustices to the underdeveloped countries. All we can do to remedy the situation is to try to reduce the negative effects of the present state of affairs and to establish the foundations for a sound world economy. The present international situation is favourable for undertaking the transformation of the economic order. . . . We have an agreement among the socialist powers. Could there not be an agreement between the former colonial and imperialist nations on the one hand and the dependent countries on the other? . . . Only the Third World with its enormous requirements can provide a fresh economic frontier for the developed nations. Only this new frontier can surpass a war economy in satisfying the productive capacity of the giant industrial conglomerates, and in creating enough jobs for the whole labour force . . .[28]

Chile collided head-on, on all sides and at every turn, with the position held by the United States in all international bodies. Divergent positions ranged from the recognition of China to the problem of the multinationals. Beyond the humanist speeches of Allende, the Nixon–Kissinger team saw in Chile a hostile rather than a non-aligned nation, perhaps even a new Soviet satellite on the Cuban model.[29]

The more militant positions fostered by Chile's representatives are chronicled in their United Nations speeches. From the position of an observer under Frei, Chile became an active member of the UN group of non-aligned nations, and an active participant in attacking the multi-nationals and calling for 200 mile maritime limits. Table 7.2 presents a summary of the evolution of the voting patterns of Chile and the United States in the General Assembly. The data highlight the growing Chilean-United States divergence at the formal diplomatic level.

Analysis of the main areas of divergence (the No votes) shows that in 1966 Chile differed from the United States only by voting to condemn Great Britain on the Oman question; in 1972 the differences concern all major international issues, including maritime rights, Portuguese colonialism, the Palestine question and apartheid. The analysis points not so much to a fundamental change between the positions taken by Frei and by

Table 7.2   *Recorded Votes of Chile and the*
United States at the General Assembly of the
United Nations

	1966			1972		
	Yes	No	Abs.	Yes	No	Abs.
Chile	18	1	—	27	1	1
United States	8	2	8	7	8	14

Source: United Nations Yearbooks, 1966–72.

Allende at the United Nations, as to an increase in the areas of friction between the United States and the Latin American group in the face of Kissinger's conduct of North American foreign policy.

There was not sufficient time for the government of Chile to complete its restructuring of externally directed actions. Nevertheless, the three years of diplomatic activity by the *UP* government effectively demonstrate a complete redefinition of international links. The pattern of relations and transactions changed significantly between the Frei era and the end of Allende's *UP* government in 1973.

Regionally, the change was perhaps less dramatic. Chile continued the main lines established in the policies of the Frei government. 'Decision 24', which authorized the screening of foreign investments and the membership of Chile in the Andean Pact, was ratified. But a double structural contradiction was to render this symbolic step impracticable and partly Utopian. An economic policy aimed at national self-sufficiency and centralization is hardly compatible with a policy that favors complementary national economies and integration of countries of differing social systems. In 1972 Chilean authorities were obliged to invoke the pact's safeguard clause concerning the protection of the domestic economy by limiting or stopping imports from other Andean countries. Having endeavored to ensure the continuity of cordial political relations with the nations of the Andean Pact, Chile's economic approach to its Andean vocation became one of progressive neglect.[30]

Continentally, Chile under Frei had maintained a policy of balanced neutrality between the American sub-empires (Brazil, Argentina and Mexico), effecting this by its alliance with the United States and regional integration. Allende chose to depart from this tradition in order to promote closer relations with Mexico and Argentina, a step which was bound to offend Brazil. Finally, Allende's relations with Cuba obviously were a source of considerable irritation to the United States and some other Latin American countries. In the short term the turn toward Argentina helped Chile, while the association with Cuba neutralized the extreme left in Chile.[31]

Just as the *UP* was unable to maintain a balance between its regional interests and its continental activity, it also oscillated between a Third World and a pro-socialist policy. Allende, who without any show of actual hostility tended to favor European over American interests domestically, scarcely profited from the contacts established between Western Europe and Chile by Frei. Neither the existence of several Social Democratic governments in Europe nor the general sympathy on that continent toward a democratic Chile would be put to advantage by his government. The Soviet Union made promises which far outstripped its actual performance: the hundreds of millions of dollars of its tied aid were not to have immediate economic effects and were not accompanied by sufficient advances in hard cash to enable Chile to surmount the crisis in its domestic economy. On the other hand, Soviet promises, Allende's trips to Cuba and Moscow, and the presence of a strong pro-Soviet communist party in the Chilean government alienated the government of China, whose offer of some tens of millions of dollars on generous terms was not used. To sum up, real diversification in Chilean diplomacy yielded only embryonic benefits which could not fill the vacuum created by the withdrawal of American credits.

The American Response

The attempt to restructure foreign policy was thus abortive in terms of cost-benefit analysis. The enterprise, although successful in the formal terms of establishing a diversified pattern of contacts and transactions, aborted because it was insufficient to respond to Chilean domestic financial needs and because the United States could not allow the policy to succeed. The Department of State under Kissinger had abandoned all imagination in its Latin American policy in favor of 'benign neglect', and of 'low profile'. But Allende's pro-Cuban and pro-Soviet orientation – added to the fear that other Latin American and even Western European countries might become contaminated by the Chilean example – angered Washington. Moreover, Chile's nationalization of the mining sector without adequate compensation (as defined by the nationalized companies) had mobilized a number of economic pressure groups, led by Kennecott and ITT, as well as sectors inside the government (the Department of Commerce) which called for retaliation. We may briefly summarize the main lines of hostile actions undertaken by the American government to pressure Chile financially, and to destabilize Allende's regime. The facts substantiate to some extent the hypothesis put forward by Petras of a central conspiracy against Chile.[32]

First, a certain number of operations were carried on by the CIA. As early as 1964 the United States, with a view to opposing Allende's candidacy, helped finance the Christian Democratic party in its victorious electoral campaign which was to bring Frei to power. The financial intervention occurred again in the 1970 presidential elections. It has likewise been established that during the Allende period the CIA channeled funds both to Chilean business associations and trade unions, as well as to some news media. These CIA operations must not make one forget about discrete diplomatic pressures on Allende, covert actions undertaken by ITT and the permanent contacts between the American military mission and the Chilean army.[33]

The failure to provide 'adequate compensation' for the nationalization of the properties of Kennecott was to provide the United States with the legal grounds to justify its measures of public economic retaliation against Chile. The United States authorities reacted strongly to the statement of the General Comptroller of Chile, declaring that since the excessive profits of the companies exceeded the book value of the mines, it followed that compensation was not called for. In October 1971 Secretary of State Rogers declared himself 'deeply disappointed and disturbed' by the Chilean decision. Three months later President Nixon threatened to cancel all loans and aid to Chile. But American assistance had already begun to decline. American and multilateral aid which amounted to $90·9 million in 1970 dropped to $19·8 million in 1971, to $10·6 million in 1972 and to $11·6 million in 1973. During the same period, the private banking sector reduced its lines of credit available to Chilean importers from $220 million to $20 million. This followed the reduction, already noted, of the trade between both countries. Finally, Kennecott arranged to have the bank accounts belonging to Chilean government agencies in the United States frozen. It also made several unsuccessful attempts to have legal embargoes on Chilean copper deliveries to Europe.[34]

It is, nevertheless, an exaggeration to state, as Allende did, that Chile was the victim of an 'invisible blockade', of a 'quiet Vietnam'. Partial accommodations were reached. Despite the confrontation between Chile, ITT and Kennecott, and despite the nationalization of the banking sector, twenty-eight private American banks agreed to refinance $160 million of private Chilean debts to the United States. The Chilean government was also able to arrange the refinancing, over an eight-year period, of 70 percent of its international debts by the Paris Club, of which the United States was a member. However, in 1973 negotiations on refinancing the portion of the national debt due that year stalled over the American insistence on compensation of the American copper companies. Finally, as already noted, American aid to the Chilean army increased.[35]

Thus, the United States continued to dangle both the carrot and the stick in the face of conflicting domestic demands and bureaucratic politics. The Pentagon obtained aid for its military allies in Chile, the State Department tried to negotiate copper indemnities, the 'Committee of Forty' provided covert assistance for the Chilean opposition to Allende, the Department of Commerce sought the economic blockade of Chile, and the Senate criticized the covert actions of the Executive. But how successful were those apparently contradictory policies in bringing about the downfall of the Allende regime? How vulnerable was Chile to American pressures?

What happened in Chile is in fact more complex and more simple than most writers maintain. As long as popular mobilization behind Allende and the *UP* was on the ascendent, the various external interventions merely reinforced Allende's position with additional fuel for his propaganda of denouncing the external enemy. But as soon as the contradictions in Allende's policies developed, the external pressures and interventions exacerbated the crisis which had developed autonomously within Chile.[36]

The American interventions particularly aggravated the consequences of the ill-conceived economic policies of Allende's advisers. They had chosen a neo-Keynesian short-term economic model of stimulating public and private consumption in order to aggregate and mobilize different social 'clienteles'. This policy led to a continuous rise in imports of equipment, replacement parts and consumer goods during a phase of decline in the world price of copper. The growth of imports led to a cumulative deficit in the balance of payments. The drastic reduction in credits from the United States, the Inter-American Development Bank and the World Bank aggravated the situation. Thus, the Chilean balance of payments dropped from a $398 million surplus in 1970 to a deficit of $98 million in 1973. International currency reserves fell from a positive balance of $348 million in 1970 to a negative balance of $437 million three years later. Tied credits from the socialist bloc and from Argentina and Mexico could only partially compensate for the simultaneous drop in American credit, the rise in consumption and the fall of the price of copper. Thus the structural victory to control the copper sector clashed with the short-term needs of the Chilean economy.[37]

The international economic difficulties induced a continuous – and sharp – currency devaluation, which in turn caused domestic inflation to soar even higher. Rising prices accentuated social unrest and helped the opposition to mobilize against Allende and his party. That mobilization was aided at the organizational level by clandestine payments from the CIA. In the context of social turmoil, economic inflation and political paralysis between Allende and his opponents, the army – permanently in touch with the American military mission – was the only institution which still retained internal cohesion and the capacity for national action. As early as 1972, at the request of both factions, it reluctantly allowed itself to be progressively drawn into the Executive until it took over the machinery of the state in 1973.[38]

Explanations

Allende's policies referred consistently to 'national', 'popular' and 'socialist' perspectives. Those ideological values stemmed from a long-established political culture in Chile. Nationalist values were prominent during the nineteenth and twentieth centuries, with Spain, England and finally the United States as popular external enemies. An anti-establishment creed developed in association with nationalism: Chile was an extraordinarily rich, endowed country ('como Chile no hay', 'si es chileno es bueno') that underwent poverty ('underdevelopment') because it was exploited by the external enemy with the complicity of the local elites, the 'oligarquia'. Hence, the underdevelopment of Chile resulted from its external subordination and its bad government. The 'people' were deprived of their share of the potential riches of Chile by the foreign and oligarchic interests. This 'national-populist' paradigm is related to the tragic fate of the nationalist President Balmaceda, who committed suicide in 1891 after he lost a civil war to the local establishment associated with British interests. It is also related to the populist leader Arturo Alessandri, expelled from the presidency in 1924 by the army.[39]

The national-populist paradigm spread progressively from the liberal sectors to the communist and socialist parties. Those organizations grew rapidly in the last fifty years, thanks to the unionization of the mining sector, the growth of urbanization and the weak but real development of industrialization. Thus, Leninist ideas of state ownership were mixed with nationalism and populism. The 'populist-Leninist' paradigm had its own historical – and heroic – reference in the ill-fated 'Republica Socialista de Chile' that existed for two weeks in 1932. Another historical symbol was the electoral victory of the 'Frente Popular' in 1938, which brought together the Radical Party (a center-left populist organization of the middle class) and the leftist parties under the presidency of Pedro Aguirre-Cerda who died before the end of his mandate. The close relations of the Chilean communist party with the Soviet Union, the real growth of American influence over the Chilean economy and the beginning of the cold war gave the United States the role of the primary opponent in the populist ideology. This role was accentuated by the 'martyrdom' of the communist militants, whose party was outlawed from 1947 to 1958. The communist party ban was a concession to the spirit of the cold war by a Chilean government pressured by the United States.[40]

The Cuban-American confrontation was the real catalyst for reviving national-populist ideology among the Chilean intelligentsia. The favorable reaction of the Chilean left and various non-communist intellectuals to the Cuban revolution was so strong that even the conservative government of President Alessandri refused to participate initially in the OAS boycott against Castro. The 1960s saw an explosion of articles, pamphlets and books proclaiming solidarity with Cuba and calling for struggle against 'United States imperialism' and 'Chilean dependence'. This ideological propaganda explains the decline of the traditional elites' influence and the necessity for moderate leaders to speak strongly in favor of national development, and against economic dependence and subordination. During the 1964 presidential campaign the two major candidates, Allende and Frei, both presented programmes of national development and struggle against dependence. Allende placed emphasis on socialism and solidarity with Cuba. Frei spoke of a 'third way' opposed to capitalism and Marxism. Frei's electoral victory reduced the effectiveness of socialist propaganda for two years, but by 1967 its appeal grew in strength as a growing number of Chileans began to be dissatisfied with Frei's policies. The Christian Democrats' policies gave rise to social aspirations and social movements among poor peasants, slum-dwellers, students, workers and even the military. The state of the economy, the continuing dependence on the world copper market, the strength of the right-wing sector inside the Christian Democratic Party were the main factors explaining the slow-down of Frei's reform policies. A communist–conservative unholy alliance in Congress also prevented the passage of important social reform legislation. The failure of the 'third way' to overcome dependence and underdevelopment, the ambiguous results of the reforms in the short term and the rise of social expectations provided good opportunities for the Chilean left.

The parties of the left denounced the insufficient speed of reforms, the limitations of the 'Chileanization' of copper, the growth of the external public debt, the continuing dependence of the economy as a whole and the multiplicity of financial, cultural and diplomatic contacts between Frei and the United States.[41]

Anti-government feelings, and pro-Cuban attitudes and social movements, were easily co-opted between 1968 and 1970 by the traditional parties of the center-left and left, the pillars of the Popular Unity. That term designated a broad and loose coalition of six parties recruiting among various strata of the petit bourgeoisie, the working class and the slum-dwellers. Ideologically, this alliance fused national-populist style and themes with socialist doctrine and Castroist apologetics. Populism was above all an emotional call to the masses promising them a better style of living; its socialism was a doctrinaire project to build a strong state-directed economy; its Castroism was a heroic call to fight against American imperialism. The two main partners of the coalition, the Socialist and Communist parties, accentuated the anti-American tendency of the Popular Unity. The fight against imperialism would return to Chile the control of its own resources – mainly the copper mines. Those resources would allow Chile to build at once a strong internal market and to raise the standard of living of the masses.

The various themes, including emphasis on the 'external enemy', paid dividends, providing Allende with a plurality of votes and a constitutional confirmation by Congress. But Allende was from the beginning a prisoner of his success, of his denunciation of Frei's ties with the United States, of his political coalition and of his own populist and rhetorical style. This demagogic style was needed to hold together a broad and permanently conflicting coalition, and to contain the rise of radical-left groups accusing Allende of 'reformism' and of 'weakness' in the anti-capitalist and anti-imperialist struggle.[42]

The highly visible Popular Unity government immediately launched its programme of constructing state socialism and restructuring foreign policy. Administrative contradictions were prominent in the government. The new staff were composed simultaneously of leftovers from the former populist governments and the young ideologues of the ruling parties. Foreign policy was managed more successfully than internal policy, thanks to the permanent supervision assumed by Foreign Minister Almeyda from November 1970 to September 1973 with a brief replacement in June and July 1973 by Orlando Letelier. Allende assumed the overall leadership and used his 'caudillo' talents to assure impressive publicity for a middle-sized power. Both Allende and Almeyda were old populist and Marxist strugglers. Even if they chose to follow a 'legal way' to socialism, their main publicly stated goal was always to create a Chilean 'popular democracy' and to emulate the Cuban experience. Both were strong admirers and close friends of Castro. Allende had been since 1967 the president of the Chilean branch of the revolutionary organization known as OLAS founded in Havana. Finally, Allende had to demonstrate his loyalty to anti-imperialist beliefs in order to avoid challenges inside and outside his government by a growing number of ultra-leftists who did not believe in his peaceful way and were advocating an immediate rupture with 'imperialism'.[43]

Allende and his team viewed the world in a parochial, simplistic perspective. For the Chilean left, Gulliver had been challenged effectively by Vietnam, and had to face growing Soviet nuclear power, and thus could no longer intervene with impunity against small states. In his own hemisphere, Gulliver had failed against Cuba and reacted weakly against the populist-military governments of Bolivia and Peru. The relative weakness of the United States, the power of the Soviet bloc and the international rise of the Third World provided an incorrect sense of security to the Chilean government between 1970 and 1973. The initial successes of his policies made Allende imprudent in challenging the United States. The case of copper is a good example of over-confident action in Allende's electoral campaign; the copper question was the concrete point of reference that sustained the nationalist, anti-American ideology. It provided so much legitimacy to the government when it proposed to confiscate American holdings in the mining sector that even the conservative Chilean senators felt obliged to support the expropriation. After the near-unanimous vote in the Chilean Congress, several legal institutions, not known for their leftist sympathies, ruled that Chile did not owe any compensation to the United States. His victories over Kennecott paradoxically placed Allende in a difficult situation: the legal decrees and rulings made it extremely difficult, if not impossible, for Chile to negotiate some form of compensation for Kennecott. So Allende was caught in a trap. The American government could now add to its covert actions an official embargo on public credits. The Soviet Union and its satellites did not or could not replace those credits. Harassed by internal difficulties, Allende was unable to invent new international tactics and went on till the end with symbolic victories.[44]

To summarize, explanations for the attempts to restructure Chilean foreign policies during the Allende period are to be found in a variety of environments, personalities and conditions. The Chilean economy faced a situation of structural dependence and economic vulnerability, particularly to the American-owned copper companies, whose decisions had significant implications for Chile's economic fortunes. With a long history of having some prominent external enemy, it was not unexpected that economic nationalism and feelings of exploitation found deep roots in Chilean society. Virtually all political parties sought to gain increased control over the Chilean economy, primarily by advocating the nationalization of the copper industries. The unpopularity of concentrating Chile's external relations on the United States was demonstrated long before Allende became President. Frei's government made systematic attempts to create balancing relations with Western European countries, but it did not take steps, beyond Chileanization of the copper industries, to reduce American penetration of the country's economy and culture.

Allende's attempts to create a largely state-run economy and to disengage from the United States represented the implementation of designs and projects Allende had long promoted in his political career. His political sympathies lay clearly with Castro-type socialism and populism; hence his foreign policy restructuring activities were predictable from his numerous campaign pledges. He found support for his actions among a variety of social and party groupings; in no way can he be accused of conducting policy 'from the top'. His restructuring activities brought few tangible results, but the political forces supporting Allende were no doubt more impressed with the symbolic meanings attached to restructuring than with financial rewards. Allende might have moved more slowly and more pragmatically had he not faced a radical-left which constantly demanded provocative anti-American actions and which was willing to institute its version of socialism at any price. Allende was a genuinely popular figure whose leadership was a necessary, if not sufficient, condition for foreign policy restructuring. His actions, although as dramatic as Burma's in the 1960s, contrast with the authoritarian manner in which Ne Win put his country into isolation. Allende's popular support lay not only within the *Unidad Popular* coalition, but also in important segments of the population which held strong anti-American attitudes, and whose political sympathies were directed more toward Castroism than European Christian Democracy. But that support began to erode as contradictory economic policies brought hyper-inflation and the seeming destruction of the petit bourgeoisie. Allende placed himself in a no-win situation. A more pragmatic approach to disengagement from the United States would probably have avoided American retaliatory measures and hence would have brought greater economic stability; but such a course of action would have prompted the ultra-left to organize a genuine socialist revolution without Allende. Only the military remained to provide strong opposition to the main directions of Allende's domestic and external policies. But the Chilean military had a tradition of abstaining from political participation and only reluctantly became involved in the political turmoil of 1973. Thus, while the military may not have actively supported Allende's efforts at external diversification and increasing contacts with the socialist states, neither did it oppose him actively. Nor is there evidence that various echelons of the bureaucracy acted to sabotage the *UP*'s foreign policy directions. Chile's foreign policy restructuring during the early 1970s was thus a *national* undertaking, one which coincided with the attitudes and sympathies of important segments of the population. The case stands in marked contrast to similar efforts by Bhutan, Burma and Tanzania, all of whose fundamental changes were instigated 'from the top'.

On paper, restructuring foreign policy may be a feasible option for many countries. But Allende forgot that in a democracy you need to be in control of your 'internal front'. You cannot challenge a great power in a harsh international environment, if you fail to control your domestic sources of support. If your fellow countrymen become deeply divided, some of them will sooner or later be co-opted by the external power whose hegemony you wish to terminate. Disengagement requires *full* public support.

Even if you believe Gulliver is a 'paper tiger', you must adopt prudent tactics to prevent his retaliation. Allende did not find a heavyweight partner on the international scene, *willing* to give active and concrete support to the disengagement effort. Symbolic requests were answered with symbolic rewards! Disruption of dependence ties left Chile economically broken, with only formal and symbolic victories. Nevertheless, Allende earned a theoretical victory: in the Chilean case, the imperial military-industrial complex was proven to exist in reality and not only in radical economic textbooks.

Notes: Chapter 7

1 Our thanks to F. Cormier, G. Laforest and G. Larochelle who helped to collect and scrutinize the available data, and to K. J. Holsti who revised and edited the manuscript.
2 On Chilean historical background, see, for example, Francisco Encina, *Resumen de la historia de Chile*: Redacción y apéndices de Luis Castedo (Santiago: Zig-Zag, 1954); Jaime Eyzaguirre, *Historia de Chile* (Santiago: Zig-Zag, 1973); Enzo Faletto and Eduardo Ruiz, *Génesis histórica del proceso político Chileno* (Santiago: Quimantú, 1972); Luis Galdames, *A History of Chile* (New York: Robertson, Russel & Russel, 1964); Frederick Gil, *The Political System of Chile* (Boston, Mass.: Houghton Mifflin, 1966); Julio César Jobet, *Ensayo crítico del desarrollo económico-social de Chile* (Santiago: Universitaria, 1955).
3 Robert Burr, *By Reason or Force: Chile and the Balancing of Power in South America 1830–1905* (Berkeley: University of California Press, 1974), p. 263.
4 On the Chilean expansionist policies, see Daniel Martner, *Historia de Chile* (Santiago: Graficos Barcelo, 1929); Francisco Encina, *Nuestra inferioridad económica* (Santiago: Universitaria, 1972); Markos Mamalakis, *The Growth and Structure of the Chilean Economy, from Independence to Allende* (New Haven, Conn.: Yale University Press, 1976).
5 On the illustration of the new pattern of relationship between the United States and Chile, see Frederick Pike, *Chile and the United States 1880–1962: The Emergence of Chile's Social Crisis and the Challenge to United States Diplomacy* (Notre Dame, Ind.: University of Notre Dame Press, 1963); Arthur Whitaker, *The United States and the Southern Cone: Argentina, Chile, and Uruguay* (Cambridge, Mass.: Harvard University Press, 1976); Frederick Pike, 'Corporatism and Latin American–United States Relations', *Review of Politics*, 36 (January 1974), pp. 132–70.
6 On Chile's role in World War II, see Claude Bowers, *Misión en Chile 1939–1953* (Santiago: Editorial del Pacífico, 1957); Michael Francis, *The Limits of Hegemony: United States Relations with Argentine and Chile during World War II* (Notre Dame, Ind.: University of Notre Dame Press, 1977).
7 Miles Wolpin, *Cuban Foreign Policy and Chilean Politics* (Lexington, Mass.: Lexington Books, 1972), pp. 89–96; Alain Joxe, *Las Fuerzas Armadas en el sistema político Chileno* (Santiago: Universitaria, 1970), pp. 99–110; Albert Michaels, 'The alliance for progress and Chile's "Revolution in Liberty" 1964–1970', *Journal of Interamerican Studies and World Affairs*, 18, 1 (February 1976), pp. 74–100.
8 James Petras and Morris Morley, *The United States and Chile: Imperialism and the Overthrow of the Allende Government* (New York: Monthly Review Press, 1975), pp. 8–9.
9 Theodore Moran, *Multinational Corporations and the Politics of Dependency: Copper in Chile* (Princeton, NJ: Princeton University Press, 1974), p. 6.
10 ibid., pp. 89–90.
11 Wolpin, *Cuban Foreign Policy and Chilean Politics*, pp. 73–86; José Rodriguez Elizondo, 'El plan Camelot', *Revista de la Universidad Técnica del Estado*, 9 (July–August 1972), pp. 49–86.
12 Armand Mattelart and Michèle Mattelart, 'Rupturas y continuidad en la communicación, *Cuadernos de la Realidad Nacional*, 12 (April 1972), pp. 100–143; A. Mattelart, *L'Idéologie de la domination dans une société dépendante* (Paris: Antropos, 1970), pp. 26, 129; Enrique Lihn, Hernán Valdés *et al.*, *La cultura en la vía Chilena al socialismo* (Santiago: Universitaria, 1971), pp. 107–11.
13 On the impact of the industrial sector on the GNP, see Max Nolff, 'Industria manufacturera', in *Geografía Económica de Chile*, edited by the Corporación de Fomento de la Produccion (CORFO) (Santiago: Talleres de la Ed. Universitaria, 1967), pp. 519–22; Oficina de Planificación Nacional (ODEPLAN), *Antecedentes sobre el desarrollo Chileno 1960–1970* (Santiago: ODEPLAN, 1971), pp. 161–71; The Economist, *The World in*

Figures (London: 1970), p. 119; Le Nouvel Observateur, *ATLASCO* (Paris, 1978), p. 61.

14 On the Christian Democratic regime and the limits of internal growth and local autonomy in a dependence framework, see Jacques Zylberberg, 'Notes sur quelques contradictions du développement national et régional Chilien 1965–1970', *Civilisations*, 21 (1971), pp. 406–24; Zylberberg, 'Intégration et désintegration de l'Amérique Latine: le Chili et le Pacte Andin 1966–1976', *Civilisations*, 26 (1976), pp. 368–86; Oscar Muñoz, 'Industrialización y subdesarrollo', *Cuadernos de la Realidad Nacional*, 12 (April 1972), pp. 26–48; Isidro Parra-Peña, 'Comparación de tres procesos globales de política económica, el Brasil, Chile y Colombia', *Trimestre Económico*, 38 (January–May 1970), pp. 101–32; Osvaldo Sunkel, 'Cambios estructurales y planificación en Chile 1938–1969', *Cuadernos de la Realidad Nacional*, 4 (June 1970), pp. 31–50; Paul Sigmund, *The Overthrow of Allende and the Politics of Chile 1964–1970* (Pittsburgh: University of Pittsburgh Press, 1977), pp. 23–76; Eduardo Frei, 'The accomplishments of the Christian Democratic government', in Paul Sigmund (ed.), *Models of Political Change in Latin America* (Toronto: Burns & McEachen, 1972), pp. 330–8.

15 Moran, *Multinational Corporations and the Politics of Dependency*, pp. 119–38.

16 On Christian Democratic foreign policy conceptions, see Manfred Wilhelmy, 'Christian Democratic ideology in interamerican politics: the case of Chile 1964–1970', in M. Blachman and R. Hellman (eds), *Terms of Conflict: Ideology in Latin American Politics* (Philadelphia, Pa: Institute for the Study of Human Issues, 1977); Manfred Wilhelmy, *Chilean Foreign Policy: The Frei Government 1964–1970*, Ph.D. dissertation (Princeton, NJ: Princeton University, 1973).

17 On the background of the Popular Unity programme, see Jacques Zylberberg, 'Rationalité et irrationalité politique: les contradictions de l'Unité Populaire Chilienne', *Res Publica*, 16 (1974), pp. 63–88; F. Debuyst and J. Garcés, 'La opción Chilena de 1970: análisis de los tres programas electorales', *Revista Latinoamericana de Ciencia Política*, 2 (August 1971), pp. 279–369; N. J. Chinchilla and W. Bollinger, 'Theoretical issues of the Chilean experience', *Latin American Perspectives* (Summer 1974), pp. 3–18; M. A. Ganero, 'Elements d'analyse et d'étude du processus politique Chilien 1970–1973', *Revista Mexicana de Sociología*, 36 (July–August 1974), pp. 513–45.

18 J. Ann Zammit (ed.), *The Chilean Road to Socialism* (Sussex: Institute of Development Studies, University of Sussex, 1973), pp. 255–6; Clodomiro Almeyda-Medina, 'The foreign policy of the Unidad Popular government', in Federico Gil, Ricardo Lagos and H. Landsberger (eds), *Chile at the Turning Point: Lessons of the Socialist Years 1970–1973* (Philadelphia, Pa: Institute for the Study of Human Issues, 1979).

19 On the ownership question of the means of production, see Oscar Garreton, 'Some preliminary facts about the management and organization of the industrial sector', in Zammit (ed.), *The Chilean Road to Socialism*, pp. 63–8; Julio Lopez, 'Sobre la construcción de la Nueva Economía', *Cuadernos de la Realidad Nacional*, 13 (July 1972), pp. 39–53; José-Antonio Viera-Gallo *et al.*, 'Materiales para el estudio del area de propiedad social', *Cuadernos de la Realidad Nacional*, 11 (January 1972), pp. 193–274; James Petras, 'Nationalization, socio-economic change and popular participation', in Arturo Valenzuela and J. Samuel Valenzuela (eds), *Chile: Politics and Society* (New Brunswick, NJ: Transaction Books, 1976), pp. 172–200.

20 Zammit (ed.), *The Chilean Road to Socialism*, p. 168; United Nations, *Yearbook of International Trade Statistics* (New York: United Nations, 1969–1973).

21 On cultural and educational problems, see Popular Unity Programme, in Zammit (ed.), *The Chilean Road to Socialism*, p. 272; Carlos Ossa, 'Pobreza, industria cultural y populismo', in Lihn, Valdés *et al.*, *La cultura en la vía Chilena al socialismo*, pp. 105–20; Hernán Valdés, '¿Prudencia o desorientacion para formular las bases de una política cultural?', *Cuadernos de la Realidad Nacional*, 8 (June 1971), pp. 254–65; Armand Mattelart, '¿Hacia una cultura de la movilización cotidiana?', *Cuadernos de la Realidad Nacional*, 10 (December 1971), pp. 49–97.

22 Petras and Morley, *The United States and Chile*, pp. 166–7; United States, Library of Congress, *Chile: A Chronology. Chile Since the Election of Salvador Allende* (Washington, DC: Library of Congress, 1973), p. 376.

23 On the external restructuring process, see Popular Unity Programme, 'The Popular government's foreign policy', in Zammit (ed.), *The Chilean Road to Socialism*, pp. 275–7; Edy Kaufman, 'La política exterior de la Unidad Popular Chilena', *Foro Internacional*, 17

(October–December 1976), pp. 244–74; Carlos Fortin, 'Principled pragmatism in the face of external pressure: the foreign policy of the Allende government', in Ronald G. Hilton and H. Jon Rosenbaum (eds), *Latin-America: The Search for a New International Role* (Beverly Hills, Calif.: Sage Center for Interamerican Relations, 1975), pp. 217–45; Tomas MacHale, 'The Chilean approach to international relations under the government of the Popular Unity', in Francisco Orrego-Vicuña (ed.), *Chile: A Balanced View* (Santiago: Gabriela Mistral, 1975), pp. 217–45; J. C. Ogelbst, 'Le Chili sous Allende: relations extérieures et problèmes intérieurs', *Europa-Archiv*, 27 (1972), pp. 581–8; Federico Gil, 'Socialist Chile and the United States', *Inter-American Economic Affairs* (Autumn 1973), pp. 538–56; Alberto Sepúlveda, 'La nueva política exterior de Chile', *Revista de Política Internacional*, 121 (March–June 1972), pp. 71–97; C. Almeyda-Medina, 'The foreign policy of the Unidad Popular government', in Gil, Lagos and Landsberger (eds), *Chile at the Turning Point: Lessons of the Socialist Years 1970–1973*; Leopoldo González Aguayo, 'La política exterior de la Izquierda chilena', *Revista Mexicana de Ciencias Políticas y Sociales*, 18 (October–December 1972), pp. 131–62.

24 Antonio Soto, 'Balance de la política exterior', *Mensaje*, 265 (December 1977), p. 690; *Keesing's Contemporary Archives* (1971–2), pp. 24871, 24620, 25417, 24388, 24873; Almeyda-Medina, 'The foreign policy of the Unidad Popular government', in Gil, Lagos and Landsberger (eds), *Chile at the Turning Point: Lessons of the Socialist Years 1970–1973*, pp. 94–8.

25 *Keesing's Contemporary Archives* (1971–2), p. 24652; 1973, p. 25825(A); *Facts on File* (1973), p. 36 E 3; *The Statesman's Yearbook* (London: Macmillan, 1970), p. 803; (1972), p. 811; (1973), p. 813.

26 On international economic relations, see United Nations, *Yearbook of International Trade*, 1970–4; Library of Congress, *Chile: A Chronology*, p. 376; Paul Sigmund, 'The invisible blockade and the overthrow of Allende', in Orrego-Vicuña (ed.), *Chile: A Balanced View*, p. 119; *Facts on File* (1971), p. 137 F 3; 617 F 3; 1020 E 2; (1972), p. 1028; (1973), p. 89 A 1.

27 Almeyda-Medina, 'The foreign policy of the Unidad Popular government', in Gil, Lagos and Landsberger (eds), *Chile at the Turning Point: Lessons of the Socialist Years 1970–1973*, pp. 91–2.

28 Jacques Zylberberg, 'De la C.N.U.C.E.D. No. 1 à la C.N.U.C.E.D. No. 3, *Civilisations*, 22 (1972), p. 459.

29 ibid, p. 459; Library of Congress, *Chile: A Chronology*, p. 378; William Buckley, 'United States policies in Chile under the Allende government: an interview with former ambassador Edward Korry', in Orrego-Vicuña (ed.), *Chile: A Balanced View*, p. 294.

30 Almeyda-Medina, 'The foreign policy of the Unidad Popular government', in Gil, Lagos and Landsberger (eds), *Chile at the Turning Point: Lessons of the Socialist Years 1970–1973*, pp. 88–9.

31 Jacques Zylberberg, 'Intégration et désintégration de l'Amérique Latine: le Chili et le Pacte Andin 1966–1976', *Civilisations*, 26 (1976), pp. 368–86; Manfred Wilhelmy, 'Christian Democratic ideology in interamerican politics: the case of Chile 1964–1970', in M. Blachman and R. Hellman (eds), *Terms of Conflict: Ideology in Latin American Politics* (Philadelphia, Pa: Institute for the Study of Human Issues, 1977), p. 134.

32 Petras and Morley, *The United States and Chile*, pp. 79–80.

33 Staff report of the Select Committee to Study Governmental Operations with Respect to the Intelligence Activities, *Covert Action in Chile, 1963–1973* (Washington, DC: US Government Printing Office, 1975).

34 Petras and Morley, *The United States and Chile*, pp. 96, 111; Jonathan Sanford, 'The multilateral development banks and the suspension of lending to Allende's Chile', in Orrego-Vicuña (ed.), *Chile: A Balanced View*, pp. 131–3; James Theberge. 'United States economic policy towards Chile during the Popular Unity government', in *Chile: A Balanced View*, pp. 157–9; Almeyda-Medina, 'The foreign policy of the Unidad Popular government', in Gil, Lagos and Landsberger (eds), *Chile at the Turning Point: Lessons of the Socialist Years 1970–1973*, pp. 90–91; Arturo Valenzuela, 'The breakdown of democratic regimes: Chile', in Juan José Linz and Alfred Stepan (eds), *The Breakdown of Democratic Regimes*, (Baltimore, Md: Johns Hopkins University Press, 1979), pp. 56–9.

35 Petras and Morley, *United States and Chile*, p. 167; Sigmund, 'The invisible blockade and the overthrow of Allende', in Orrego-Vicuña (ed.), *Chile: A Balanced View*, pp. 118–19.

36 Jacques Zylberberg, 'Le Chili, l'Amérique Latine et les Etats-Unis', *Etudes Inter-*

nationales, 6 (December 1975), pp. 555–62; Zylberberg, 'Rationalité et irrationalité politique: les contradictions de l'Unité Populaire Chilienne', pp. 80–1.

37 Edward Glab, 'A political and economic overview of the Popular Unity government', in Orrego-Vicuña (ed.), *Chile: A Balanced View*, pp. 183–4.

38 Zylberberg, 'Rationalité et irrationalité politique: les contradictions de l'Unité Populaire Chilienne', pp. 82–7; Manuel Garretón and Tomás Moulian, *Análisis coyuntural y proceso político: Las fases del conflicto en Chile 1970–1973* (San José: Editorial Universitaria Centro-Americana, 1978).

39 Jacques Zylberberg, 'Les limitations du développement Chilien, I: Le poids du passé', *Civilisations*, 22 (1972), pp. 198–218; Ricardo Donoso, *Las ideas políticas en Chile* (Mexico: Fondo de Cultura Económica, 1946); Frederick Nunn, 'Military rule in Chile: the revolution of September 5, 1924 and January 23, 1925', *Hispanic American Historical Review*, 47 (February 1967), pp. 1–22; Hernán Ramirez-Necochea, *Balmaceda y la contra-revolución de 1891* (Santiago: Editorial Universitaria, 1969).

40 Atilio Borón, 'Notas sobre las raíces histórico-estructurales de la movilización política en Chile', *Foro Internacional*, 16 (July–September 1975), pp. 64–121; Digna Castañeda-Fuertes, 'Algunas características de la clase obrera Chilena entre los años 1925–1970', *Casa de las Américas*, 15 (September–October 1974), pp. 106–11; Jack Ray, 'The socialist republic of Chile', *Journal of Interamerican Studies*, 6 (April 1964), pp. 203–20.

41 Jacques Zylberberg, 'Notes sur quelques contradictions du développement national et régional chilien 1965–1970', *Civilisations*, 21, (1971), pp. 406–24; Arturo Valenzuela, 'The breakdown of democratic regimes: Chile', in Linz and Stepan (eds), *The Breakdown of Democratic Regimes*.

42 Zylberberg, 'Rationalité et irrationalité politique: les contradictions de l'Unité Populaire Chilienne', pp. 71–2, 75–80.

43 Salvador Allende, *Nuestro camino al socialismo: La vía Chilena*, ed. Joan Garcés (Buenos Aires: Ed. Papiro, 1971).

44 Jorge Arrate, 'The nationalization of copper', in Zammit (ed.), *The Chilean Road to Socialism*, pp. 145–50; Francisco Orrego-Vicuña, 'Some international law problems posed by the nationalization of the copper industry by Chile', in *Chile: A Balanced View*, pp. 262–5.

8

Restructuring Foreign Policy: A Comparative Analysis

K. J. Holsti

Social scientists have long debated the benefits and limitations of the case study method. The basic trade-off is between in-depth understanding and capacity for generalization. By including eight cases we do increase the capacity for generalization, but certainly not sufficiently to argue that foreign policy realignment is *regularly* caused by x, y, or z, or some combination of them. Nevertheless, understanding of the phenomenon is increased by looking at each case in depth, rather than by trying to collect data over a large number of cases. The perceptions of a Ne Win, the ideological aspirations of Allende, or the nationalism of certain bureaucratic organizations in Ottawa in the early 1970s do not lend themselves to precise measurement. While the case studies may lack rigor and precision, they do reveal the calculations, fears and aspirations that underlay key decisions leading to foreign policy change.

From the point of view of foreign policy theory, we regrettably cannot explain why some states restructure their foreign policies while others, facing similar domestic and external problems, do not. Here is the crux of the problem of creating valid generalizations: we can say that conditions x, y, z combine to help explain why a particular government restructured its foreign policy; we can go even further and show how *similar* conditions resulted in similar behavior in other states. We find some regularity in both independent and dependent variables across the sample, but this must be largely a function of the selection of cases. All did, obviously, restructure their foreign policies, and hence the probability that x, y, z are related vastly increases. But we cannot infer from these similarities – even in a probabilistic sense – that *most* states, when x, y, z combine in the same way, would behave similarly. We lack a control group of states which, facing similar domestic and external conditions, did *not* change their foreign policy patterns. Kenya's post-independence development and external policies have been fundamentally different from Tanzania's, yet the two countries' overall situation and their domestic characteristics bear similarities.

The problem of generalization relates to time as well as to lack of control groups. The main characteristics of the Canadian-American relationship were not significantly different in the 1950s compared to the late 1960s. Yet in the former period Canadians were overwhelmingly satisfied with the relationship, while a decade later increasing numbers began to perceive American economic and cultural penetration as a threat. When we recognize that similar conditions – the independent variables – do not always, or even often, lead to the same form of foreign policy behavior among different states, or even in the same state at different times, then our generalizations must be very modest indeed. This concluding chapter therefore can do no more than suggest that certain conditions, particularly dependence, vulnerability, perceptions of weakness and massive external penetration, *predispose* some governments to restructure their foreign policies and that sometimes the major residues of dependence and interdependence are seen as threats which, in turn, compel governments to build moats and create more 'distance' between themselves and their mentors. Comparisons and generalizations derived inductively from our case studies must be understood in a probabilistic sense. We can suggest that countries facing conditions such as those found in our studies might choose to alter radically their patterns of externally directed activities and their policies regarding foreign influence – and that is about all. We cannot predict with any degree of certainty either that they *will* do it, what forms of restructuring might be involved, or when it would be undertaken.

Types of Causal Statements

Each of the chapters has listed conditions which help 'explain' the various decisions to restructure foreign policy. We have used the most traditional and common form of causal analysis, where $a, b, c \ldots n$ 'cause' the various forms of restructuring. This is the commonly used 'pressure model' where, in a sense, an independent variable explains policy-makers' actions. The most obvious example from our cases is China's military activities in the Himalayas which compelled the key policy-makers of Bhutan to turn to India for assistance. Causality, however, can also be conceived in an 'in order to' sense.[1] Nyerere, Mao, Ne Win and others were not simply responding to a set of conditions from which they wished to escape; they were also designing policies to reach a *more valued state of affairs*. This teleological form of explanation emphasizes future goals and objectives rather than present domestic and external conditions. In fact, both forms of explanation are intertwined. Ne Win's isolationist behavior may be accounted for both by his objective of creating a relatively classless, socialist society in Burma, and by his attempts to 'escape' from the legacies of colonialism. We will not point out where both forms of explanation are being used, for our purpose is not to assess their utility, but to analyze foreign policy behavior.

Several more introductory words are in order. Discussions of 'disengagement' and 'collective self-reliance' have become fashionable in recent diplomatic rhetoric. Many of the developing countries have sought to fashion foreign policy strategies that would increase their bargaining strength against the industrial nations. These have taken the form of regional trade arrangements (Andean Pact), coalition-formation in United Nations fora (UNCTAD), calls for a new international economic order and the creation of cartels. Some of these strategies may have been responses to the increasing popularity of academic dependence theory, a set of hypotheses about north–south relations which pictures the world in hierarchical and exploitative terms. From the analyses of Galtung, Frank, Furtado, Amin and others, it follows that if the developing nations wish to increase their economic capabilities and end exploitation, they will have to reduce their links with the industrial world and, if possible, band together to reverse the terms of trade which have increasingly favored the rich and the powerful. Whatever the current popularity of dependence theory – and its attraction is certainly understandable in an age where equality has become a prime transnational value – it is clear that none of the case studies in this volume can be understood as implementing some academic theory. The studies cover time periods when dependence theory was still in its infancy, invented, nurtured and understood only by a few academics in Latin America. There is no evidence, outside of the possible exception of Chile, that any of our decision-makers was familiar with the broad outlines of the theory. The decisions and actions examined in this volume were taken in the context of concrete economic, social and military problems related to each particular country. None of the personalities was attempting to test some academic analysis or to demonstrate that others should follow the path they had taken. Finally, dependence theory provides only a one-sided view of the problems faced by the governments of our cases. Its economic reductionism, while certainly pertinent for understanding Chile, Canada and Tanzania, fails to account for restructuring where military and cultural factors offer more powerful explanations.

Foreign Policy Restructuring: Changing Patterns of Relations

In six of the cases, fundamental reorganization of the countries' external relations is clearcut. When we compare the pattern of relations at t_1 and t_2 – usually involving a two- or three-year hiatus – significant differences emerge, differences that are not typical of states which adjust incrementally and pragmatically to changing domestic and foreign conditions. The most dramatic changes, as indicated by the pattern of externally directed activities and policies toward foreign penetration, are Bhutan, Burma, China I, II, III, and Chile's abortive attempts to cut loose from the American hegemon. With the exception of Chile, and China which shifted policy orientations several times in succession, the others were of a reasonably lasting character. Burma's extreme form of isolationism has been altered somewhat in recent years, but the main lines of policy – exclusion of foreigners and low levels of external activity – have characterized the country's foreign policies since 1963. Bhutan became and remains, in effect, a dependency of India, although it continues to promote programs aimed at reducing the Indian role in the country and maintains some 'screens' against Indian penetration.

Tanzania and Canada represent examples of countries which were fully committed to foreign policy restructuring at the rhetorical level, but which over a period of years achieved only mixed records of recasting their external ties. Both sought to reduce vulnerability by diversifying foreign trade, but the statistics over a ten-year period indicate only marginal success in this objective. For those who propose that dependent countries simply cut their links with their traditional trade partners in order to foster 'self-sufficiency',[2] these two examples and Burma illustrate the difficulties involved. Given Canada's proximity to the United States, similarities on their legal and economic systems, and traditional ease of conducting business across a highly permeable border, a truly effective policy of diversification would require massive government intervention into private economic decision-making, a policy which would probably encounter significant domestic resistance. Vigorous Canadian government programs to diversify trade, particularly to the EEC and Japan, have paid some dividends, but they have not cut into the essential structure of imports and exports. Whatever the motives of the Canadian government, its policy of diversification could succeed only with the active assistance of the new trade partners. There is no evidence that the members of the EEC or Japan were eager to purchase Canadian products merely to satisfy Canadians' concern with their vulnerability.

Similar conclusions pertain to Tanzania. The east African country's domestic policies have generated considerable international curiosity, sympathy and enthusiasm. But as Chapter 3 demonstrates, efforts to diversify trade have borne few fruits. For years after Arusha, Tanzania remained an exporter of raw materials and an importer of manufactured goods. While geographic trade concentration declined marginally, Tanzania's economic fortunes remain largely tied up with Western industrial markets and sources of supply. One reason for the relatively slight change in the trade pattern may be similar to those relevant to Canada: Tanzania's vulnerability has not been exploited by the industrial countries, and alternative markets achieved through diversification may provide fewer, not greater opportunities. To put it in economic terms, the opportunity costs of trade diversification may be higher than the costs of continued dependence.

But trade diversification is not the only, or perhaps even the most important, component of foreign policy restructuring. The domestic dimensions, or policies to establish or maintain political, economic and cultural autonomy, may be equally significant. Tanzania successfully gained control of its indigenous economy and has become capable of directing its meager resources toward nationally determined priorities. Canada's various 'border-screening' devices, as well as activities by voluntary associations and provincial governments, successfully reduced or managed the scope and extent of American penetration. Nevertheless, foreign ownership of Canadian economic resources continues at a level unmatched elsewhere, a phenomenon that has mixed blessings. Whatever the balance between costs and advantages, it is clear that by the 1980s the Canadian population for the most part has ceased to regard the United States as a major threat to national autonomy, whether in the economic, cultural, or political spheres. The internal dimensions of restructuring in these two countries must be judged as significant and, from the nationalist perspective, largely successful.

The Independent Variables

External Factors

The introductory chapter proposed that governments often restructure their foreign policies to cope with non-military threats. These perceived conditions may range from extreme economic vulnerability (trade concentration toward a single market, for example) to concerns about cultural 'pollution' through excessive contact with foreigners. Given the advances of transportation and communication facilities during past decades, it is understandable that some peoples might feel that their society, or segments of their culture, could be absorbed or destroyed by an influx of aliens and their ideas. While a nationalist response to asymmetrical cultural contacts is hardly new in history, the scope of external penetration today is multiplied greatly by technology. It is not entirely surprising, then, that most nationalist moat-building exercises have flourished as contacts with others broadened. Communications – particularly when they go predominately in one direction – may create fear rather than mutual understanding. Much of the literature on international integration, which places communication as a key factor explaining the development of mutual empathy, seems either irrelevant or incorrect when placed in the context of relations between inherently unequal partners.[3] Some of the case studies confirm that non-military threats are more important in helping to explain restructuring efforts than are other variables. In Burma, Canada, Chile and Tanzania the 'foreigner', predominately in his non-military guise, was the perceived threat. In these cases, a prime object of policy was to increase autonomy and to reduce, control, or even eliminate the foreign presence.

Perceived military threat was an important source of foreign policy restructuring only in the case of Bhutan, and China III; it was a marginal consideration for Burma. China's military activities in the Himalayas during the late 1950s were virtually a sufficient condition explaining the decisions to abandon rigid isolationism and to invite the Indians to provide for Bhutan's defense and modernization. But even in this case, Bhutan's leaders feared the costs of opening up the country and, as a result, imposed a variety of 'border-screening' devices to maintain control over the influx of Indians. By the late 1970s, some influential Bhutanese saw India as a greater threat than China and began to demand the rapid 'Bhutanization' of the country's civil service. China III also offers an example of a fundamental shift in policy, largely prompted by fears of military pressure. Finally, in the case of Burma, the desire to avert any possible spill-over of the Vietnam war into Burma, as well as concern about foreign involvement in the various ethnic and communist rebellions, were factors that help explain that country's turn to rigid isolation. But the extreme degree of isolation prior to and after the Vietnam war suggests that the restructuring policies had sources other than traditional security concerns.

Domestic Factors

Internal threats – rebellions and civil wars – do not loom important in any of our cases except Burma and China II. In Burma, the rebellions and secessionist movements had reduced government control over the country to the small central sector, and government officials occasionally explained that foreigners could not enter the country because their safety could not be guaranteed. While this explanation deserves some consideration regarding aspects of 'moat-building', it does not help us understand the drastic reduction of Burma's external activities or the expulsion of all foreigners, whether or not they inhabited unsafe districts. Other countries facing similar uprisings seldom adopted draconian measures such as those decreed by Ne Win in Burma.

In China, the internal threat was felt by both top decision-makers and ordinary citizens. Mao Tse-Tung and his followers feared that the Chinese version of Soviet revisionism had by 1965 become so strong that only violent action from below would succeed in dislodging it. Mao therefore deliberately perpetrated domestic disorders and rebellion, which by 1967 had gotten so far out of hand as to resemble civil war and threaten the territorial integrity of the country as a whole. It was the disunity spawned by the Maoists' initiatives that caused Russian precautionary military moves in 1967 and 1968 and that resulted in early 1969 in violent clashes at the Sino-Soviet border.

Domestic economic vulnerability was a serious consideration in Canada, Chile, Tanzania and China I. The first three governments perceived that their opportunities for autonomous industrialization and capital formation were hampered by the structure of foreign trade and the pattern of foreign investment. In Chile and Tanzania, the 'commanding heights' of the economy were foreign-owned, trade patterns emphasized exchange of raw materials for manufactured goods, with declining terms of trade, and they had no influence over the world prices of their export commodities. Economic decisions having vital impact on their opportunities for gains were made by those who remained largely outside the control and influence of Chilean or Tanzanian officials. In the case of Canada, the amount of foreign investment was also perceived by many as a threat, but the solutions turned around efforts to screen investment and takeover bids rather than to nationalize foreign assets. The potential costs of a trade pattern where 70 percent of a country's exports go to a single market were driven home in August 1971 when the Nixon administration imposed a 10 percent surcharge on imports to the United States, a decision which had significant impact on Canadian employment levels. This action changed many Canadian policy-makers' images of Canada as a potentially vulnerable country, to Canada as a victim.

In China, vulnerability to Soviet economic control of the advanced industrial sector and hence of the country's economic future was graphically evidenced upon Soviet withdrawal of advisers in 1960 and total cessation of trade and assistance thereafter. The industrial sector went into an immediate depression from which it did not recover for a half-decade. China was forced to depend entirely on its own resources, since Beijing's extremely cold relations with the United States and its Asian and European allies prohibited a swing toward the West. Burned severely by the consequences of overdependence, China's leaders vowed never to be placed in such a situation again and struck out in the direction of total self-reliance, from which they would not deviate for another decade-and-one-half.

Domestic factions – groups vocally pushing the government toward various forms of restructuring – were prominent only in Canada and Chile. In the former, the New Democratic Party capitalized on the growing nationalism in the country and pushed strongly for some of the restructuring policies. The Liberals, who had only a minority government in 1972–3, adopted some measures, such as a commitment to establish a foreign investment screening device, in part as a means of staying in office. The position of the NDP was hardly a sufficient condition to explain all of the restructuring policies, but without their hue and cry, the policies might otherwise have been much milder and some of them might not have been introduced at all. Several Liberal Cabinet ministers did promote the idea of a visible Canadian independence and development of border-screening devices, but their advice was not heeded until other sources of pressure, the American surcharge, the NDP and bureaucratic initiatives, came to play a significant role.

In Chile, radical factions within the *UP* and proto-guerrilla organizations such as the MIR advocated measures that went far beyond nationalization of some foreign-owned industries and external diversification. While the main lines of Allende's foreign policy restructuring were personal creations reflecting his Marxist world view, it is likely that the timing and severity of several key decisions were influenced extensively by pressure from the far left.

The Chinese case is an intermediate one. In each of the three transitions, factions were a prominent feature of domestic politics and, in each case, foreign policy changes were advocated by the challengers to Mao Tse-Tung's leadership. Thus, P'eng Teh-Huai in 1959 advocated less stringent opposition to Moscow; Lu Jui-Ch'ing in 1965 reportedly pressed for a return to Soviet-Chinese cooperation against the United States in Vietnam; and Lin Piao is accused of touting the Soviet line in 1970–1. But none of these challengers had their way; all were defeated by Mao. Nor did any of them make foreign policy the major element in their anti-Maoism. Finally, China did not change its foreign policy because of their advocacy, even after their respective downfalls. It was Mao's own personal proclivities and pressure from the Soviet Union that drove China to make the three translations noted in Chapter 6.

In the remaining countries – Bhutan, Burma and Tanzania – social and political groups in the society apparently played no direct role in formulating the restructuring decisions.

Traditional Cultural Factors

Few areas of political analysis have been so difficult to explore as the relationship between cultural norms and practices, national traditions and foreign policies. Theories of national character have long been held in disrepute, and the links between concepts as diffuse as culture, tradition and political behavior are extremely difficult to establish with precision. A few studies, such as Bamba's comparative examination of two Japanese statesmen representing different generations and cultural traditions,[4] are notable because of their rarity. And because we cannot establish direct causal relationships with the sort of unsystematic evidence available here, this discussion will not employ a causal model, but will simply point out to what extent restructuring policies were or were not *consistent* with certain traditions or cultural norms cited in the literature. The analysis must thus be tentative and hypothetical rather than determinative. Our notion of traditional-cultural factors is loosely defined as relevant and widely held attitudes or images of national history, of the outside world and of particular international relationships. Negative attitudes toward a former colonial tutor, widely held over a period of time by large segments of the population, offer one example.

Among our cases, cultural-traditional attitudes were consistent with the foreign policy restructuring decisions of Burma, Chile and China. The study of Burma reveals well-established anti-foreign sentiments throughout the political strata, highly ambivalent attitudes about modernization under foreign tutelage and notable concerns and fears about contacts with foreigners and their cultures. Ne Win's personal xenophobia was not typically Burmese, perhaps, but the policy of isolation was consistent with Burma's historical traditions and with the Burmese nationalists' longing for a return to a golden age unsullied by contacts with foreigners.

An external enemy – first Spain, followed by England and then the United States – has been a traditional factor in Chileans' portrayal of their history. Although not a colony since the beginning of the nineteenth century, many Chileans have seen their country as a victim of others' actions and economic presence. The American-owned copper mines and their prominence in the Chilean economy helped to provide a cause around which nationalists of various political persuasions could unite. The policies of Chileanization and external diversification were not, after all, the unique creation of Allende and the various Marxist-Leninist groups which surrounded him. Efforts to reduce American influence in the country – to disengage from a hegemon – were attempted in various guises during the 1930s and during the Frei presidency. Allende's policies were doctrinaire and less subtle than Frei's, but his goals were similar and consistent with the views of both Marxists and non-Marxist nationalists. Unlike Burmese xenophobia which was directed against *all* foreigners, the traditional attitudes operating in the Chilean case were directed specifically at the United States. If they did not compel Allende to act as he did, at least they created a 'mood' among politically important segments of the population which allowed him to diversify and nationalize without strong opposition.

China offers an excellent illustration of the correlation between tradition, culture and 'style' on the one hand, and foreign policy decisions and changes on the other. The first two instances of Chinese foreign policy restructuring evidence strong linkages between this set of domestic conditions and foreign policy outputs. Four traditional attitudes, in particular, informed each of the transitions: anti-colonialism; Sino-centricity; guerrillaism; and one-man leadership. Anti-colonialism prevented the Chinese from approaching the Western powers, particularly the United States, sooner as a counterweight against the Soviet Union. Sino-centricity drove the Chinese away from the Soviets sooner and into self-reliance more completely than would have been the case for a nation more closely inte-grated into the international system. Guerrillaism – the tendency for the Chinese communist leadership to respond to latter-day challenges on the basis of lessons learned during the formative Kiangsi-Yenan period – precipitated the Cultural Revolution and was a major factor in the Chinese strike at Soviet border forces in early March 1969. Finally, the apparent need of the Chinese people as a whole for a single, omniscient, all-powerful leader obviated any possibility of replacing Mao Tse-Tung before his natural demise.

The evidence regarding Tanzania does not allow any generalization. There is little to suggest that the types of traditional-cultural variables listed in our framework were relevant to Nyerere's decisions. Tanzanian independence had come without a war of liberation; while some among the political elites may have held anti-British sentiments or lamented the neo-colonial situation of the country in the mid-1960s, neither a general xenophobia nor a widely articulated critique of England was a prominent characteristic of Tanzanian life after independence.

In the Canadian case, the restructuring and border-screening policies were, if anything, inconsistent with traditional-cultural conditions. Anti-American sentiments have reappeared throughout Canadian history, but it would be difficult to argue that they are either widespread or constitute an unbroken tradition in Canadian political life. Unlike the Chileans, Cana-dians have not defined their national-historical experience in terms of struggle against an external enemy. Polls since the end of World War II indicate an overwhelmingly favorable attitude of Canadians toward Americans, as well as broad-based support for the traditional regime of free flow of goods, people, money and communications between the two countries. The perception of an increasing threat emanating from the United States arose clearly in the late 1960s and early 1970s, but from a historical perspective this mood was an exception, an aberration from the norm. Yet the Trudeau government certainly responded to it; hence, even if an aberration, it was a significant consideration in the restructuring decision-making process. The virtual demise of the 'third option' in the late 1970s and the short-lived Clark government's popular foreign policy subordination to American leadership in 1979–80 reveal the extent to which the more traditional sentiments reasserted themselves.

The remaining cases also went clearly against tradition and were incon-sistent with widely held attitudes and options. Bhutan's abandonment of isolation, in such a short period of time, would not have been predictable given the views of most of the country's political and religious elites. While some of them understood that modern communications technology would eventually render isolationism obsolete, few of them enthusiasti-cally overturned a policy which had provided peace and tranquillity to the country for several generations. The Prime Minister was not a typical Bhutanese and his visions of Bhutan's future could only have raised apprehensions among the political-religious notables. The residues of attitudes which are consistent with isolationism can be seen in the king's very cautious approach to the Indians, and in the strict regulations developed to control the types and extent of Indian activity in the country. Our conclusion must be that the foreign policy innovations of the late 1950s in Bhutan were inconsistent with traditional-cultural variables.

China III seems at first another instance of this sort. Rapprochment with the United States and Japan, and opening China's economy to imperialist-like penetration in the 1970s, does go against the grain of China's long tradition of xenophobia, Sino-centricity and anti-colonialism, to say nothing of the anti-Americanism of the previous two decades. Yet there were other traditions, augmented by leadership styles, that worked at cross-purposes. One was a still-living tradition of friendship with the United States, the only major Western country that treated China with a considerable degree of equality in the twentieth century. The other was the habit of the United Front strategy and the tendency to seek safety in three-sided coalitions, both learned during the quarter-century of struggle for power in China ending in 1949. It was thus relatively easy to rationalize the quick movement toward the United States: in the face of the Soviet military threat, there was no other choice; and past experience indicated that such a strategy could work.

Decision-Making Variables

In only one case, Canada, did the bureaucracy play a prominent role in promoting, defining and implementing a set of policies which dramatically sought to alter traditional patterns of relations. Bureaucratic pressures were hardly a sufficient condition for the restructuring activities of the Canadian government, but without the vigorous leadership of segments of the Department of External Affairs, the CRTC and the secretary of state's office, efforts to monitor and control transnational influences and to subsidize Canadian institutions would probably have been less notable. The Department of External Affairs' attempts to act as a coordinator for all relations with the United States, and its declared willingness to enter into conflicts with the southern neighbor, must also be noted.

In Bhutan, decisions were made at the top. No doubt some advisers warned against the perils of abandoning isolationism, but certainly the initiative to accept India's offers of aid came from the Prime Minister and the king.

The bureaucracy and military in Burma were probably split along numerous lines; but as their opinions were seldom solicited by Ne Win and his closest associates, it is doubtful that their views, if in opposition, were in any way influential, much less decisive. The influence of the bureaucracy becomes more apparent in the 1970s when the extreme isolationism of the country had proven to be economically disastrous. While it is impossible to gauge the extent to which the military or bureaucracy enthusiastically supported Ne Win's initiatives and decrees, there is some evidence in Chapter 5 that Ne Win's anti-foreign sentiments and fears were shared by others in the political strata.

The Chilean bureaucracy was split by political feuds; in some sectors bureaucrats were involved in political and revolutionary initiatives. In others, such as those dealing with financial matters, Allende no doubt received much advice suggesting that his domestic policies and his relations with the United States were helping to provoke an economic crisis. But the initiatives of disengagement and diversification came from the top; the only question was the extent to which the bureaucracy would implement the decisions vigorously or haltingly. In Tanzania as well, the policy initiatives came from Nyerere, with little or no input from administrative cadres. If anything, it is remarkable that there was not more overt bureaucratic resistance to Arusha because its implementation proved financially burdensome to government officials.

The three Chinese cases are all instances of which basic decisions were taken by a single person, Mao Tse-Tung, with little bureaucratic involvement. This is somewhat surprising, given the traditionally large role the bureaucracy has played in China, even in the post-1949 era. And it is true that there were bureaucratic rumblings in each transition, and that Mao had to overcome intra-party opposition at the top, with factional support for his several opponents – P'eng Teh-Huai, Lin Shao-Ch'i and Lin Piao – extending far down into the party and the army. But in the end it was Mao who made the choices and it was Mao who had his way, not the bureaucratic or party opponents.

The perceptions, values, preferences and objectives of key decision-makers assume critical importance in all cases except Canada, where the 'third option' and the institution of various border-screening devices went against some of the philosophical predilections of the Prime Minister and the leaders of his party. In Bhutan, Burma, Chile, China and Tanzania the key decisions were made by single leaders, occasionally (as in China) after consultations with a few important advisers. The policies were not usually developed as a result of lengthy debate in bureaucratic or parliamentary institutions, nor did they always follow recommendations of professionals, whether academic or governmental, who had carefully weighed alternatives, costs and benefits. A few edicts and commands were sufficient for Burma; the government never even published an explanation or apology for its drastic reversal of U Nu's foreign policies. In Bhutan, agreements with Indian officials – made more or less secretly – overturned traditional policy. The main domestic consultations came only after the commitments had already been made. Allende had publicized the directions his domestic and foreign policies would take in numerous campaign speeches and the *UP* party platform. But aside from the copper mine nationalizations, other facets of foreign policy restructuring were not the subject of extensive congressional scrutiny or debate. In addition to Allende, Foreign Minister Almeyda was a doctrinaire Marxist of a particularly radical persuasion, a devoted admirer of Mao and outspoken critic of the United States. The anti-American and pro-communist flavor of Chile's restructuring no doubt stemmed partly from Almeyda's leadership, but his views were certainly not inconsistent with Allende's cosmology and political programs. Chile's foreign policy activities in the early 1970s were largely predictable from the views expressed by both men prior to gaining office.

Nyerere formulated the main principles of the Arusha Declaration by himself, based on his perception of the increasing class formations growing in the country, as well as his conclusion that the neo-colonial relationship with Great Britain was demeaning and preventing Tanzania from exercising diplomatic influence in Africa.

Mao Tse-Tung was always his own man, as noted previously. His 'thought' and his personal rule had been made official as long ago as 1945 and was a fact by 1935. This is, of course, typical of communist politics in their early years, but it went farther in China. Most analyses of Chinese politics and foreign policy tended over the years to be reduced to inquiry into Mao's personality and his biography. Whether or not one takes a neo-Freudian approach, it seems clear that, of all Chinese, he best understood the nature of the Chinese psyche, and only he was able to play upon that psyche to get all others to do his bidding – even when it seemed quite out of keeping with generally accepted facets of Chinese national character.

All the leaders except Allende operated relatively pragmatically. The Chilean leader came to office dedicated to disengagement and restructuring; none of the others did. Ne Win, as a caretaker Prime Minister in 1958, had carried on U Nu's foreign policy lines. Once in office for about one year, after the 1962 coup, however, he began initiating policies that assumed the pattern of isolationism. To the extent that these policies were ever justified publicly – and they seldom were – they express strong perceptions of threat emanating from a hostile outside world, as well as perceptions of Burmese weakness. Indications of xenophobia were seen in Ne Win's personal habits – his avoidance of publicity, his rare public appearances, non-contact with foreign ambassadors and secretive reliance on a few advisers. Although Ne Win claimed to be constructing socialism according to a rather mystical program, aside from the nationalizations there is little in the two major dimensions of foreign policy that smack distinctly of socialism.

Likewise, Bhutan's turn toward India was not planned. The king and Prime Minister simply reacted to a military threat in the only way they could conceive: obtain assistance from the closest (and only) friendly neighbor. Nyerere acted on the basis of his disillusionment with the post-independence experience – he 'learned', adapted and ultimately made a critical choice based on his reflection on trends in the country. There was no element of textbook ideology or even patterning Tanzania's future on some other country's model or example. Not only to escape a situation defined as neo-colonial, his objectives were to increase the latitude of choice in economic policy, divest foreigners of their power over the 'commanding heights' of the economy and reduce the country's vulnerability to economic and military pressures placed by Great Britain and, potentially, by other Western nations. His own position as a spokesman for the liberation of southern Africa would also be enhanced if he were seen to be the leader of a genuinely independent state.

Mao's policy lines were in fact a mixture of ideology, reaction to outside pressure, his own vision of China's future and the necessity to do battle constantly with his internal opponents. Mao did not have to react so strongly to what he perceived as Soviet ideological errors in the 1950s; it was his own *Weltanshauung* that caused him to do so. It was reaction to the Soviet cut-off of economic relations in 1959–60 that, together with subsequent Sino-centerism, caused Beijing to adopt a policy of extreme self-reliance in the early 1960s. It was the disjunction between Mao's vision of China's ideal future and his realization that China was evolving in quite a different direction that caused him to unleash the forces of the Cultural Revolution. And it was, at least partly, the resolution of the conflict with Lin Piao in the early 1970s that enabled Mao to lead China into détente, and then coalition, with the United States against the Soviet Union.

Canada's 'third option' foreign policy developed in a decidedly piecemeal and pragmatic fashion. Decisions concerning the content of television and radio were made as early as 1968; subsidies to Canadian institutions, particularly in the arts and communication, as well as removal of the special tax exemption for advertising in *Time* magazine, came later. The policy of trade diversification was not launched until 1972, and the Foreign Investment Review Agency did not start its operations until the sixth year of Trudeau's leadership, in 1975. None of these measures represented the implementation of a clearly articulated foreign policy philosophy. Trudeau had barely mentioned foreign policy issues in the 1968 campaign, and even the formal policy review, *A Foreign Policy for Canadians*, published in 1970,[5] did not outline measures for diversification, vulnerability reduction and creation of border-screening devices. Mitchel Sharp's essay of 1972 was the closest to a conceptual statement on the need for diversification. It formally launched the 'third option', but many important aspects of border-screening were already in place, the result, primarily, of bureaucratic and private initiatives.

Chile violates our selection rule that restructuring must occur through an incumbent government and not as a result of revolution or other form of government change. Chile is included, nevertheless, because it is important to examine a case where restructuring efforts were resisted by a hegemony power. Allende came to power committed to a fundamental reordering of the nation's orientation toward the outside world, and to disengagement from the United States. Aside from the nationalizations and increased diplomatic contacts with socialist states, however, not much was spelled out in detail. But closer identification with Third World countries, admiration for Cuba and distrust of the United States were certainly predictable from Allende's often announced commitment to socialism and his electoral alliance with the communists of Chile.

Table 8.1 summarizes the relative influence of the independent and decision-making variables for all the cases. Naturally, assignment of scores is based on incomplete evidence and judgement rather than carefully developed indicators and formal measurements. On the traditional-cultural variables, only consistency or inconsistency between restructuring and widely and long-held opinions, attitudes and standards is noted. What patterns, if any, can we derive from the layout?

Looking first at the domestic factors, it is clear that internal threats were seldom relevant, and that foreign policy restructuring was rarely a response to the importunings of domestic factions. Only in the cases of Canada, China II and Chile can we argue that foreign policy change was, in part, a response to domestic pressures. Economic vulnerability, however, was germane in at least four of the cases. The vulnerabilities arose out of

Table 8.1 *The Sources of Foreign Policy Restructuring*

Countries	External Variables		Domestic Variables			Traditional-Cultural Factors	Decision-Making Variables	
	Non-military threats	Military threats	Internal threats	Economic vulnerability	Factions	Widely held and historically significant attitudes and perceptions	Bureaucratic pressures or initiatives	Personality and perceptual factors
Bhutan	0	+ +	0	0	0	▽	?	+ +
Burma	+ +	+	0	+	0	△	0	+ +
Canada	+ +	+ +	+	+ +	+	▽	+	+ +
China I	+	0	0	+	+	△	0	+ +
China II	0	0	+	0	+	▽	−	+ +
China III	0	+	0	0	+	▽	0	+ +
Chile	+ +	0	0	+ +	+	▽	?	+ +
Tanzania	+ +	0	0	+ +	0	?	−	+ +

Key: Very significant; powerful explanation = + +
Moderately significant = +
Not relevant = 0
Pressures against adopted policy = −
Consistent with policies adopted = △
Inconsistent with policies adopted = ▽
No judgement or insufficient information = ?

contacts with the outside world, so this is not, strictly speaking, a domestic variable. Of the traditional-cultural factors, no pattern emerges either. Burma's, China's I and II, and Chile's restructuring and disengagement efforts were consistent with widely held attitudes. A knowledge of these countries' history and public perceptions would allow the observer to predict that restructuring would be a probable choice of some government. Canada is a marginal case; perceptions of American threat were widely held in the late 1960s and early 1970s, but these views did not have deep historical roots. In the remainder of the cases, government policies contradicted our expectations.

Bhutan and China III represent examples where external threats are extremely important in explaining foreign policy restructuring. While the eight cases do not constitute a representative sample of postwar foreign policy restructuring, it is clear that the introductory chapter's hypothesis concerning the importance of non-military threats and economic vulnerability finds considerable support.

In Burma, Canada, Chile, China I and Tanzania, policy-makers expressed strong concern about the extent of foreign penetration, their vulnerability to outside economic decisions, the weakness of their cultures in the face of foreigners and modern communications media, and their lack of autonomy in government decision-making, particularly in the economic realm. In all of them the domestic dimension of their restructuring featured moat-building and border-screening devices, expulsion of foreigners and nationalist economic policies. Their externally directed activities, except in the cases of Burma and China I, sought to diversify economic and other contacts. Various disengagement policies against a hegemon were notable as well in the Chilean, China I and Tanzanian cases.

Writers on international relations have often assumed that growing interdependence is a phenomenon that influences all societies equally; nothing could be further from the actual state of affairs. Communication flows, penetration, trade vulnerability and strengths of societies are distinctly unequal. The persistence, and possibly even the growth, of nationalist sentiments based on fear of outsiders can, to a certain extent, be explained as a response to the 'shrinking world'. A major conclusion from this study must be that the various processes which bring societies closer together and which bind their economies may breed counter-reactions in the form of autonomy-seeking behavior. This is not a generalization which applies to all countries at all times, of course, but the proposition that the world is heading for a regime of free flow of goods, communications and peoples is also wide of the mark. Edward Morse[6] has claimed that there is an inherent incompatibility between national autonomy and modernization. This observation appears persuasive – and certainly the Burmese case suggests that one cannot achieve economic growth (if that is how 'modernization' is defined) through isolation. Yet, as our other studies and other examples (for instance, Iran, Cambodia, Albania) suggest, the search for modernization *with* autonomy goes on. Given a reasonably free choice, few governments today are willing to place themselves in the hands of a tutor and open up the society to an unfettered flow of foreign advisers, cultural artifacts and communications. The fear of cultural or language pollution or loss of national identity were strong perceptions in the minds of many of our policy-makers and shared widely among segments of the population. Nationalism appears to come from perceptions of social, economic and military *weakness*, whereas much of the traditional literature on the phenomenon correlates it with growing national strength. Policies of dependence reduction, moat-building and increased autonomy probably do contradict the requirements of economic logic, but the policy-makers of our cases apparently thought either (*a*) they could have autonomy and growth, or (*b*) they would sacrifice growth for the sake of autonomy when the two were not compatible. Although each of the countries adopted different mixes of policies, ranging from extreme isolationism and expulsion of foreigners to trade diversification, the impetus for their actions was basically similar: overreliance on others, dependence, vulnerability and external penetration. We turn, finally, to some speculations about why the various restructuring policies took the form they did. Why, for example, did not Tanzania adopt an isolationist orientation? Why did Burma not diversify instead of sealing itself off from the rest of the world?

For Bhutan, the options were extremely limited. In the face of a perceived military threat to its independence, there was only one possible source of support for the country's miniscule, sword-bearing army – India. As a non-entity in the international system which had had only sporadic relations with the southern neighbor, Bhutan had no possibilities of seeking assistance elsewhere. Even for the objective of modernization, the alternatives were limited by India's sensitivity to Bhutan's contacts with the rest of the world. Whatever the merits of the case, Indian governments clearly dealt with Bhutan as a protectorate and for all practical purposes determined who could have access to the landlocked country and with whom Bhutan could have external relations. When Bhutan entered the world – long after the Chinese threat had subsided – it did so through portals opened by the Indians. The Prime Minister and the king of Bhutan chose dependence because they had no available alternatives.

Burma's change to isolationism reflects characteristics of Burmese attitudes toward foreigners, widely held antipathy against colonialism and all its destructive consequences in Burma, a romanticized image of a golden age of Burmese purity in isolation, and Ne Win's perception of Burmese social and cultural weakness in the face of the foreign onslaught. Burma's colonial legacy, its pre-colonial history, Ne Win's attitudes and personal predilections all point to a policy of isolationism. U Nu's internationalism had been tried and failed in the sense that it transformed Burma into an arena of cold war competition. While the variables are not as determinative as in the Bhutan case, isolation appears a natural, perhaps even rational, response to Burmese perceptions of their situation. What remains to be explained is the extremity of the policies (much as Cambodia during the Pol Pot regime), rather than the orientation. The answer seems to lie in Ne Win's personality and his reliance on several key advisers. Other options, such as diversification, dependence or switching partners, would not have solved Burma's problems as they were defined by the military government under Ne Win.

Canada developed a strategy of selective border-screening device creation, subsidies to national institutions and external diversification; it was roughly in keeping with the liberal democratic tradition of the country. Given Canada's history of international involvement, its extensive trade and cultural links with Europe, Japan and the United States, and its generally favorable record in international diplomacy, the most feasible and least costly option would be to develop counterweights to the United States, rather than to disengage. The border-screening policies were not exclusionist in the sense that Burma's were, but were designed only to provide facilities for monitoring and controlling external penetration, not abolishing it. Any policies which might have deviated notably from the liberal paradigm of state–economy relations would have generated intense opposition at home and probable American retaliation. The Canadian approach combined nationalism with a large dose of business-as-usual on the economic front. Policies of self-sufficiency, radical disengagement from the United States, or isolation would have been disastrous for a country which earns more than a quarter of its GNP through trade. The remaining option, 'switching partners', could not be contemplated for obvious reasons.

Like Canada, Chile had been traditionally a trading nation, but its sense of exploitation by foreigners was much more pronounced. Disengagement and diversification were highly predictable given Chile's history and widespread anti-Yankee sentiments. That it would take the form of emphasizing ties with the socialist states is explained by doctrinaire considerations. The notion of exploitation by a foreign-comprador bourgeoisie alliance and underdevelopment caused by structural dependence were familiar to the leaders of the *UP* as well as to many leading intellectuals even in Frei's time. What distinguished Frei's orientation from Allende's was that he operated from the assumption that Chile was essentially a European-Christian country, a part of the West, while Allende and his supporters viewed theirs as a Third World country whose position in the international economy demanded a socialist goal and identity. Isolation would have been highly incongruous, given Chile's history, its reliance on trade and the *UP*'s socialist identification. Another option, switching partners, may have had some appeal, but Allende must have had doubts about cutting off ties with Europe, particularly since the Soviet Union did not appear eager to establish a relationship with Chile based on the Cuban model. Given more time, however, a strong pro-Soviet orientation might have unfolded. Had Allende survived and paid heed to the radical left, his increasing involvement in promoting revolutionary causes in Latin America would have led to strong reliance on the socialist countries.

China's three foreign policy restructurings took three of the four possible forms open to the country: orientation to the Soviet Union in opposition to the United States; self-reliance within the communist camp leading in the end to total diplomatic and economic isolation; orientation to the United States in opposition to the Soviet Union; and balance between East and West. Each orientation lasted approximately a decade and each was tried in turn: the 1950s was the decade of the military, economic and ideological alliance with the Soviet Union; the 1960s was devoted first to self-reliance and then during the Cultural Revolution to isolation; the 1970s saw reorientation to the West, in particular to the United States. Only the last option remained untried, and it is in that direction, true independence through balance, that China ultimately seems headed. In each of the three restructurings, China felt it had no reasonable other options at the time. The other interesting point is that Beijing never looked back to resuscitating a previous policy – compromising with Moscow in the 1970s, for example. Perhaps, once the fourth option is tried and found satisfactory because of the growth of Chinese power, the major swings of the previous decades will cease. Insufficiency of power, after all, has been at the root of Chinese foreign policy instability.

Desiring to escape a situation with all the trappings of neo-colonialism, what were the options for Nyerere? While he helped popularize the notion of self-reliance, his many attempts to explain the meaning of the term were not entirely successful. If development is the prime priority, then self-sufficiency hardly makes sense to a country which has one of the lowest per capita incomes in the world. Self-reliance must mean a policy which invites foreign participation, but clearly on the host's terms, with identifiable benefits accruing to Tanzania. It does not mean isolation or self-sufficiency in the sense practiced by China after its break with the Soviet Union. Certainly Nyerere was no replica of Ne Win; he had an international following and was deeply engaged in the political and diplomatic problems of southern Africa. Nor did Tanzania possess the resources of China; self-reliance could not be self-sufficency. It turned out, rather, as diversification, combined with disengagement from a rather indifferent Great Britain. A non-doctrinaire socialist, Nyerere could hardly be expected to 'switch partners' unless faced with a direct military threat and no alternative sources of support. The policy directions of Tanzania are strikingly similar to those of Canada, with about an equal record of successes and failures. Given Nyerere's objectives – domestic development, egalitarianism, increased autonomy and international political influence – and his international stature, the forms of restructuring he adopted seem appropriate.

Foreign Policy Restructuring and International Conflict

The most notable postwar cases of restructuring have generated serious international conflicts and crises. Yugoslavia's and China's break from the Soviet bloc, Cuba's reorientation toward the Soviet Union, Albania's walk out of the socialist camp, Chile's disengagement from the United States and Iran's anti-American stance in 1979 led to serious diplomatic complications, attempted coercion and occasional intervention. In particular, where a hegemon has been challenged by a dependant, violent responses are likely to follow. Only Albania escaped major coercive efforts, primarily because the hegemon lacked military access to the breakaway, or because of potential counter-measures by the smaller party.

Our cases suggest that over a period of years, nations come to occupy roles and functions in the international system which become well-established.[7] Except for peripheral countries which have only weak or intermittent external ties, others become enmeshed in complex networks of obligations, patterns of interaction and mutual expectations. These all change subtly over time as new items come on the bilateral and multilateral diplomatic agendas and as the power of the country waxes or wanes; but their basic configurations remain relatively stable. Attempts significantly to change obligations, relationships and expectations are seldom greeted with indifference among those who benefit from the established patterns. This is no less true in international politics than it is in interpersonal relations. We all more or less successfully accommodate to gradual change. Major alterations, disruptions, or separations of established roles are likely to result in quite different behavior. The most typical response, we can hypothesize, is for the status-quo party to remonstrate and to try to re-establish the old relationship. If these efforts fail, coercion becomes more prominent; when that fails, the probability of violence increases. It is impossible to state at which point a relationship becomes disrupted – some partners show more tolerance than others and the stakes involved in any relationship are seldom the same – but when the phenomenon of restructuring is involved, a critical point has been reached and conflict results. To the extent that autonomy-seeking behavior is likely to increase as a consequence of growing interdependence, we could predict that foreign policy restructuring and role reversal are likely to become increasingly prominent forms of diplomatic behavior, resulting in increased international conflict.

China's break with the Soviet Union and its later reorientation toward the United States represented not only a dramatic disruption of the conventions of socialist solidarity and all the rules of behavior those imply, but changed the country from a strategic ally to a strategic opponent, a direct security threat to the Soviet Union. All the obligations, pattern of relations and expectations, as seen from Moscow, were brutally violated and terminated, culminating in the non-renewal of the 1950 mutual security treaty and Deng's visit to the United States in 1979. China's punitive expedition against Russia's Vietnamese ally in the spring of the same year highlighted the extent to which there had been a complete role reversal from the old days of fraternal party relations. China's actions constituted no less than a diplomatic revolution.

Chile's actions were hardly as dramatic, but they were greeted in Washington with great concern. Henry Kissinger in his memoirs[8] makes it clear that the American government was scarcely concerned about protecting business interests against nationalization. Rather, the officials saw Allende as another Castro, and believed that Chile would become a bastion of the Latin American revolution, the spearhead of an anti-American crusade on the continent. American national security, not the profits of corporations, were at stake. Had Allende proceeded in a manner emphasizing nationalism and diversification, rather than socialist solidarity and revolution, the level of conflict between the countries would have remained muted – as was the case of America's relations with nationalist regimes in Peru and Bolivia during the same period and with Nicaragua after 1979. Not only did Allende abrogate treaties with the United States, disrupt the traditional pattern of relations and destroy any expectations about continuing the old relationship, he also defined the United States as Chile's principal enemy. It was not just the divorce, but the coupling with America's adversaries, that proved intolerable to Washington.

Since Bhutan had no relations with any other nation prior to 1958, its change would not likely provoke conflict. However, the involvement of India in Bhutan after 1958 undoubtedly extended the Sino-Indian conflict to a new geographical domain. Bhutan was a pawn of this larger rivalry, but its remoteness and lack of strategic value prevented its restructuring from having repercussions abroad. Burma's change was similarly greeted with relative equanimity. Since Burma's behavior implied losses (such as they were) to all parties equally, no one could claim that it was being singled out for special treatment. In terms of world politics, moreover, Burma was a peripheral actor; no country had a significant stake there, and none was harmed economically or strategically by Ne Win's hermit policies. The costs of restructuring accrued almost entirely to the Burmese alone.

Canada's diversification and border-screening policies caused some concern in Washington, but as the policies were implemented it became clear that Canada was not seeking to disengage from the southern neighbor, nor to single out the United States for exclusionist treatment. The Americans did not have large stakes to lose by the policies, and although they protested on occasion against some policies which went against the traditional rules of the Canadian-American game (for example, Saskatchewan's nationalization of American-owned potash mines), few obligations, relationships and expectations were seriously challenged. Some American policy-makers also believed that the 'third option' involved a certain amount of posturing for electoral purposes, and assessed that in the long run Canada could not effectively diversify its trade relations. Some of the border-screening devices angered select groups in the United States (the broadcasting industry), but none affected all Americans, and none unilaterally introduced new rules for conduct, or harmful precedents. When a senator from an American agricultural state introduced a resolution condemning Saskatchewan's nationalization policies, it was adopted unanimously by the handful of senators who bothered to appear for the debate on the issue![9] In brief, while Canada's restructuring efforts were visible enough and involved important changes, they did not add up to a fundamental challenge to the main outlines of the traditional relationship. As with Burma, the costs (if there were any) were borne by Canadians, not Americans.

Finally, Tanzania's diversification strategy had few repercussions abroad. That country's reliance on China for building the Taraza railway created some concern in Western capitals, but as there was no evidence of increased Chinese influence in the diplomacy or internal politics of Tanzania, those fears subsided. Great Britain terminated its aid programs to Tanzania in pique, but the former colonial tutors did not launch a major effort at coercion to re-establish the early post-independence relationship. No doubt the British by the late 1960s had become fully accustomed to giving up lost causes without recourse to extreme measures. Tanzania's increased contracts with the Scandinavian countries, Canada and some of the LDCs must also have assuaged any fears about a security threat. Tanzania remained essentially a Western-oriented country, if not a British protégé.

Foreign policy restructuring by relatively peripheral states which choose orientations that do not threaten the perceived security interests of bloc leaders or other hegemons are thus likely to succeed without generating high levels of conflict. Other conditions are no doubt relevant, as the Eyptian turn toward the West suggests, but lack of strategic significance is a critical condition. Role reversal and reorientation in other cases are likely to exacerbate international tensions and to result in a variety of coercive, punitive and violent responses by former hegemons.

In an age where independence and equality stand as major international values, the search for autonomy and breaking away from dependent relationships will continue, sometimes in unexpected places. Regimes which become too closely identified with any single sponsor, tutor, or protector are open to the claim that they are selling out to foreigners and opening up the country to unwanted foreign influences. Such countries often become international pariahs. In these circumstances, the Khomeinys and Khaddafys of the world can appeal to nationalist or xenophobic tendencies and obtain support for radical departures in foreign policy directions. As governments of developing countries survey the international environment, they perceive a variety of threats, not all of which are military. The postwar European urge for integration and the dazzling growth of 'interconnectedness' between societies has desensitized us to the continuing importance of nationalism and to the fears of those who see their languages, cultures and real or imagined national identities threatened by the onslaughts of foreigners. Whatever may be said about a growing world culture, it is clear that the growth is neither universal nor uni-directional. Political solidarity and integration have not resulted from it. Quite the contrary. International disintegration and autonomy-seeking behavior are at least equally prominent phenomena of our age. In future, we will see not only more new states originating from the political fragmentation of multi-ethnic societies, but also increased efforts of highly penetrated countries, occupying subordinate and dependent roles in the international system, to restructure their foreign policies in order to create more economic, cultural and political autonomy. Sometimes these efforts will be relatively unobtrusive, pragmatic and involve few costs or sacrifices; for others, such as Iran, the characteristics of restructuring will be doctrinaire, inflexible and antagonistic to those who are seen as corruptors and exploiters. The Chiles, Chinas and Irans are to be expected in a world where hierarchy, dependence and domination continue as central features of the system.

Notes: Chapter 8

1 Richard C. Snyder, H. W. Bruck and Burton Sapin, *Foreign Policy Decision-Making* (New York: Free Press, 1962), pp. 83–4, 144.
2 This strategy for developing countries has become fashionable among academics, following the policy implications of Andre Gunder Frank's theory of underdevelopment. See his

Latin America: Underdevelopment or Revolution (New York: Monthly Review Press, 1969), esp. ch. 1.

3 See K. J. Holsti, 'Change in the international system: interdependence, integration, and fragmentation', in Ole R. Holsti, Randolph Siverson and Alexander L. George (eds), *International System Change* (Boulder, Co.: Westview Press, 1980), pp. 23–54.

4 Nobuya Bamba, *Japanese Diplomacy in a Dilemma* (Vancouver: University of British Columbia Press, 1972).

5 Secretary of State for External Affairs, *A Foreign Policy for Canadians* (Ottawa: Queen's Printer, 1970).

6 Edward L. Morse, *Modernization and the Transformation of International Relations* (New York: Free Press, 1976), p. 111.

7 K. J. Holsti, 'National role conceptions in the study of foreign policy', *International Studies Quarterly*, 14 (September 1970), pp. 232–309.

8 Henry A. Kissinger, *White House Years* (Boston, Mass.: Little, Brown, 1979), ch. 17.

9 Maureen Appel Molot and Jean Kirk Laux, 'The politics of nationalization', *Canadian Journal of Political Science*, 12 (June 1979), pp. 236–7.

Index